The Arras Culture

I.M.STEAD

To the memory of
George Francis Willmot
lately Keeper of the Yorkshire Museum,
who pursued original research throughout Europe
and encouraged many an aspiring archaeologist,
this book is gratefully dedicated

CONTENTS

Cover: *Head on the hilt of the North Grimston sword.*

LIST OF FIGURES

LIST OF PLATES

(The photograph on the Cover, and Plates 4-7, 8a and 9 are by A. L. Pacitto; Plates 1, 8b and 10 are reproduced by courtesy of the Trustees of the British Museum; Plate 2 is from photographs taken by the Royal Commission on Historical Monuments (England); Plate 3a is taken from *Trans. East Riding Ant. Soc.*, *xviii*, 1911; Plate 3b is by T. C. M. Brewster; and Plate 8c by the Department of the Environment).

PREFACE

The La Tène Cultures of Eastern Yorkshire (Yorkshire Philosophical Society, 1965) was the greater part of a post-graduate thesis, the research for which was undertaken between 1959 and 1961. It had not been written with a view to publication, but when the opportunity arose it seemed better to publish despite the shortcomings rather than to leave it in typescript in a university library along with far too many other theses, unread and virtually inaccessible. Sales of the volume have justified the decision of the Yorkshire Philosophical Society to publish, and when the stocks were almost exhausted the writer was approached with a view to the preparation of a second edition. But research in this field has advanced considerably in the last decade, and most sections demanded thorough re-writing. It was soon apparent that the book would have to be completely re-cast, starting with the title — for what had seemed a clear distinction between two cultures has now been eroded: the material belongs to a single culture, the Arras Culture.

Apart from incorporating new discoveries, the information previously available has been thoroughly re-worked; all the artefacts have been re-examined, more fully described, and re-measured. Metric measures have been used except where other writers have recorded in imperial units, and there conversions have been added. The material remains of the Arras Culture are mainly in three collections, and for help in the recent study of them the writer is grateful to Elizabeth Hartley and Peter Hall, Yorkshire Museum, York; John Rumsby, Hull Museum; and colleagues at the British Museum. Material from Wetwang Slack, generously made available by John Dent, is mentioned in the text but no pieces have been illustrated or discussed in detail pending the full excavation-report. Most of the illustrations are the work of Gillian March and Robert Pengelly, and most of the photographs were taken by Tony Pacitto.

Despite the considerable advances in research, the Arras Culture is still known almost entirely from its burials and grave-goods, so the basic arrangement of this book is quite similar to that of its predecessor. It differs in placing less emphasis on Champagne: the Champagne material was included originally because it had been studied in detail by the writer, but its exclusion from the present work leads to a more balanced approach. Also omitted is the brief section on settlements, for advances in the field of aerial photography have produced very many settlements, mainly undated, and shown how unrepresentative is the small sample available from old excavations. The air photographs are being correlated and plotted by H.G. Ramm and his colleagues at the York office of the Royal Commission on Historical Monuments (England), and a rapid general survey has recently been undertaken by the Humberside Joint Archaeological Committee. The work of these bodies is providing a sound basis for planning selective excavation in order to study domestic sites as well as burials. The stage is clearly set for an even more impressive advance in our knowledge of the Arras Culture in the course of the next decade.

British Museum
July, 1977.

THE SITES

1. Arras.

The main road from York to Hull leaves the Vale of York at Market Weighton and climbs sharply up the western edge of the Wolds. Gradually it then loses height, and eventually, after Beverley, the chalk gives way to boulder clay, and the road turns south following the River Hull to the Humber. At the highest point (138m above sea level), on the escarpment of the Wolds, a group of large Bronze Age barrows explored by Greenwell towards the end of the last century is still visible despite the onslaught of modern agriculture. But almost 2km further east, where the road runs between the farms of Arras and Hessleskew, an extensive barrow cemetery in the fields on both sides of the road has now been completely levelled.

The Arras barrows were only small, and they must have escaped ploughing in Romano-British and Medieval times, for they were still in existence at the start of the nineteenth century. In Medieval times the land would have belonged to the now deserted village of Arras, and the barrows would have been protected in pasture close to the village. This name of Arras has no connection with the town in northern France, for it was derived from "Erg" and passed through "Herges" and "Erghus" to become Arras in the sixteenth-century (Smith 1937:230) — by which time little would have remained of the village. Like many villages in the area Arras was depopulated in the fifteenth century when much of the Wolds was converted to sheep farming, and the barrow cemetery then enjoyed the protection of pasture until the time of the agricultural revolution. Thereafter, in common with the rest of the Wolds, Arras suffered from the ravages of ever more heavy agricultural machinery, and the toll of antiquity is exceptionally well-documented. Of about a hundred barrows visible in 1815, only 31 could be plotted when the Ordnance Survey produced their first 6-inch map of the area in 1855, and when that map was revised in 1910 continuous ploughing had reduced the number to only 13. The present writer surveyed the area in 1959, when three barrows could be seen — with the eye of faith; today there is not one.

The barrows at Arras were quite thoroughly explored between 1815 and 1817 by a group of local gentry. The reason for this excavation is not recorded — and indeed there is precious little record of the results. Perhaps the resumption of agriculture on the Wolds occasioned disturbance of some of the antiquities, or it could be that the gentry were inspired by the interest in antiquarian matters which had been developing throughout the previous century: indeed, more than a century earlier, in 1699, Abraham de la Pryme had noted the Arras barrows and recorded his intention to excavate them (Jackson 1869:200). The excavation team in 1816 included the Rev. E. W. Stillingfleet, Barnard Clarkson, and possibly Dr Thomas Hull, little-known names because they failed to broadcast the results of their work. Stillingfleet, the vicar of South Cave, came from a famous family of clerics, and was also involved in unpublished excavations of barrows at Skipwith in 1817 (p.103); Wharram-le-Street, 1820 (Wellbeloved 1875:75); and Kilham, 1824 (Wellbeloved 1875:137; York Catalogue 1846:11); on his death in 1865 he bequeathed his archaeological collection to the Yorkshire Museum. Clarkson lived at Holme House, Holme-on-Spalding-Moor, and his collection of antiquities was dispersed at auction after he had been declared bankrupt in 1832. Thomas Hull, M.D., had a practice in Beverley; he is not recorded as an excavator at Arras, but he certainly received some of the finds (Oliver 1829:4) and he is known to have dug barrows at Bishop Burton (Ibid.: 7).

The first published account of the 1815-17 excavations seems to have been in 1829 in a general History of Beverley (Ibid.: 3-4), where a letter written by Dr Hull to Hinderwell, the Scarborough historian, is quoted at length. Hull's was probably an eye-witness account, and it sounds more reliable than the garbled version derived from Clarkson which is given in the same work (Ibid.: 4, note 7). Stillingfleet's account (Stillingfleet 1846) was also written in the form of a letter, dated 28th January, 1847 — thirty years after the excavations — and published in 1848 as part of the proceedings of the 1846 York meeting of the Archaeological Institute, where some of the Arras finds had been exhibited. He also left a manuscript to the Yorkshire Philosophical Society, which was still in their library when Greenwell was preparing his work on Early Iron Age burials in Yorkshire (Greenwell 1906:255, note b) but does not seem to have been seen since then. Greenwell also refers to a manuscript letter from Hull, dated 2nd October, 1827, in the Yorkshire Philosophical Society collection (Greenwell 1906, 275, note a; also mentioned by Davis & Thurnam 1865:2, note).

Another relic of the 1815-17 excavations, which has only recently come to light is a manuscript plan discovered by C. S. Briggs in a volume of drawings in the Department of Medieval and Later Antiquities, British Museum. It has now been transferred to the Department of Prehistoric and Romano-British Antiquities. This plan, (Pl.I) dated 5th August, 1816, is signed by one William Watson, and must have been a version of the one which accompanied Stillingfleet's manuscript in the Yorkshire Philosophical Society collection (Greenwell 1906:303, note a). Watson (1784-1857) was a well-known local land-surveyor who lived nearby at Seaton Ross and whose work included large-scale plans of both Pocklington and Market Weighton (Harris 1973). The Arras plan shows that the turnpike road from York to Beverley bisects the cemetery, with 55 numbered barrows to the north and 33 to the south. Curiously it does not include all the barrows that can be documented, for there were certainly another 12, to complete the century (p.98). The discovery of Watson's plan also solves a minor mystery connected with the Arras site, for some of the finds in the Yorkshire Museum are labelled as from 'Barrow W.17', 'W.24', etc. Presumably these are Watson's barrow numbers.

Apart from showing the general arrangement of the barrow cemetery Watson's plan includes notes against six of the barrows. An isolated and un-numbered barrow some 250 yards (230m) south-west of the cemetery is marked "Indian ornaments" a description most likely to be applied to the Bronze Age jet beads (p.81) to which Stillingfleet (1846:27) refers "as still worn by uncivilized tribes". W.7 and 28, labelled "nothing", need no further explanation; W.4, "excavations in the rock" is obscure; the un-numbered "cross barrows" near the east edge of the plan could refer to a sheep bield (one of Mortimer's "embankment crosses") but W.36, "the round thing" may perhaps be correlated with an item of grave-goods. W.36 is shown as a very small barrow, and the most likely explanation of "the round thing" is in the account of the discovery of an iron mirror which seems not to have been recognised as such by Stillingfleet: "the round iron instrument, which we familiarly termed the oat cakes baker" was found "with a skeleton in a small barrow" (Greenwell 1906:294, note a, quoting the Stillingfleet manuscript). Perhaps this object was found at the time that Watson was surveying the site, in August, 1816, which would account for it being noted on the plan when other more distinctive features were not recorded.

Stillingfleet concentrates his description on only three of the graves, but they were the richest and most interesting of his discoveries. These three barrows were not numbered in his account, and cannot be identified on Watson's plan; instead, they were named: the Queen's Barrow, the King's Barrow and the Charioteer's Barrow. The Queen's Barrow (Stillingfleet 1846:27-8), was excavated a month after Watson's survey, on 4th September

1816 according to a label in the Yorkshire Museum; it was on the Arras side of the road (Barrows 1-55), of small diameter and about 3ft (1m) high. In a shallow grave only 1ft (30cm) deep was a crouched or contracted skeleton ("her feet gathered up") with the head to the north. The grave-goods consisted of a necklace of glass beads, an amber ring, bronze brooch, bronze pendant, two bracelets, a toilet-set and a gold finger ring.

The King's Barrow (Stillingfleet 1846:28-30) was also on the north side, but on the very edge of the turn-pike road. Watson's plan has been annotated fairly recently in pencil, "43 or 55 King's?", and these are the two barrows nearest the position described. But as the grave-group from W.43 survives in the Yorkshire Museum, it seems likely that Watson's no.55 was the King's Barrow. Stillingfleet records its diameter as 8 to 9 yards (8m), its height as unkown because it had been partly levelled, and its grave as being 11 or 12ft (3.5m) across and nearly circular. Here too the skeleton was orientated with the head at the north, but it was on its back, apparently with the legs flexed, and accompanied by the remains of a vehicle and two horses.

The third named barrow, also with the remains of a vehicle, was the Charioteer's Barrow (Stillingfleet 1846:30-1). Its location is given merely as on the Hessleskew side of the road (i.e. Barrows 56-88), and it was recorded as only 8ft (2.5m) in diameter. The position of the skeleton was not noted, but for its skull being towards the north (Greenwell 1906:281).

The excavators say little of the un-named barrows in their published accounts. Stillingfleet notes that the position of the skeleton in the Queen's Barrow (crouched or contracted) and its orientation (skull to the north) "were frequent, if not general features, in the interments of this group" (Stillingfleet 1846:27-8). Hull confirms the orientation, and adds that each barrow contained a single skeleton in a shallow grave about 2ft (60cm) deep (Oliver 1829:3). Other details of the Arras graves can be gleaned from Greenwell's published account, based on the Stillingfleet manuscript. Thus, whilst the skeletons were usually crouched or contracted, some were extended; the skull was normally at the north end, occasionally at the south, but never to the east or west (Greenwell 1906:275). Some graves rested on the chalk, and a few were even above the chalk (Ibid., 268, note b, and 275). Some details of three other grave-groups are given (Ibid., 301-3), and Greenwell comments on the rarity of animal bones and pottery (Ibid., 264 and 276).

Further excavations at Arras were carried out in the middle of the nineteenth century, by a more responsible body — the Yorkshire Antiquarian Club — a field club whose primary object was to excavate.

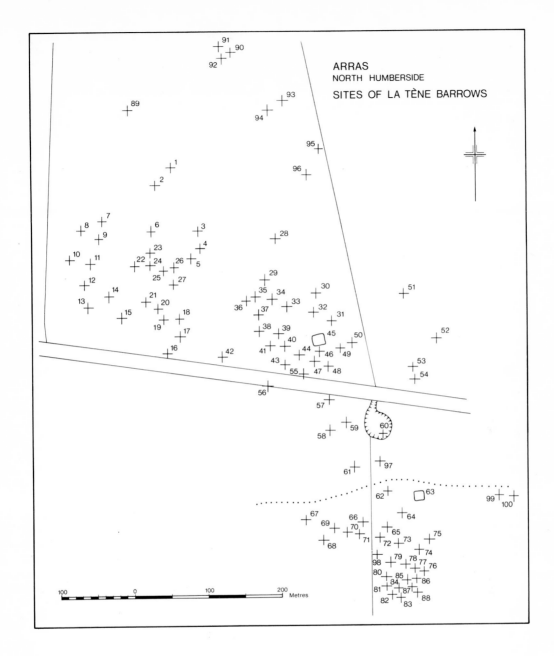

1. *Plan of the Arras cemetery, incorporating information from the Ordnance Survey maps, the Yorkshire Antiquarian Club's plan, Watson's plan of 1816, the 1959 excavation, and aerial photographs.*

Its inception in 1849 followed three years after the Archaeological Institute's York meeting, when the Arras finds were exhibited and local interest was stirred (Ramm 1971:68-9). The Yorkshire Antiquarian Club had William Proctor, a surgeon, as secretary and its membership included John Thurnam, one of the greatest of nineteenth-century archaeologists. They visited Arras in May, 1850, and excavated three barrows, two of which seemed to have been disturbed by their predecessors (Proctor 1855:182). The third barrow had an undisturbed grave containing a skeleton in good condition: contracted, on its left side and orientated north-south. The only grave-goods were pig-bones, found near the skull. The skull from this grave was published in detail (Davis & Thurnam 1865) in an account which included a plate of grave-goods from the 1815-17 excavations and a description of those excavations based on published sources. In the Yorkshire Philosophical Society's collection there is a manuscript account of the Yorkshire Antiquarian Club's activities, which at least in part seems to have been copied from the published version (Proctor 1855). But the manuscript is accompanied by unpublished sketches, including a plan of Arras showing eight numbered barrows and two without numbers (Pl. 2a). It could be that this plan was intended to supplement Watson's 1816 plan — for the eight numbered barrows are all to the north of those plotted by Watson. The one intact grave found in 1850 was presumably one of the eight, whereas one of the disturbed graves "on the Hessleskew side of the road close to the hedge" is presumably one of the un-numbered barrows on their plan, which seems to correspond to Barrow 56 on Watson's. In his report on the excavation, Proctor noted "a tumulus being surrounded by a square instead of a round fossa" and it took more than a century for that remark to be fully appreciated.

Watson's plan shows a chalk pit on the Hessleskew side of the road — and it still survives. During work in that pit in 1876 the third Arras vehicle burial was unearthed, and Greenwell was soon on the scene to question the workmen, examine the grave and collect the antiquities (Greenwell 1877:454-7; 1906:279, 284-6). The barrow had been 14ft (4.3m) diameter, 1½ft (45cm) high, and had covered a 12ft (3.6m) diameter circular grave cut 3ft (1m) into the chalk. The skeleton, said to have been female, was extended, on its left side and orientated north-south and surrounded by vehicle remains and harness.

The most recent excavation at Arras took place in 1959, when a proton magnetometer survey was organised in an attempt to locate burials and to see if any remained undisturbed (Stead 1961:44-7). At that time, unfortunately, Watson's manuscript plan had not been re-discovered, although the positions of 34 barrows were known from the early Ordnance Surveys and the Yorkshire Antiquarian Club's plan. About three hectares were surveyed with the proton magnetometer, comprising four areas — three of which were in the central part of the cemetery and covered the sites of 19 barrows, as we now know. But the magnetic anomalies were surprisingly weak, and only two barrows were detected. In each case the barrow was represented by a surrounding ditch, square in plan, of which the magnetometer detected only three sides. Subsequent excavation distinguished the ditch on all four sides, with no apparent difference in section between the six sides located by geophysics and the other two.

The 1959 survey was a disappointment, but it did draw attention to the distinctive form of barrow — the barrow with a square-plan ditch — of which an isolated example had been noted in 1850. The two barrows excavated, one on each side of the road, seem to be correlated with Watson's numbers 45 and 63, both of which are shown on the 1855 and 1910 editions of the Ordnance Survey (although W.63 is plotted slightly differently on the two editions). Barrow W.45 was 40 to 42ft (12 to 13m) across and defined by a ditch 6 to 8ft (2m) wide and 3ft to 3ft 6in (1m) deep. The central grave, not detected by the magnetometer, was 3ft (1m) deep below present ground level; it had been previously excavated, but the remains showed that the skeleton had been orientated south-north (skull fragments at the south end of the grave) and an iron penannular brooch had been overlooked.

The barrow on the Hessleskew side of the road, probably W.63, was slightly smaller, 34 to 36ft (10 to 11m) across with a ditch 6 to 7ft (2m) wide and 3ft to 4ft (1m) deep. A magnetic disturbance near the centre was not a grave, and no grave was discovered; this could have been one of the barrows with a grave on or above the level of the chalk (cf. Greenwell 1906:275).

The only other recent development at Arras is in the field of aerial photography. The site has been viewed by aerial photographers many times, but it has proved remarkably unresponsive. In the summer of 1974 some of the barrows appeared briefly, and only very faintly, but it was sufficient to support the accuracy of Watson's 1816 plan. Some barrows showed as lighter patches with dark surrounding ditches, whilst others were represented only by the ditches; 17 barrows were photographed by A.L. Pacitto, and at least five (including W.45) had square-plan ditches (details p.97).

The material from the 1815-17 excavations was divided between the excavators, and apart from a few oddments in the British Museum, only the Stillingfleet collection in the Yorkshire Museum survives. Even Stillingfleet's share is not entirely intact, for the gold ring from the Queen's Barrow was not given to the Yorkshire Museum, and its present location, if it survives, is unknown. Some indication of the lost objects is provided by Stillingfleet who had eight bracelets in his collection but who could still say "we found several much finer bracelets; but they did not fall to my share" (Stillingfleet 1846:27). Dr Hull possessed some bones and grave-goods including an anklet and a bracelet, found, allegedly, in the same grave but on the bones of different individuals (Oliver 1829:4, and pl. opp., no.7). Barnard Clarkson's collection of antiquities, dispersed at auction, included bracelets, brooches, beads and a cart-tyre (Stead 1965a:119). The only major finds since the Stillingfleet excavations came from Greenwell's cart-burial, whose grave-goods were purchased by A.W. Franks and presented to the British Museum.

Arras is still one of the most important of a group of La Tène cemeteries, and a comparatively rich example in terms of its bronze grave-goods and vehicle-burials. It is the obvious type-site for a culture that can be defined by its burials and that is still known by little more than its burials. The culture can be considered in terms of grave-goods and burial-rites, and of the latter there are three distinctive features: (i) large cemeteries of small barrows, (ii) some barrows defined by square-plan ditches, and (iii) some barrows covering vehicle-burials. The distribution of these aspects of the Arras Culture will be considered in detail in the following chapters, followed by an account of the grave-goods.

2. Barrow Cemeteries

Two barrow cemeteries, apart from Arras, survived into the nineteenth century — and, indeed, to the present day — and were investigated by early barrow-diggers. Danes Graves, near Driffield, attracted the attentions of both Mortimer and Greenwell, and Mortimer also opened some of the mounds at Scorborough, near Beverley. But aerial photography has shown that these three sites are chance survivors representative of many more cemeteries whose barrows had been flattened by ploughing. Three such sites came to light in the course of large-scale top-soil removal: one at Eastburn, during the construction of Driffield aerodrome in the 1930s, and two nearby at Garton/Wetwang Slack in advance of gravel extraction in the 1960s and 1970s. Other cemeteries, smaller groups and individual barrows are being subjected to constant erosion by ploughing and it was this threat, unspectacular in the short-term but devastating over the years, that prompted

the Inspectorate of Ancient Monuments, Department of the Environment, to organise the planned excavation of a typical site.

The chosen site lies between Burton Fleming and Rudston. This area was one of the outstanding prehistoric centres in England, with the Rudston monolith — the tallest standing stone in Britain — the Burton Fleming henge and no fewer than four cursus monuments bearing witness to its importance as early as the third millenium (Dymond 1966). The barrows on Woldgate, the enormous Willie Howe on low ground just west of Burton Fleming village, and the many ring-ditches between the two are the sites of Neolithic and Bronze Age burials. Crop-marks reveal Iron Age burials and settlements in profusion, and the archaeology of the area extends beyond prehistory to include a Roman villa with remarkable mosaic pavements at Rudston, and a fine example of a Deserted Medieval Village at Argam. Not only is it rich in archaeology, but a remarkably complete picture of that archaeology is available because the Rudston area is extremely responsive to aerial photography, and in the last 20 years considerable attention has been paid to it. Aerial photography guided the selection of a cemetery, first noted by St. Joseph in 1964, whose extent was more or less known before excavation started; surrounded by crop-marks of settlements to which it might be related; but not unduly complicated by earlier or later features.

The cemetery between Burton Fleming and Rudston, centred in a field called 'Makeshift', appears to be entirely on gravel, and mainly in the valley of the Gypsey Race. This stream, a rare occurrence of running water in the area, rises in the Great Wold Valley and runs eastwards to Burton Fleming, where it turns sharply to the south as far as Rudston, from whence it resumes its eastwards course to the sea at Bridlington. Between Burton Fleming and Rudston the Gypsey Race flows (intermittently, for it is usually dry as far as Rudston) through glacial gravels which fill a once steepsided chalk valley.

The 'Makeshift' cemetery is bounded on the east side by the Gypsey Race and on the south side by a dyke which follows the bottom of a subsidiary dry valley known as Springdale. The distribution of the barrows is in the form of a reversed 'L', following the two gravel valleys and avoiding the chalk; its extent is about 700m in the one direction, almost 800m in the other, and there are more than 300 barrows. But only 300m to the north are two smaller groups: the first, with 18 graves, was excavated in 1976; and the second, with about 25 barrows, most of them excavated in 1972, is cut by the parish boundary between Rudston and Burton Fleming

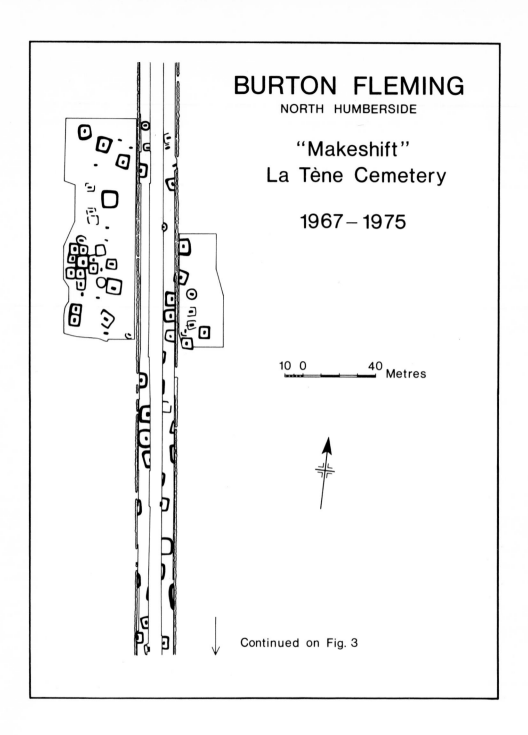

BURTON FLEMING
NORTH HUMBERSIDE

"Makeshift"
La Tène Cemetery

1967 – 1975

10 0   40 Metres

Continued on Fig. 3

2.   *Plan of the northern part of the 'Makeshift' cemetery, Burton Fleming (continued on figure 3).*

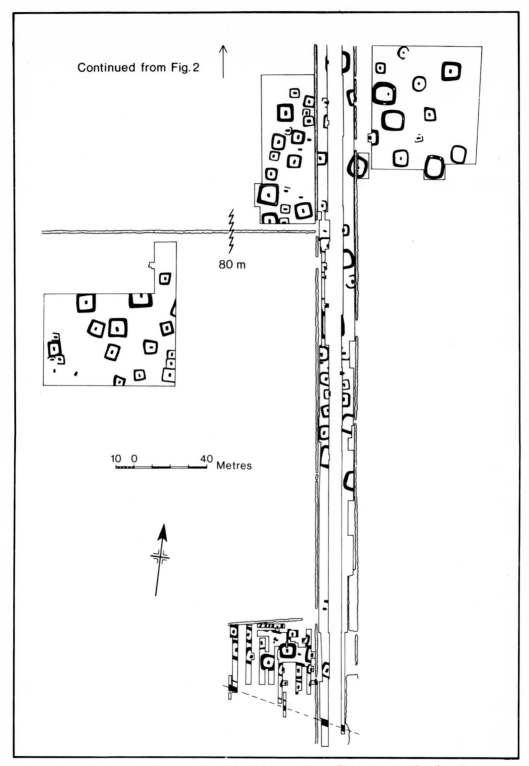

Continued from Fig. 2

80 m

10 0   40 Metres

3. *Plan of the southern part of the 'Makeshift' cemetery, Burton Fleming (continued from figure 2).*

which is here represented by a pit-alignment. A more scattered group of square barrows is only 450m north-east — near the henge monument. Still further is a branch-valley, Bell Slack, which houses a cemetery of more than 200 square barrows arranged in two groups; whilst northwards along the main valley there are more than 200 square barrows in two further groups on either side of the Gypsey Race east and south-east of Burton Fleming village. In an area of approximately 2km by 3km there are at least 800 square barrows (Stead 1977:fig.5).

So far six separate areas of the 'Makeshift' cemetery have been examined, with a concentration along the road-sides where the excavated areas have been usefully linked by the strips along the grass-verges (Figs. 2 and 3). In nine major seasons of excavation (1968-76) 207 burials have been excavated in this cemetery and the two groups to the north.

The normal burial rite accords well with the scrappy information available from earlier excavations of Arras Culture burials: crouched or contracted inhumations (Pl. 4a and b), orientated north-south, and each at the centre of a small barrow. So far 153 north-south orientated graves have been excavated, and the vast majority held crouched or contracted inhumations; only 18 of these skeletons were flexed, and none was extended. The usual rite (94 skeletons) was with the skull at the north end of the grave facing east; with a much smaller number (33 skeletons) having the skull at the south end facing west: all these 127 skeletons were on their left sides. Skeletons on their right sides were far more unusual — 22 skeletons, of which 15 had the skull at the north end of the grave. In four of the north-south graves no human remains had survived. Almost half of these burials had grave-goods, and the limited range of objects comes as no surprise in an Arras Culture context: 58 brooches, 34 pots, seven bracelets (four of bronze — including a pair — and three shale), four glass beads, two bronze rings and a ring-headed pin. Some of these burials had been placed in wooden coffins — at least 20 examples were identified by soil-patterns, but none had metal nails or fittings.

Whilst the normal burial rite came as no surprise, a second series of burials was quite unexpected. These too were each at the centre of square-plan ditches, but the orientation of the graves was in the opposite direction (Pl.5) — east-west — and instead of being crouched or contracted, they were normally extended (Pl.4c) or flexed. Of these graves 54 were excavated: 31 had skeletons with the skull at the east end, 22 at the west end, and in one grave the skeleton had not survived. 29 skeletons were extended, 19 were flexed, four crouched and one

contracted. The sharp distinction in orientation and position was further emphasised by the range of grave-goods, for there was not a single pot with these east-west burials, and the only brooch was of a quite different type from those found with the north-south burials. Instead, 10 skeletons were accompanied by swords and six of them also had spearheads; two had spearheads but no swords; and other graves produced five knives, three spindlewhorls, a shield and a toe-ring.

The difference between these two types of burial is one of the most important results of the Burton Fleming excavations. Superficially it might appear that the north-south burials with pots and brooches could be female, whereas the east-west ones with swords and spearheads might be males: but examination of the human remains, by Sheelagh Stead, has shown that there are males and females in each group. It would seem that two different populations were using the cemetery — or perhaps two different sects. That there was some relationship between the two is suggested not only by their use of the same cemetery, but by their mutual use of square-plan ditches, and their respect for each other's burials. It is important to establish whether or not the two rites were contemporary, but this is not easy when the ranges of grave-goods are mutually exclusive. If it could be shown that the east-west burials were earlier, then a broader signifi-cance could be attributed to them, for one of the curious differences between the Yorkshire and continental La Tène cultures is that the former have crouched burials in contrast to the latter's practice of extended inhumation. But the evidence from Burton Fleming will not support this, for the few relevant facts suggest that the east-west burials were later than the north-south. Those facts are: (i) of the 59 brooches from the site, the only one with an east-west burial is the only one of distinctively La Tène III form (Fig.26, no.6), and (ii) in the only instance of one burial cutting another, it is a north-south burial which has been disturbed by an east-west burial. This evidence does not conclusively place all east-west burials at Burton Fleming later than all north-south burials, but it suggests that if the difference between the two is chronological, then the east-west burials are the later. The east-west burials from Burton Fleming cannot be matched as a group in any other Arras Culture cemetery, although an extended east-west burial was found at Garton Slack (A.E. 1970:13), and there is a single flexed east-west burial from Wetwang Slack (Dent, personal letter).

Apart from the two major groups of burials at Burton Fleming, some minor variations are worth noting here. The rite of barrow burial seems to have been virtually invariable: some of the east-west burials did not have barrow-ditches, but the ditches with that type of burial were so shallow that they might well have been completely removed by ploughing. Only one typical north-south burial lacked a barrow-ditch, and there seems a reasonable case for supposing that it never had one, for that was the only grave to have been cut by a later grave. Not all the barrows had central burials, and in particular there was one distinctive form — with a large rectangular barrow-platform — which lacked central burials but had secondary burials in the ditches. In all there were 13 barrows without central graves, eight secondary burials in barrow-ditches, and two other secondary burials. Seven ring-ditches were found amongst all the square-plan ditches, four had east-west graves at their centres, two had north-south graves, and two lacked central burials.

Burials of children and adolescents were extremely rare (5 skeletons), and it is obvious that some other burial-rite was in general reserved for those under the age of about seventeen. Only one child was found alone in a primary position, although two others were in a primary grave, super-imposed and in turn covered by an adult skeleton. The fourth child was one of the secondaries in a barrow-ditch, whilst the fifth one was in a unique position. It adjoined the only north-south burial which lacked a barrow-ditch, and one is tempted to regard it as a secondary burial. Perhaps the burial-rite for children was as secondaries in the body of the mound, for in the only instance where there was not a barrow any secondary grave would have had to cut into the natural gravel and would thus survive ploughing.

There were five examples of multiple burial, one of which, an adult and two children superimposed, has already been mentioned. Another was odd in that a skeleton had been disturbed by a later skeleton in the same grave, but the other three examples were large graves with skeletons side by side. One was north-south orientated and held crouched skeletons arranged in opposite directions; the second was east-west and had one crouched and one extended skeleton; and the third was east-west and held two extended inhumations — one with a spearhead which had entered the body from the back and remained somewhere near the heart. Two other corpses had been buried still containing the weapons which had killed them — one embedded in the pelvis and the other in the vertebrae.

In a cemetery with an obvious linear arrangement, it might well be expected that the earlier burials would be found in one area and that there would be a gradual progression to later burials at the opposite end. No clear chronology is yet apparent, but there are differences between the areas: a group of burials at the north is entirely north-south orientated, has a richer collection of metal grave-goods, but few pots; in the central area are more or less equal numbers of east-west and north-south burials, but the former dwindle considerably to the south. The burials at the south end of the site have produced more pots and brooches than those in the centre, where one distinctive and close-packed group of barrows lacked any grave-goods. The significance to be attached to these differences remains to be seen, and it is unfortunate that the position of burials within the cemetery cannot be compared with a detailed typology of grave-goods to establish a chronology. The grave-goods vary little and are not numerous — only amongst the brooches is there any prospect of typological classification.

The Burton Fleming site may be disappointing from the chronological viewpoint, but its position relative to contemporary sites is potentially of great importance. In close proximity there are many Iron Age cemeteries, groups, and isolated barrows whose relationship to one another warrants close examination. Furthermore, because of aerial photography, these burial sites can be seen amongst contemporary settlements and fields; within this area one could break new ground by exploring the settlements of a culture known so far only from its burials.

The situation of the Burton Fleming cemetery, in a gravel-filled valley within the chalk, is by no means an unusual location for a cemetery of the Arras Culture. South of Rudston many narrow tongues of gravel stretch westwards from Holderness up the chalk valleys, and one of the most prominent of these, once followed by the Malton and Driffield Junction Railway, is currently being worked for its gravel. This is the valley, or slack, which houses at its eastern end, near Driffield, another Gypsey Race, and which then extends westwards through the parishes of Garton and Wetwang; the archeologists working in advance of gravel excavators have named their site successively Garton Slack, and then Wetwang Slack. This was the scene of considerable activity by Mortimer — he included 35 barrows in his Garton Slack Group (Mortimer 1905:208-70) — and it was the impending destruction of one of his barrows which re-established interest in the site in 1965. That barrow, and some other features, was excavated for the Inspectorate of Ancient Monuments by T.C.M. Brewster, whilst other material including the remains of an extensive La Tène cemetery was rescued from the quarry face by C. and E. Grantham. From 1968 onwards the work at Garton Slack warranted a full-time team, which was directed by Brewster until his retirement from the field in 1975, when the work was taken over by J.S. Dent (p.103 for further details). Several small groups and isolated La Tène burials were excavated by Brewster, and in Dent's first season another extensive square-barrow cemetery was reached.

This is not the place for a complete survey of the Garton/Wetwang Slack discoveries, for the work has yet to be concluded and the excavators have to publish their reports. But it would be wrong to ignore the site, and some of the finds must be briefly mentioned. The Grantham's cemetery was not particularly rich in grave-goods, but their collection includes a fine swan's-neck pin, four brooches and other pieces (p.102). The groups and odd barrows excavated by Brewster were more productive, an outstanding discovery being the first vehicle burial of the Arras Culture to be excavated in modern times (p.20). Another barrow produced a skeleton accompanied by an iron mirror. On a rather more mundane level, it is interesting to note secondary burials in barrow-ditches — including several infants. Dent's cemetery was also comparatively rich, with 30 brooches, 13 bracelets (7 of iron), 5 necklaces, an iron sword and a piece of a shield, but only 4 pots (Dent, personal letter 29/6/77). There were no east-west orientated extended or flexed primary burials in this cemetery — the sword was found with a typical north-south orientated crouched skeleton — but one of Brewster's square barrows had a central grave with an east-west extended skeleton (A.E. 1970:13).

The excavators at Garton/Wetwang Slack have had to work without the assistance of aerial photography because the thick soil cover over the gravel has blanketed the effect of growing crops over archaeological remains. To this disadvantage is added the restrictions imposed by the threatened area, for the narrow strip of gravel is to some extent out of context, and the further difficulty of correlating the work of different excavators. But from an Iron Age point of view — other periods are also represented by important material — the site is significant for the quality of some of the finds, and even more so for the opportunity of seeing the relationship between cemeteries and isolated burials as well as other contemporary features (ritual houses, enclosures, pits, and domestic material including dwellings and granaries are mentioned in the published notes).

While awaiting the full publication of the Garton/Wetwang Slack sites, it is instructive to return to the excavations of an earlier age, at Danes Graves. Again the cemetery is in a gravel valley, indeed the burials extend beyond the edge of the valley, for whilst most were on gravel (Greenwell 1906:260), some were cut into the solid chalk rock (Mortimer 1911:41). The valley here, Danesdale, is a slight one, and is sited almost midway between Wetwang and Rudston. By chance a considerable number of barrows — 212 have been plotted —

survive in a plantation where they are ravaged by tree-roots and rabbits. It was apparent even in the last century that the cemetery had once been considerably larger, the clues being provided by the observation of soil-marks (Greenwell 1906:255) as well as some probing (Mortimer 1911:40-1; Mortimer rarely used the probe — much favoured by his contemporaries in Champagne — because he concentrated his activities on surviving barrows). Today, aerial photography has shown that about half of the site is under plough, and there must have been about 400 barrows originally (Ramm, personal letter).

Although the barrow cemetery here is one of the few surviving monuments of the Arras Culture, it is not a site to be recommended to the visitor, for not only is it so overgrown with brambles and nettles as to be virtually inaccessible for most of the year; far worse, its neighbour is a processing plant for condemned carcases and the reeking of rotting flesh is enough to daunt the most ardent of archaeologists. But last century it was devoid of industry — "a charming spot" according to Mortimer (1897:5) — the antiquaries flocked there, and there can be few barrows not dug at one time or another.

The earliest recorded excavation appears to have been in 1721 when a party beating the bounds of the parish of Kilham — Danes Graves is at the junction of Driffield, Kilham and Nafferton — "came nigh the Danes Graves in Driffield field where out of curiosity we caused a man to dig in one of the said graves" (Mortimer 1899:287; Greenwell 1906:254, note a). Several other barrows were dug and left virtually unrecorded before the Yorkshire Antiquarian Club — already met with at Arras — opened six barrows in 1849, and a further 14 were excavated by Greenwell, in two days in March, 1864. These early excavators evidently paid as little attention to their back-filling as they did to their reports, and when Mortimer, in 1871, requested permission for a further excavation an angry owner (W.H. Harrison-Broadley, who had recently been elected M.P. for the East Riding) responded that "the investigations have been conducted so recklessly, so carelessly, and even so indecently — the graves were not even filled up again — that I have determined not to again allow them to be disturbed" (Mortimer 1899:294-96). It is typical of the rivalry between the two that Mortimer should publish this letter discrediting Greenwell. In 1881 Mortimer seized the opportunity to excavate a couple of mounds disturbed when trees were uprooted in a gale, but it took a further 16 years, and the death of Harrison-Broadley before large-scale excavations were allowed. The chance of further excavations at Danes Graves inspired a rare bout of co-operation between

Greenwell and Mortimer who, together with Thomas Boynton (Pl.3a) jointly excavated 53 burials in 1897-98. Mortimer (1911:30) records the division of responsibility between the co-directors: "the Canon taking notes; whilst Mr Boynton and I assisted in excavating... I also took notes"! After 1898 the field was left to Mortimer, who dug a further 26 burials between 1899 and 1909.

Within the cemetery the barrows "are not arranged with any regularity" (Greenwell 1906:259), although Mortimer observed that at the western end of the wood they were roughly in lines (1897:1) which accords well with Burton Fleming. Mortimer also noticed that the northern barrows had fewer grave-goods than those to the south

skeletons were orientated north-south and on their left side. At Danes Graves 66 skeletons were on the left side, 23 on the right; 62 were orientated with the skull between north-east and north, and 24 at the opposite extreme, between south-west and south; only 12 had their skulls in other directions (see **Appendix, pp.99-101; Greenwell 1906:261,** recorded slightly different figures). These figures are quite similar to those from the comparable north-south graves at Burton Fleming, the main difference being more skeletons on their right sides (26% at Danes Graves, 14% at Burton Fleming). Comparison between the grave-goods of the two groups (i.e. excluding the Burton Fleming east-west burials) is also close:

	Recorded Skeletons	Brooches (%)	Pots (%)	Bracelets (%)	Beads (%)	Pins (%)
Danes Graves	114	30‡ (26)	17 (15)	6 (5)	2 (2)	1 (1)
Burton Fleming	153	58 (38)	34 (22)	7 (5)	4 (3)	1 (1)
‡ (14 definite brooches, to which I have added 16 unidentified objects of bronze or iron)						

(1911:45-6). According to the measurements of the antiquaries, the barrows varied from 10ft (3m) to 33ft (10m) in diameter and in height up to 5ft (1.5m) (Proctor 1855:183) although few were more than 3ft (1m). Of the larger barrows, no.41 (barrow numbers are those used in the Appendix, p.99) was 33ft (10m) diameter and had a skeleton with the wheel-headed pin; no.46 (30ft; 9m) had a multiple burial; and no.43 (27ft; 8m) had a cart-burial. Greenwell refers to shallow ditches round the barrows (1906:260) and Mortimer in one instance specifies "a distinct circular trench" (1911:32). No square-plan ditches were observed, but it would be particularly difficult to recognise a square in the undergrowth, and air photographs show distinctively square examples in the adjoining ploughed fields. Each barrow had a single central burial in a grave sometimes no more than a scoop in the original top-soil (Greenwell 1906:260); Mortimer records graves only 6in (15cm) and 8in (20cm) deep (1911:38), and "once the body had been laid on the original surface soil" (Greenwell 1906:260). The average depth of grave was 1ft 6in (45cm); 3ft 6in (1m) was an "unusually great depth" (Mortimer 1911:39), although one grave 4ft 6in (1.37m) deep was recorded (*Ibid*: 43).

The skeletons were crouched or contracted — "all laid in a contracted position" (Greenwell 1906:260), and although Mortimer uses the word 'flexed' occasionally, it seems to have been regarded as a synonym for 'crouched' (e.g. Mortimer 1911:43). Never, it would seem, was a skeleton extended. After reading the Burton Fleming account, it will come as no surprise that the vast majority of

The Danes Graves grave-goods were limited to the same range as Burton Fleming, with the exception of a cart-burial (p.20) and a single spindle-whorl. At Burton Fleming the spindle-whorl was an accompaniment of extended east-west graves, but here it was found with a crouched or contracted inhumation whose skull was to the north-east (Mortimer 1911:33). Coffins were absent, or unobserved (Greenwell 1906:261). No weapons were found with the skeletons, and unlike Burton Fleming and Garton Slack there were no spear-heads embedded in skeletons — although Mortimer does mention a couple of skulls with deep gashes (1897:8, table, no.15; 1911:45).

Multiple burial was a rarity: four graves held two adult skeletons, side by side (no.67, Mortimer 1911:34, and no.93, *Ibid*:40), superimposed (no.56, *Ibid*:32-3) and arranged at right angles to one another (no.43, Fig.5), whilst in another there was an adult and a small child (no.85, *Ibid*:38). More complex was the arrangement in no.46 (Mortimer 1897:4-5) where five skeletons were found: skeletons E and D were on the floor of the grave, aligned but in opposite directions; C was superimposed on D, but the opposite way round; in one corner was a young child (B), with another (A) at the top of the grave. The burials of children were extremely rare, for apart from those just mentioned there was one in a secondary position in the body of a mound (no.15, Greenwell 1865:110) and three primary burials (no.70, Mortimer 1911:34; no.37, Mortimer 1897:8, table, no.7; and no.105, Mortimer 1911:45).

Pig-bones, usually the humerus but occasionally other parts, were found with several of the skeletons at Danes Graves, as at Burton Fleming. In one grave (no.73, Mortimer 1911:34-5, and fig.2) two complete skeletons of pigs were found — one on either side of the crouched human skeleton — and the skeletons of two goats, also one on either side of the human, completed the group. Another Danes Graves burial had goats arranged in a similar way (no.19, Greenwell 1865:110), and a small Calais Wold barrow excavated by Mortimer (1905:163-4, and fig.411) with a pig and two goats alongside a crouched burial, is almost certainly La Tène (p.99).

Although more recently excavated, the cemetery at Eastburn gives much less information: the site was discovered during the construction of Driffield aerodrome just before the Second World War and the rescue excavations were incomplete and not fully recorded. Burials were found in a stripped area 100 yards by 60 yards, and Thomas Sheppard, Director of the Hull Museums, observed 50 graves there, each surrounded by a circular trench (Sheppard 1939:37). These graves were rapidly emptied, the skeletons were in poor condition and grave-goods were few. There were 'occasionally' two skeletons in a grave, but only one of these is detailed — an adult and a child (*Ibid*:36, figure, C). An iron involuted brooch, part of another, and a pot were found. Further discoveries were made a year later, but the details are even more vague. The skeleton of a female, better preserved than the others, was removed to Hull Museums where it is still on exhibition (*Ibid*:39, and pl.ii; p.36, figure, E — about 70 yards from the stripped area). The published plan shows the positions of two other isolated skeletons (*Ibid*:36, figure, F and L) as well as an area excavation some 100 yards by 25 yards, which is not mentioned in the text. Within this second area three points are marked, two pots (J and K), and H "jet ring and ornaments". The pots are presumably two of the three listed and illustrated (*Ibid*:39-40, and pl.iii) each with a pig humerus inside and each having accompanied a skeleton. There is no mention of the jet ring in the text, but there is a list of other objects: a bronze bracelet, bronze tube (shield fragment) and brooch are specifically stated to have been found with burials; a spear-head, sword, a second tube and two other bronze objects were also found and the implication is that they too were found with burials. It is apparent from the report that these excavations were not closely observed, but there is no mention of an extended skeleton (except for a Saxon burial) and the crouched burial which was photographed and lifted was regarded as having the "characteristic attitude" (*Ibid*:39). It would seem that the sword and shield(s) were found with crouched burials; the spearhead, of course, could have been left in a fatal wound.

The cemetery at Scorborough has been investigated twice, but few barrows have been excavated and no grave-goods recovered. Nonetheless it is interesting and remarkable being without doubt the finest surviving monument of the Arras Culture and one of the best-preserved barrow cemeteries in the country. The site is on damp and heavy clay-land which has never been used for anything other than pasture, and it adjoins medieval fish-ponds — which might have removed some of the barrows — in a field south-east of Scorborough Hall. At least 120 small barrows survive (Fig.4), and have recently been surveyed at the same time as steps were taken to ensure their preservation (Stead 1975).

Above half the barrows are only 4m to 5.5m in diameter and between 15 and 30cm high. Some are even smaller — 2 to 3m diameter and 8 to 12cm high. It is interesting to see that the very small barrows are concentrated in a group (nos.107-120) at one end of the cemetery, which recalls the position at Arras, where several of the very small barrows are at the south-east end of the site (nos.76-8, 82-4, and 86-7). One of the small examples at Scorborough was excavated in 1970 in order to prove that such small features were indeed barrows. It produced a contracted inhumation, with the skull at the south-east end, in a grave only 40cm deep. The condition of the skeleton was extremely poor, and this recalls Mortimer's experience when he dug six mounds here in 1895. The skeletons he found were contracted; three of them were on the left side with the skull at the north end — the most usual Arras Culture position; two had their skulls towards the south; and of the other no bones had survived (Mortimer 1895). Nine of the Scorborough barrows are scarred with the marks of previous excavations, and it has proved possible to identify those dug by Mortimer (Stead 1975:5).

The largest Scorborough barrows extend up to 15.6m diameter, and there are 14 barrows with diameters in excess of 7m. Some of these are curiously flat (*Ibid*:6, fig.3, profile F) — the barrow with the largest diameter is only 34cm high; and the most impressive barrows on the site (nos.64 and 65, respectively 68cm and 75cm high and 11.5m and 10.4m diameter) are distinctively square in plan.

The excavations in the barrow cemeteries have produced very consistent results, and there can be no doubt that these sites belong to the same culture. Danes Graves has produced a vehicle burial and air photographs have revealed many square barrows there; Scorborough has at least a couple of square barrows; and the two sites most thoroughly excavated under modern conditions, Burton Fleming and Wetwang Slack, have produced the remains of masses of square barrows.

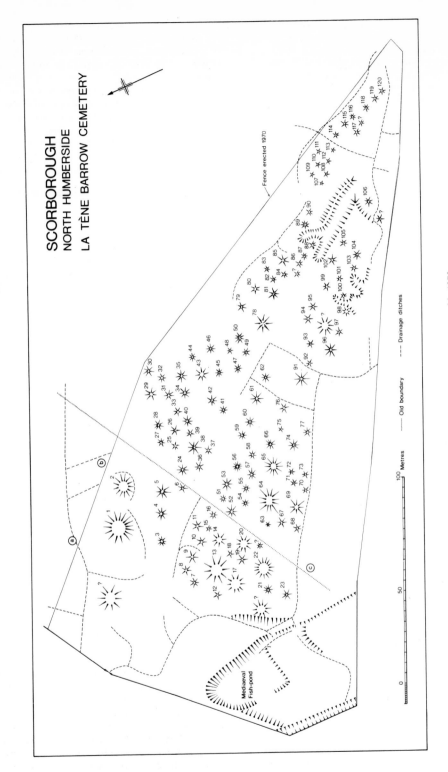

4. *Plan of the Scorborough cemetery, surveyed in 1970.*

19

3. Cart-Burials

'Vehicle-burial' is used here as a general term to cover both 'cart-burial' (two wheels) and 'waggon-burial' (four wheels). Vehicle-burial can thus be used to translate exactly the French 'sépulture à char' and the German 'Wagengrab' in instances where it is not clear whether four or two wheels were found, or where the term is used to cover both cart-burials and waggon-burials. 'Chariot-burial' has been discarded because it has often been taken to imply that the vehicle was a war-chariot. The well-known engravings of cart-burials in Champagne, showing the skeleton accompanied by weapons, naturally suggest that the vehicle was also part of the warrior's panoply. But not all cart-burials are associated with weapons — even in Champagne — and in Yorkshire weapons are absent. Furthermore, on the continent there is a continuity in tradition between burials with Hallstatt waggons and La Tène carts (pp.26 and 28), and the waggons are unlikely to have been used in war. Both Hallstatt and La Tène vehicles were probably regarded in the same light when placed in the grave, possibly in a limited funerary capacity carrying the corpse to the grave, or perhaps going beyond that and speeding the journey to the other world.

The Yorkshire cart-burials may be divided into two groups: those in which the vehicle has been dismantled; and those in which it has been buried complete. The former group is the better documented, for in 1897 an example was excavated at Danes Graves by Mortimer and Greenwell and a fairly detailed account with a plan was published (Fig 5); recently, in 1971, another was excavated with very great care by Brewster, at Garton Slack, and useful interim notices have been published, although the full report is not yet available.

The Danes Graves cart-burial (Mortimer 1897: 3-4; 1898:121-4; Greenwell 1906:276-8) was under a mound 27ft (8.2m) diameter and 3ft (1m) high, in a grave 8½ft (2.5m) by 7½ft (2.3m) and 2½ft (75cm) deep. The main axis of the grave was north and south; in the western half were the remains of two wheels, flat on the floor; and in the eastern half there were two skeletons. The wheels were represented by iron tyres and iron nave-hoops, and there were two linch-pins and various harness rings nearby. Mortimer (1897:4) notes "a clear and distinct cavity, two inches (5cm) wide, in the soil filling the grave close above the wheels. This cavity extended horizontally more than 4 feet (1.2m) in a curved direction, and was caused unquestionably by something which had gone to decay — probably the curved frame of one of the sides of the chariot". Of the skeletons, the more northerly was crouched, orientated south-west to north-east, on its right side, and accompanied by an iron and bronze brooch and

some pig-bones. The second skeleton was also crouched, but orientated north-south, on its left side, and without surviving personal possessions.

The Garton Slack cart-burial (Brewster 1971) had been at the centre of a square barrow; all trace of the mound had disappeared, but the surviving ditch showed that it had measured 10.4m square. The central grave was trapezoidal, 3.6m long by 1.8m wide at the one end and 3.2m wide at the other. The two wheels had been dismantled and flattened — very similar to Danes Graves — but the skeleton had been set over the top of them (Pl.3b). The inhumation had been flexed on its left side, orientated north-south, and with the skull at the north end facing east. It was accompanied by pig-bones; two horse-bits were found over the body; and five terrets, two strap-links, and the remains possibly of a whip were also found. The wheels had each had twelve spokes — identified by stains in the grave-filling — and metal remains included four nave-hoops (three of bronze and an odd one of iron) but, curiously, no linch-pins. Fragments of sheet bronze with traces of wood attached were found in the filling of the grave, and the excavator suggested that this could have belonged to the body of the vehicle, which might have been inverted over the grave. One of the most interesting features of this burial was the surviving traces of a cart-pole.

More than twenty years before the discovery of the Danes Graves cart-burial, Greenwell had excavated one at Beverley, in 1875, under a barrow 21ft (6.5m) diameter and 2ft (60cm) high (Greenwell 1877:456; 1906:278). The grave was orientated north-south and measured 6¼ft (1.9m) long by 4½ft (1.4m) wide and 2¾ft (84cm) deep. Soil conditions had destroyed any trace of bone, and the only finds were objects of iron in poor condition. "About the middle of the grave, towards the east side, were the tires of two wheels, laid flat, side by side, each having within it a ring, the hoop of the respective naves... on the west side of the grave were two snaffle-bits" (Greenwell 1906:278).

The three cart-burials found at Arras employed the same rite — in one, recorded by Greenwell, the wheels were clearly flat on the floor of the grave and, perhaps like Danes Graves, at one side of the grave, alongside the skeleton. The two cart-burials excavated by Stillingfleet and party had the skeleton central to the two wheels, a position similar to Garton Slack, although the wheels were 'inclining' from the skeleton. Greenwell's Arras burial, the Lady's Barrow (named by Fox 1958:6, in keeping with the titles given by the excavators to the other three important Arras grave-groups) was found by chance in the course of excavating a chalk-pit, and was recorded by Greenwell (1877:454-7; 1906:279,

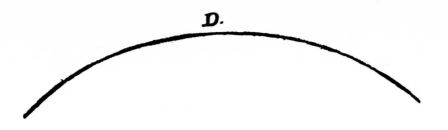

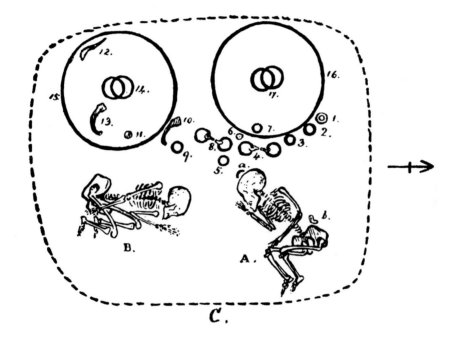

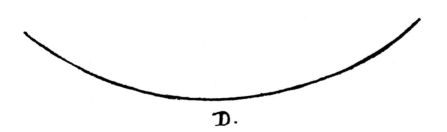

5.   *Plan of the cart-burial at Danes Graves; from J.R. Mortimer 1897: pl.ii.*

284-6). Under a barrow 14ft (4.3m) diameter and 1½ft (45cm) high was a huge circular grave, 12ft (3.6m) diameter and 3ft (1m) deep. About the middle of the grave was the skeleton of a woman (identified by Rolleston, see report in Greenwell 1877:457) on its left side, with the head at the north end (Greenwell 1906:284, but at the *west* end in 1877:454) and accompanied by bones from two pigs. According to the workmen who uncovered the grave the skeleton had been extended; beyond that it is not clear how much of the layout of this grave Greenwell himself observed and how much he learnt from the workmen. "Underneath the head of the woman was a mirror. Behind the back were the iron tires of two wheels laid partly the one over the other, and within each tire were two bronze hoops, those of the corresponding naves, and a circular piece of iron. In front of the face were two bits laid slightly above the bottom of the grave" (Greenwell 1906:284-5). A small bronze object, possibly from the shank of a whip, was also found in the grave, and in examining the spoil thrown out by the workmen, Greenwell discovered a terret.

The King's Barrow, Arras, (Stillingfleet 1846:28-30) had been almost levelled, but its diameter was 8 to 9 yards (8m) and it covered a circular grave 11 or 12ft (3.5m) diameter and only about 1½ft (45cm) deep. The description of the skeleton ("that of an old man") is obscure — it might have been flexed or crouched — but it was certainly orientated north-south, and near the skull were the skulls of two pigs (complete skeletons of the pigs were depicted in the Stillingfleet MS, Greenwell 1906:279, note a). "Inclining from the skeleton, on each side, had been placed a wheel... each of these wheels had originally rested on a horse... the head of each horse being not far from that of the charioteer". To the west of the human skeleton was a pair of linch-pins, and other items of harness seem to have been found on the same side — two harness rings, five terrets and two horse-bits.

The Charioteer's Barrow (Stillingfleet 1846:30-1) was less than 2ft (60cm) high and only 8ft (2.5m) diameter. The measurements of the grave are not recorded, nor are there any details of the skeleton, although by implication it was orientated north-south. "Inclining from the body of the British warrior, both on the western and on the eastern side, had been placed a wheel and a bridle bit, with iron rings which had belonged to the chariot, or to its trappings". The remaining items from this grave are oddities: a bronze disc, interpreted by the excavators as a shield-boss, which had been in contact with the under part of the skull, as well as a bronze case and two antler objects which were found on top of the skeleton.

In contrast to this practice of burying a dismantled vehicle in a grave, is the rite observed at Pexton

Moor, where a cart had been buried entire, the wheels in an upright position. The circumstances of this discovery were not ideal: the barrow was opened in 1911, when one iron tyre was excavated (Kirk:1911), it was re-examined 24 years later when the other tyre and further features were recorded, and another 24 years had to pass before the report was published (Stead 1959). Unlike the burials discussed so far, on or adjoining the chalk wolds, this one was on the limestone hills, and its barrow was composed mainly of sand. It was surrounded by a square-plan barrow ditch and had been 17ft (5.2m) across and, at the time of its first excavation, about 4ft (1.2m) or 5ft (1.5m) high. There was no grave, but the cart-wheels had been buried in two shallow pits, some 10in (25cm) deep, orientated almost diagonally to the square-plan ditch. No bones survived, and the only other find was a horse-bit, discovered some 5ft (1.5m) in advance of one of the wheel-holes.

Only 8km away from the Pexton Moor cart-burial another had been found in the middle of the nineteenth century, at Cawthorn Camps. Several features recall the Pexton Moor burial, and it seems likely that this cart, too, had been buried upright. The grave had been excavated by Thomas Kendall, of Pickering, and the only published account is given by Mortimer (1905:361) who obtained his information from Kendall and his foreman — some years after the excavation. The barrow had been built mainly of sand, and was about 3ft (1m) high. "One of the chariot wheels was pressed down nearly flat, and the decayed wood of the spokes, which numbered only four, was shown very clearly. The other wheel stood upright, and nearly reached to the top of the barrow... the pole reached eastwards about 7 feet (2m) from the body of the chariot, and at the terminal end were decayed hooks and rings of iron and brass (bronze)". No human or animal bones were found, and there was no grave — the vehicle "seemed to have been placed on the old surface line under the barrow".

The only other vehicle-burial from which part of a grave-group survives cannot clearly be assigned to either the dismantled Arras or the intact Pexton Moor types. It was found by chance at Hunmanby in 1907, and had been badly disturbed — half of it had slipped away in a fall from the edge of a quarry — but Sheppard was able to examine the site and excavate the surviving part of the grave. His description (Sheppard 1907) is obscure in places, and he did not publish a plan of the remains. The burial was under a slight mound, in a grave cut into natural gravel to a depth of 3ft 6in (1.1m). Sheppard records that the grave was "basin-shaped" and measured 11ft 6in (3.5m) at the top; Greenwell (1906:311) in a post-script to his paper, refers to this measurement as the diameter, so presumably Sheppard's basin-

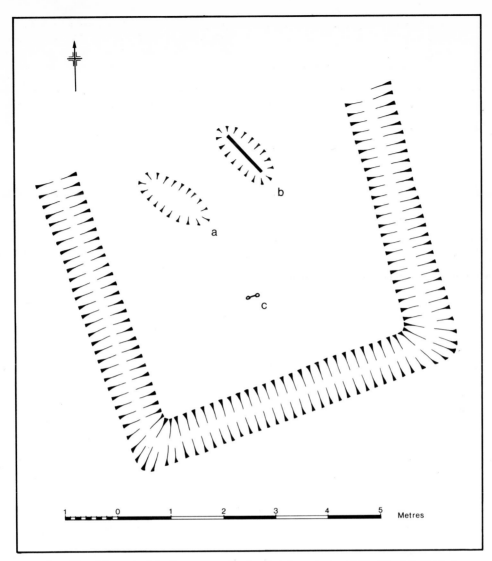

6.   *Plan of the cart-burial at Pexton Moor; based on the information provided by Miss A.E. Welsford.*

shape means that the grave was circular rather than referring solely to its profile. The grave had sloping sides, and the base was not quite horizontal, being about 6in (15cm) deeper at one end than at the other. The only surviving tyre (fragments of the other were found at the bottom of the quarry) had been buried in an upright position and had collapsed so that its upper part was only a foot (30cm) from the bottom of the grave, leaving the nave-hoop sandwiched between the upper and lower portions of the crushed tyre. Other grave-goods included bronze fragments, possibly from a shield, a horse-bit, terret and rein-ring, but their positions relative to the tyre are not recorded. The only bones

mentioned in the report, "a fragment of bone and parts of two teeth of a horse, in an advanced state of decay" were found immediately below the surviving tyre. The Hunmanby burial has one feature of the Arras-type cart-burials — it was in a large apparently circular grave; on geographical grounds it would also be reasonable to link it with the burials on the Wolds. But the surviving tyre was certainly not flat on the floor of the grave, and Sheppard was of the opinion that "the position of the iron demonstrated that the wheel, and presumably the chariot also, had been buried in its normal standing position". Upright wheels do not necessarily mean that the vehicle was intact — at Vix, for instance, the vehicle

23

had been dismantled but the wheels were upright in the grave (Joffroy 1958:106).

There are other references to vehicle-burials in the area of the Arras Culture, and in one instance (Middleton-on-the-Wolds) a linch-pin has survived to give further credence to the account. Mortimer (1905:358-60) records this possible Middleton cart-burial, along with equally vague references which might be interpreted as vehicle-burials at Seamer (but see Rutter & Duke 1958:62) and Huggate. In the Yorkshire Antiquarian Club MS., at the Yorkshire Museum, there is also a reference to barrows at Huggate "examined many years since by Lord Burlington who was said to have found in them the wheel of a chariot", and the Morfitt MSS. in the same collection raise the faint possibility of a cart-burial at Hornsea (Stead 1965a:93-4). But these accounts are of very little significance.

Various writers have referred to cart-burials elsewhere in England, but not one will stand up to critical examination, and there is little point in reciting the list. For a cart-burial there must, at least, be evidence for a couple of iron tyres, and it seems clear that in England all the well-documented examples are restricted in distribution to within 35km of Garton Slack. On the continent the rite is also found, in some numbers in Champagne and the Middle Rhine, and in smaller groups elsewhere. These continental examples will be examined briefly in order to establish points of similarity and difference.

The largest group of cart-burials found on the continent is that in Champagne, where some 140 examples can be listed and many others have doubtless been excavated without record (see Joffroy & Bretz-Mahler 1959 for a general account). The River Aisne defines their distribution on the north and the east, whilst to the south there are few beyond the valley of the River Marne, and on the west side the main distribution is defined by the hills to the south of Rheims. Most of these burials are on the great chalk plain of Champagne, centred on the River Vesle, and mainly in the department of Marne, although they extend into the southern part of Ardennes. To the west there is a scattered distribution of cart-burials, particularly along the valley of the River Aisne. Many of the Champagne burials were excavated in the second half of last century, along with thousands of more ordinary burials found in the same cemeteries; it has been estimated that more than 12,000 Iron Age burials had been excavated in Champagne up to 1929 (Favret 1929:15, note 1). Excavation techniques were primitive and publication was usually ignored, so from these extensive excavations there is in fact very little real information. In fairness to the nineteenth-century excavators of Champagne, though they deserve little sympathy, it is worth noting that at least a third (probably more, but the records are so inadequate) of the cart-burials had been previously disturbed.

It seems that always the cart-burial was found in a cemetery; some were very extensive — 270 burials at Mairy-sur-Marne, including 14 cart-burials (Favret 1913) — but others in so far as they were explored seem to have been quite small. Most of the graves in these cemeteries seem to have been flat, without covering barrows, but several of the cart-burials had surrounding circular or square-plan ditches which probably defined barrows long since ploughed away. The standard of excavation does not allow one to appreciate how many of these enclosures or barrows there were in each cemetery, but a well-excavated cemetery at Manre, "Mont Troté", (Ardennes) had a circular ditch round the only vehicle-burial and the excavator suggested that this represented a barrow (Quatreville 1972:16-18). Two comparable circular enclosures and two small square enclosures were also found at Mont Troté, but the vast majority of the 104 graves in the cemetery were unenclosed. Most barrows in Champagne have been ploughed flat, but some still survive, and one at Epoye, "La Motelle", (Marne) covered a cart-burial (Bosteaux-Paris 1892).

The plans of the Champagne cart-burials varied in shape, with the most elaborate form being like Somme Bionne, "L'Homme Mort", (Marne), (Morel 1898:pl.7; cf. Smith 1905: pl.ii). This grave was large and rectangular, 2.85m by 1.8m and 1.15m deep, with separate holes cut below the floor to receive the wheels, a shallow central trench in front for the cart-pole, and at the end of the pole-trench a cross-trench to house the harness. The grave was at the centre of a circle 16m diameter, defined by a ditch 1m deep. Only three other plans are known to conform with this, although other examples could have been only partly excavated. Certainly the simple rectangular grave, lacking the pole-trench and harness-trench, seems to have been far more common (see sketch plans, Stead 1965a: 11-12, figs.5 and 6). Another variety had a trapezoidal grave, comparable to that at Garton Slack, and one of the best examples of this form, from Somme Tourbe, "La Gorge Meillet", (Marne), had clearly never had separate pole- and harness-trenches for the harness was found on a wide ledge at the foot of the grave (Fourdrignier 1878:pl.i). One constant feature of the plans of all these Champagne vehicle-burials is that the wheels had been sunk in separate holes, a feature noted at Pexton Moor, although the parallel with Pexton Moor cannot be pushed far, for all the Champagne cart-burials were in grave-pits.

The principal vehicle remains were iron tyres, the nave-hoops of the wheels and linch-pins, as in Yorkshire; although the Champagne wheels differed

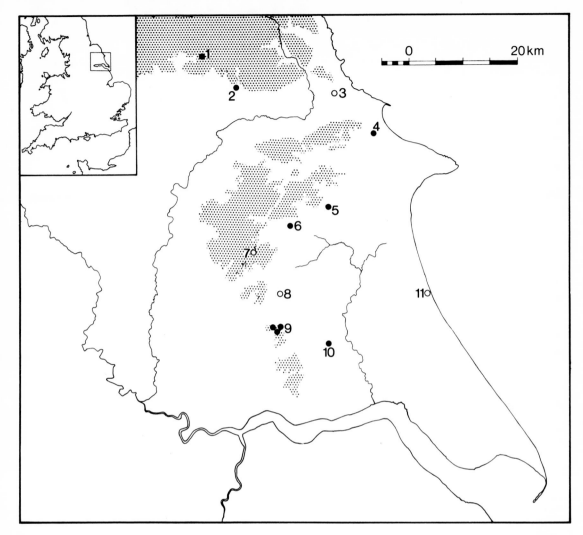

7. *Distribution of La Tène cart-burials in Yorkshire and Humberside: 1, Cawthorn Camps; 2, Pexton Moor; 3, Seamer; 4, Hunmanby; 5, Danes Graves; 6, Garton Slack; 7, Huggate; 8, Middleton-on-the-Wolds; 9, Arras; 10, Beverley; 11, Hornsea. (land over 120m stipled).*

in having iron fittings apparently used to join a single-piece felloe (Stead 1965b:261, fig.2a and b). Other iron rings, and pieces interpreted as swingle-tree fittings (*Ibid*: fig.2c; see now Haffner 1976) regularly occur in these graves. Harness includes horse-bits, but not specialised terrets or yoke-fittings, only simple harness rings.

The Champagne cart-burials were often lavishly equipped with a variety of pots, sometimes metal vessels, as well as personal ornaments and quite often a range of weapons. The opulence of these grave-goods makes their Yorkshire counterparts seem particularly poverty-stricken, although a familiar note is struck by the frequent occurrence of

pig-bones. Grave-goods are really the only means of establishing the sex of the skeletons which accompanied these vehicles, for the human bones were not studied, and none have survived. The frequent appearance of weapons confirms the obvious, that men were commonly buried with the carts — indeed this is the main reason for regarding the vehicles as war-chariots — but there are reasonable grounds for supposing that some of the skeletons were female. Certainly at Prunay, "Les Commelles", (Marne), (Favret 1929:23-5) and Juniville, "Le Mont de Croupsault", (Ardennes), (Fourcart 1909) the skeletons were decorated with torcs and bracelets, and at the latter site a pair of

25

gold ear-rings was also found. Nicaise (1885) went to some length to show that in Champagne torcs were found only with women. There are several examples of two skeletons in the one grave, either side by side or superimposed; such double, and even triple, burials are frequent in Marnian cemeteries. Sometimes an adult was accompanied by a child, and in a cart-burial at Bouy, "Les Varilles", (Marne), (Nicaise 1884:38) an adult had been buried between two children. The skeletons in these Champagne burials were invariably fully extended, and normally orientated west-east.

Most cart-burials in Champagne seem to date from La Tène I; none is associated with La Tène II grave-goods. There are at least two two-wheeled vehicles with Late Hallstatt brooches, and one particularly interesting burial at Chouilly, "Les Jogasses", (Marne), (Favret 1936:65-9) where a waggon had been interred. The waggon had wheels set in four wheel-holes, and it came from the Late Hallstatt part of the Chouilly cemetery; it is clearly the immediate fore-runner of the Marnian cart-burial tradition.

La Tène II/III vehicle-burials do exist in France, mainly to the west of Champagne, and they have something in common with a site well to the north, in Belgium. These north-western sites may be loosely grouped, and considered together; unfortunately their common factors include the lack of properly recorded excavation and incompletely surviving grave-groups, but some outstanding objects remain. The recent re-publication of the remains of a vehicle-burial from Attichy, (Oise), (Duval & Blanchet 1974) has served to link the principal sites in this area, and has considerably strengthened the argument for a Paris provenance for an important group of harness and cart-fittings now in the Musée des Antiquités Nationales (Cowen 1934; Jacobsthal 1944: 184; Stead 1965a:15). From Attichy there are two undecorated terrets and the base of a third — a different type, with elaborate plastic ornament. The undecorated terrets match exactly an example from Leval-Trahegnies, "La Courte", (Belgium), (Mariën 1961:51, no.53) — a site which also produced a fine pair of linch-pins (*Ibid*:40-5, nos.54 and 55). The Leval-Trahegnies linch-pins, with strong plastic faces, are very reminiscent of that said to have been found at Paris (Jacobsthal 1944: no.163); and with the Paris linch-pin is a pair of terrets with which the decorated fragment from Attichy may be compared. The close links between these three sites are unmistakeable. Another site, on the outskirts of Paris, Nanterre, may be compared with this group on more than geographical grounds. It had large iron tyres (1.3m diameter, according to Hubert 1900:411) considerably larger than those found in Champagne, but more comparable with the fragments from Attichy

(1.1m to 1.2m). Furthermore, the Nanterre linch-pin, with large box-head, is of the same general type as the Paris linch-pin although it lacks the plastic decoration; a decorated example from Niederweis, near Trier, (Jacobsthal 1944:no.161) brings the comparison closer, for it shares with the Nanterre linch-pin a bronze clip below the head. Finally, Nanterre has a terret — a type unknown from Champagne but represented, in rather different forms, at the other three sites considered here. Duval and Blanchet would add the Armentières, (Aisne), vehicle-burials, as well as Inglemare, Belbeuf, (Seine-Maritime), (Duval 1975), to this group on the grounds that they have bronze nave-hoops which are unknown in Champagne but present at Nanterre. Armentières is the only French vehicle-burial associated with La Tène III brooches.

A quite different group of vehicle-burials is sited to the east in the wooded hills of the Belgian Ardennes. It has been established entirely on the basis of very recent excavations — not a single vehicle-burial was known here 20 years ago, but now there are a dozen (Cahen-Delhaye 1974 and 1975). The group is also remarkable in having a very tight distribution, for all sites fall within a radius of 9km to the north and east of Neufchâteau, in Belgian Luxembourg. Presumably the bodies were inhumated, but soil conditions have destroyed all trace of the bones. With one exception the burials are under barrows; often the barrows cover more than one grave, and the vehicle-burial is not always central. The vehicles are always in graves, never on the old ground surface, and the graves tend to have irregular shapes with some approximating to oval and trapezoidal forms. Wheel-holes are regular features, whilst pole-trenches and harness-trenches are sometimes found — features which, along with some of the vehicle fittings and other grave-goods, indicate close contact with Champagne. The grave-goods show that these burials belong to an early stage in La Tène I — considerably earlier than the finds from Leval-Trahegnies.

The nearest vehicle-burials to the Neufchâteau group are those in the Forêt des Pothées (Maubert-Fontaine) in the French department of Ardennes (Fromols 1955) some 70km away to the west, whereas the nearest cart-burials of the Champagne group are about 80km to the south-west. The cart-burials in the Forêt des Pothées may be compared with the Neufchâteau group in that they belong to a barrow cemetery, and the presence of wheel-holes links them with both Neufchâteau and Champagne; but there are few other points of comparison. The pottery from Maubert-Fontaine has been compared with Hunsrück-Eifel rather than Marnian types, and they are usually assigned to a La Tène II date.

The next important group of La Tène I vehicle-

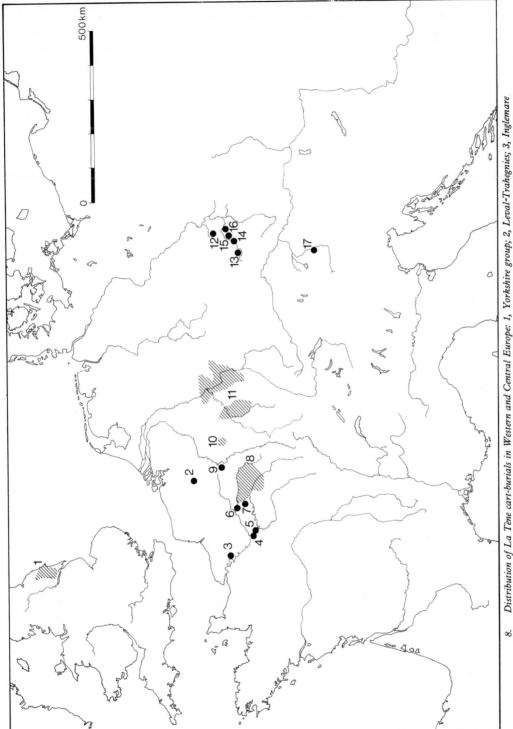

8. Distribution of La Tène cart-burials in Western and Central Europe: 1, Yorkshire group; 2, Leval-Trahegnies; 3, Inglemare (Belboef); 4, Nanterre; 5, Paris; 6, Attichy; 7, Armentières; 8, Champagne group; 9, Maubert-Fontaine; 10, Neufchâteau group; 11, Hunsrück-Eifel groups; 12, Hořovičky; 13, Mirkovice; 14, Maneìn-Hrádek; 15, Sedlec-Hůrka; 16, Želkovice; 17, Dürnburg-bei-Hallein.

burials is in the Middle Rhine area, extending from just north of Koblenz to Mannheim, and westwards into the Mosel valley and the upper reaches of the Nahe. The distribution here falls into two parts, separated by the highland of the Hunsrück, but the burial-rite is the same. A cart-burial in the cemetery at Kärlich, (Kr. Koblenz), seems to be fairly typical, with a rectangular grave, 3.2m by 1.6m and 1.5m deep, in which was found an extended skeleton, orientated west-east (Günther 1934). By the feet were a bronze beaked flagon, two iron spearheads, six amber beads, some gold bands and decorated gold sheet. The vehicle was represented by two iron tyres, whose lower parts were still upright on the floor of the grave — not sunk in separate trenches. The wheels seem to have had eight spokes, iron nave-bands, and bronze axle-caps; there were other metal fittings of the vehicle, but harness was absent. The grave was bordered by a narrow trench, possibly a bedding-trench for a timber cover, and was central to a large barrow 26m diameter, whose ditch alone survived (Rest & Röder 1941). This burial (Kärlich 4) was one of six cart-burials in a large La Tène I cemetery, and one of the others (Kärlich 5) also had a wooden burial-chamber (Ibid., with a plan, fig.41). The cart-burials from the western province of the Hunsrück-Eifel Culture have recently been collated, and the publication includes four useful grave-plans (Haffner 1976: figs.31, 36, 41 and 43).

Burial under barrows seems to have been a general feature in the Middle Rhine, and there are other instances of wooden chambers or covers. Vehicles seem to have been buried complete, with wheels upright, and usually the rite was one of inhumation. Harness was usually absent (but there is a single iron horse-bit from Waldalgesheim, aus'm Weerth 1870: pls. v and vi, fig.14; and a pair from Freisen, Kr. St. Wendel, Haffner 1976: 34, 174), and grave-goods were often rich with gold objects and imported bronzes (Harbison 1969:37-8). As in Champagne, the earliest stage is represented by a waggon, for at Bell, (Kr. Simmern), a four-wheeled vehicle had been buried in a wood-lined grave-chamber, 2.5m by 1.8m and 1.25m deep, under a barrow 22m diameter and 1m high (Rest 1948). It was the largest of 29 barrows excavated in this cemetery, and it seems clear that it was the earliest barrow in the cemetery as well (Driehaus 1966). Bell is particularly interesting for comparison with the Late Hallstatt waggon from Chouilly, "Les Jogasses", (Marne), particularly since the wheels at Bell were sunk in holes below the floor of the grave — a practice common amongst the cart-burials of Champagne. In the Middle Rhine there is certainly one cart-burial with wheel-holes — very shallow holes only 15cm deep at Gransdorf (Kr. Wittlich) (Haffner 1976:176 and fig.31) — but it seems to be a unique example.

Apart from Bell these Middle Rhine burials are La Tène I, and the third and second centuries B.C. seem devoid of vehicle-burials. But the rite re-emerges in La Tène III in the same area — at Plaidt there are La Tène I and III vehicle-burials within little more than 100m of one another (Joachim 1969:93). Apart from the chronological break there are other major differences, for in La Tène III the burial rite is cremation in flat graves, and the vehicles are represented by fragments scattered in the grave — no complete vehicle had been buried (Ibid.).

Beyond the Rhine there is a small group of cart-burials in Western Bohemia, including one recently excavated in the cemetery at Manětín-Hrádek (Soudská 1976). The grave, large (3.1m by 3.5m) and shallow (35cm), had probably been covered by a stone cairn and was enclosed by a trench which defined a squarish area 5.6 by 6.1m. Towards the northern end of the grave were two shallow hollows which had held the wheels — but the remains consisted only of iron nails; in the western half were five phalera; and to the east of the centre was a pile of calcined bones along with shreds and fragments of brooches. The cremated bones were apparently those of a child, but the excavator considered the possibility that there had originally been a central inhumation — if so, soil conditions would not have been favourable for its preservation. Other cart-burials have been found in the vicinity, the nearest being at Sedlec-Hůrka where two burials — the upper one with the remains of a cart — had been covered by a barrow. Three other sites produced cart-fittings and harness (Ibid.; Harbison 1969: 57), including Hořovičky where two iron-bound bronze phalera were decorated with human heads (Megaw 1970: no.47; Jacobsthal 1944: pl.218 g). The Sedlec Hůrka burial has been dated Hallstatt D, but the others are La Tène I.

South of this Bohemian group there are two cart-burials in the important Early La Tène cemetery at Dürrnberg-bei-Hallein, near Salzburg, Austria (Burial 44, Penninger 1972:76-80; Burial 112, Moosleitner, Pauli & Penninger 1974:76-8), and still further east isolated examples have been recorded in Hungary, Roumania and perhaps even Bulgaria (Harbison 1969:38-9, 57-8).

So far in the discussion two-wheeled Early La Tène vehicles have been traced across Europe. Four-wheeled Late Hallstatt vehicles have entered as the precursors of the La Tène tradition in Champagne, at Les Jogasses, and in the Middle Rhine, at Bell; whilst in Bohemia one two-wheeled vehicle has been dated to Hallstatt D. But the tradition is represented throughout Hallstatt C and D, mainly in the form of waggon-burials, which occur in the same area as the cart-burials in Bohemia, from whence they extend south-westwards through territory to the south of the La Tène cart-burials — from Bavaria, through the upper reaches of the Danube to Switzerland and into Burgundy. This distribution appears to have chronological significance, for the earlier, Hallstatt C, waggon-burials are in Bohemia and Bavaria, whilst further to the south-west they belong to Hallstatt D (Schiek 1954:158, fig.6); the trail then extends to the north-west, in new areas, in the La Tène period.

Whilst the Hallstatt vehicle-burials in Bohemia and along the Danube have four wheels — where the records are sufficiently detailed to determine the number (*Ibid*:163-5) — in Switzerland there seem to be some with only two wheels. The Hallstatt D burial-rite on the Swiss Plateau was mixed, with cremation giving way to inhumation, often in large barrows covering a number of burials on the old ground surface or in very shallow graves, with secondary burials higher in the mounds. Unfortunately many of the barrows here were explored long ago, and no vehicle-burial has been recorded in a modern excavation. However, there are vehicle remains from 26 barrows, including dismantled wheels, and the vague records suggest at least as many two-wheeled as four-wheeled vehicles (Drack 1958:4-9, 45; 1974a:24-9). Among the Hallstatt vehicle-burials in Eastern France there might well have been carts as well as waggons, but again the excavations were carried out many years ago. One such might have been the burial at Grandvillars, Territoire de Belfort, where the plan indicated two wheels but the surviving tyre fragments seem to add up to more (Joffroy 1958:52-4); another was the famous Tumulus de la Garenne, Sainte-Colombe, Côte-d'Or. That huge mound, 70m diameter and 4m high, was removed by a farmer in 1845-6, and immediately afterwards the site was excavated by local antiquarians. The accounts of this excavation, collected by Joffroy (*Ibid:* 57-70), are far from complete but they include a reference to the skeleton resting on two wheels side by side, which recalls the situation at Garton Slack (Pl.3b). Surviving debris includes a distinctive piece of a Late Hallstatt brooch (*Ibid:* fig.15, no.11), whilst the most important find from this grave is a sixth-century Greek bronze cauldron (*Ibid:* fig.12).

The Yorkshire cart-burials share features with their continental counterparts, but nowhere is the burial-rite precisely comparable. The Pexton Moor and Cawthorn Camps burials are perhaps closest to Europe: there the vehicles had been buried complete and upright, like most continental cart-burials. The presence of wheel-holes at Pexton Moor recalls the practice in Champagne, although in Champagne graves were always excavated in contrast to the Pexton Moor burial on the old ground surface.

Harness was found at both Pexton Moor and Cawthorn Camps but personal grave-goods were absent in market contrast to most of the continental cart-burials; and it is worth noting that the position of the skeleton in these two graves is unkown — no skeleton has been recorded from a La Tène burial north of the Vale of Pickering (soil conditions would have destroyed any trace of inhumation in most cases, although cremations should have survived).

The more common Yorkshire rite, in which the cart had been dismantled, cannot be matched in a La Tène context on the continent; a burial at Husby, Kr. Flensburg, Schleswig-Holstein, held a dismantled cart but it was accompanied by a cremation and is well beyond the geographical limits of La Tène culture (Raddatz 1967). Other La Tène III cremations contained parts of vehicles, but there can be no question of a direct link with Yorkshire. Dismantled carts do seem to occur in Late Hallstatt times, in Eastern France and in Switzerland, but the records are unfortunately inadequate. It has been suggested that there two wheels might have been placed in the grave to be representative of a four-wheeled vehicle, but this argument seems far-fetched; certainly there is no record of a single wheel having been buried to represent a two-wheeled vehicle. But if two-wheeled dismantled carts do occur in this area, other aspects of the burial-rite are quite different from Yorkshire: their large barrows, often with multiple burials contrast with the Yorkshire rite of single graves under small barrows, and harness, which is regularly found in Yorkshire is only rarely recorded in Burgundy and Switzerland.

4. Square Barrows.

The excavations at Burton Fleming and Garton/Wetwang Slack have located square barrows in their hundreds, and these features, virtually unobserved by the early antiquaries, have now become one of the most distinctive elements of the Arras Culture. The excavated examples do not stand alone, for they are but a small percentage of the many hundreds discovered by aerial photography in the last decade. They occur in large cemeteries (Pls.6b and 7), small groups (Pl.6a), and in isolation; there cannot be a parish on or adjoining the Wolds without its square barrows, and in some areas one looks with disbelief at fields which apparently lack them. As the vast majority are known from aerial photography, there are seldom traces of a mound, and the feature is represented by a grave at the centre of a square-plan ditch. But there are examples surviving as mounds and there can be little doubt that originally each one was a barrow; no excuse is made for adopting here the short-hand term 'square barrow' to describe the type.

The square barrow was recognised as a distinctive element of the Arras Culture following the 1959 excavations at Arras (Stead 1961), and the only antiquarian reference to a similar feature on the Wolds was also at Arras, seen by the Yorkshire Antiquarian Club (Proctor 1855:218). On the limestone hills, north of the Vale of Pickering, barrows tend to be better preserved — certainly before the activities of the Forestry Commission — and examples with square-plan ditches were noted by Mortimer, at Cawthorn Camps; by Greenwell, on Hutton Buscel Moor; and by Hinderwell, on Seamer Moor (Stead 1961:47-8). The observant Yorkshire Antiquarian Club also noticed two groups of square barrows at Skipwith, on scrub-land in the Vale of York (Pl.2b; Proctor 1855:187-9). But it is not easy to recognise these features in the field, particularly when the barrows are small, because the corners are soon eroded. The most obvious upstanding examples are the two at Scorborough (p.18) whose measurements (10 to 12m diameter) are greater than those of most Arras Culture barrows. Another very fine and large example is the named barrow, Loft Howe, in Wykeham Forest, shown to the writer by Douglas Smith, who has identified others in the vicinity. With smaller barrows it is easy to let ones imagination create squares out of circles and vice versa: but in the large cairn-field at Iron Howe, Snilesworth, near Helmsley (McDonnell 1963:39) several of the more substantial mounds appear to have straight sides. Firmer ground is provided by aerial photographs, although it is still not always possible to distinguish clearly between a square and a circle. Square barrows in the northern part of the Wolds have been listed by Ramm (1973; 1974) and for North Humberside by Loughlin & Miller 1979. Ramm very kindly made his distribution-map available to the writer in advance of publication (now Ramm 1976: fig. p.61), and with minor variations it forms the basis of Fig.9.

The most reliable evidence for square barrows is that of excavation, starting with the only two square barrow cemeteries to have been excavated in any detail, Burton Fleming (Pl.5) and Wetwang Slack. In the cemetery at Skipwith four barrows were examined prior to destruction in 1941, but no burials were found and their identification as barrows was disputed (Stead 1961:50). Of the Cowlam group, six square barrows from 7m to 14m across, were excavated in 1969 and 1972 (p.99); four had been previously explored by Greenwell, including one with an Early La Tène grave-group which establishes Cowlam as the site of the earliest square barrows in Yorkshire. In an isolated square barrow dug at Grindale in 1972, Manby found traces of a previous excavation which might well have been where Tindall found three brooches in 1857 (p.102). When the cart-burial at Pexton Moor was excavated for the second time, in 1935, the excavator traced three sides of a square-plan ditch defining an area 17ft (5m) across (Stead 1959:215, fig.1 and pl.xxi, b). The only other excavation of an isolated square barrow in Yorkshire was in 1970 at a site about 1km from the Scorborough cemetery; that barrow was about 10m diameter, had been levelled shortly before the excavation, and no grave was found.

Unlike the cart-burials, square barrows can be compared with related features elsewhere in England, and even in Scotland. Without doubt the most closely similar group of square barrows in Britain is that recently discovered from the air by Gordon Maxwell, Royal Commission on the Ancient and Historical Monuments of Scotland, in the valley of Lunan Water, between Forfar and Montrose, in Angus, Scotland. Several sites there have both large and small square barrows as well as ring-ditches, and there are definite central graves in the squares.

Closer to Yorkshire are the small squares observed on air photographs of the Trent Valley — a good example of six or eight squares south-east of Derby was photographed by Pickering and displayed at a symposium in London in 1974. These features occur singly or in small groups, but never in large cemeteries, and obvious central graves seem to be very rare. One example, at Aston-upon-Trent (Derbyshire) has been excavated, but without positive results (May 1970). The Aston square, one of a small group of five or six, measured 27ft (8.3m) across and its ditch produced pottery which might have been Iron Age, but excavation failed to locate a central grave. Nonetheless, it might have been a square barrow, because some of the undisputed Arras-type barrows are assumed to have had burials on the old ground surface (Arras, p.8; Cowlam, p.36; Danes Graves, p.17; Scorborough, above). But until they produce burials the squares of the Trent Valley, and others known from aerial photography in southern England, will remain in the 'possible' category.

Small surviving barrows within larger square earthworks have been noted at Cowleaze, Winterbourne Steepleton (Dorset) (28ft, 8.5m, and 35ft, 10.7m, diameter barrows; 70ft, 21m, square) and Didling Hill (Sussex); and an excavated example at Leckhampton (Gloucestershire) (35ft, 10.7m, diameter barrow; 80ft, 24m square) failed to produce dating evidence (Stead 1961:52). Another Dorset barrow, at Handley, was 29ft (8.8m) diameter and at the centre of a 50ft (15m) ditched square; excavation produced a scattered cremation on the original ground surface, associated with sherds from an undistinguished jar, and from the rapid silting of the ditch there was a Romano-British rim-sherd (White 1970). These small barrows may

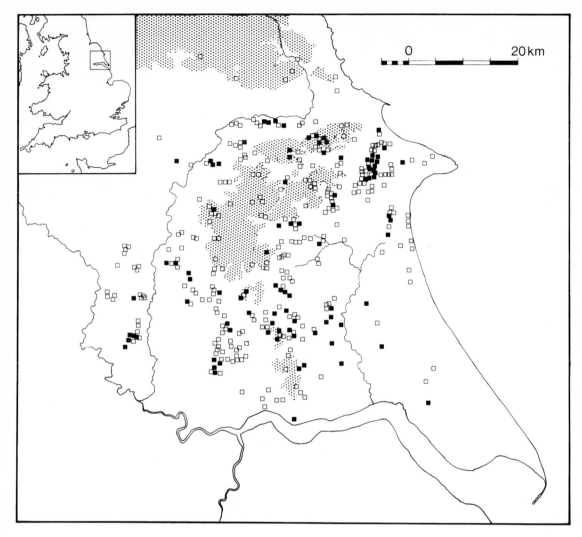

9.   Distribution of square barrows in Yorkshire and Humberside; after Ramm 1976: fig.p.61.

well be Iron Age, but none of the Yorkshire examples have similar banked enclosures, nor cremations (with the possible exception of Skipwith, p.37).

Square or rectangular enclosures associated with cremations are known in the Aylesford Culture in southern England. The extensive cemetery at King Harry Lane, St. Albans, (Herts.) produced 463 burials and seven ditched enclosures. Each enclosure seems to have had an exceptional central burial surrounded by satellites, and the largest enclosure measured some 45ft (14m) by 55ft (17m) and held 45 cremations (Stead 1969:47-50, and fig.3). The King Harry Lane cemetery was in use for about fifty years and came to a close about the time of the Roman conquest. At Baldock, (Herts.), a ditched enclosure 8m square had a single central cremation (Stead 1975b:128). This feature might well have been more usual in the Aylesford Culture, but most of the burials were found by chance and not excavated under ideal conditions, so slight ditches might well have passed un-noticed. The recent excavation at Owslebury, (Hants.), produced a small La Tène III and Early Roman cemetery with one inhumation and 18 cremations grouped in two rectangular enclosures adjoining a boundary-ditch; each enclosure had a distinguished central burial, recalling the King Harry Lane cemetery (Collis 1968:23-8).

On the continent the most impressive collection of

31

La Tène funerary enclosures is to be found in Champagne. Vast cemeteries of small square barrows cannot be matched here, but there is a range of funerary squares extending throughout the La Tène period. The most useful information is provided by recent excavations, which enable the occasional records of the earlier excavators to be set in context.

The important excavations by Rozoy at Manre and Aure, (Ardennes), have produced plans of two La Tène I cemeteries, each with a wealth of enclosures. At Manre, "Mont Troté", a cemetery of 117 inhumations (Rozoy 1970; Quatreville 1972), there were two small squares (one 7.3m square and the other 9m along one side — half had been destroyed by ploughing) each with a central burial and secondaries in the ditches. In the same cemetery there were three small circular enclosures (two similar, with diameters of 8.8m and one rather smaller, 6m to 7m across) again with central burials. One of the circles enclosed a cart-burial, and had almost certainly been a barrow; the other four small enclosures may also have been the sites of barrows, but two much larger features must be regarded in a different light. A large circle, 17.5m diameter, had a single marginal burial, perhaps unrelated; and a curious enclosure (MT.76) in the form of an elongated oval, 60m by 25m, lacked any burial.

Circular enclosures predominate in the cemetery at Aure, "Les Rouliers"; 11 circles range in diameter from 7m to 20m and in their midst is an oval, 30m by 12m and a small square. The latter, only 4m square, had a central burial and seemed to have been covered by a barrow into which two shallow secondary inhumations had been inserted (Quatreville 1973).

Small square enclosures may well have occurred in many of the La Tène I cemeteries in Champagne, but there is no reason to suppose that they were more common than at Manre and Aure. Records are few, but the following La Tène I examples may be noted: Mairy-sur-Marne, in a cemetery of 270 burials, two squares and 11 circles, each with a central burial (Favret 1913:110); St.-Rémy-sur-Bussy, "La Perrière", 10 circles (three with cart-burials) and two squares (Chertier 1972); Vert-la-Gravelle, "Le Charmont", 30 square and circular enclosures including a square with a central La Tène I cart-burial (Goury 1954:151); and Witry-lès-Reims, a square with central burial recorded by Abel Maître (Stead 1961:59-61 and fig.5).

The square enclosure with a single central burial is also found in La Tène III in Champagne, and there is every reason to suppose continuity throughout the La Tène period. Recent excavations at Ménil-Annelles and Ville-sur-Retourne, (Ardennes) have produced several examples with central La Tène III cremations (Flouest & Stead 1977) and many more sites could be listed.

Already in La Tène I there are squares enclosing several burials, and this is a feature of La Tène II and III, particularly in the region of Epernay. Three La Tène I burials at Etoges were enclosed by a square-plan ditch (Bretz-Mahler 1971:191), and nearby at Normée, "La Tempête", a rectangular enclosure about 8m by 9m held 11 La Tène II burials whilst there were three graves in an adjoining, slightly smaller, enclosure (Brisson, Loppin & Fromols 1959). Other squares enclosing several La Tène II burials were found at Fère-Champenoise, "Faubourg de Connantre", where six enclosures each about 9m square were themselves surrounded by a boundary-ditch (Brisson, Hatt & Roualet 1970). At both these sites, and at Ecury-le-Repos, "L'Homme Mort" (Brisson & Hatt 1955) burials started in La Tène II and continued into La Tène III or Gallo-Roman times.

Small funerary squares are known in the areas surrounding Champagne, particularly to the south where several have been recorded from the air but few have been excavated. There are good examples in the departments of Yonne and Côte d'Or (Parruzot 1954 and 1960; Goguey 1968:51-5 and photo 24), and some in the Seine valley at Gravon (Seine-et-Marne) are La Tène I, but in a cemetery which extends back into Urnfield times (Scherer & Mordant 1972). To the west, in Picardy, a small ditched enclosure 6m square was excavated at Allonville (Somme) in 1965 and found to contain a large shallow grave, 2.5m square, with cremated bones and pottery which has been dated towards the end of La Tène II (Ferdière & al. 1973). Small isolated square enclosures have been found in this area and elsewhere in France, wherever there is good air coverage (e.g. Agache 1976: fig.38, no.3) but excavation is needed to prove that such features are funerary and to demonstrate their date. North of Champagne, in Belgian Luxembourg, there are squares associated with La Tène III cremations at Tontelange (Bonenfant 1961).

Further south, in Burgundy, aerial photography has produced enclosures usually in the range of 15 to 25m square, and three examples have now been excavated (Joffroy 1975). The most interesting was a 13m square whose central La Tène II cremation was surmounted by a stela whose upper part had been removed in the course of agriculture but which was still standing 80cm high. Nearby, a larger enclosure, 23m square, had an empty central pit and a La Tène I brooch in the filling of the ditch.

Square ditched enclosures — some of which certainly had barrows at the centre — are found in the lower Moselle valley and the Neuwied Basin, that same Middle Rhine area with the La Tène cart-burials. As in Yorkshire, the numbers of known

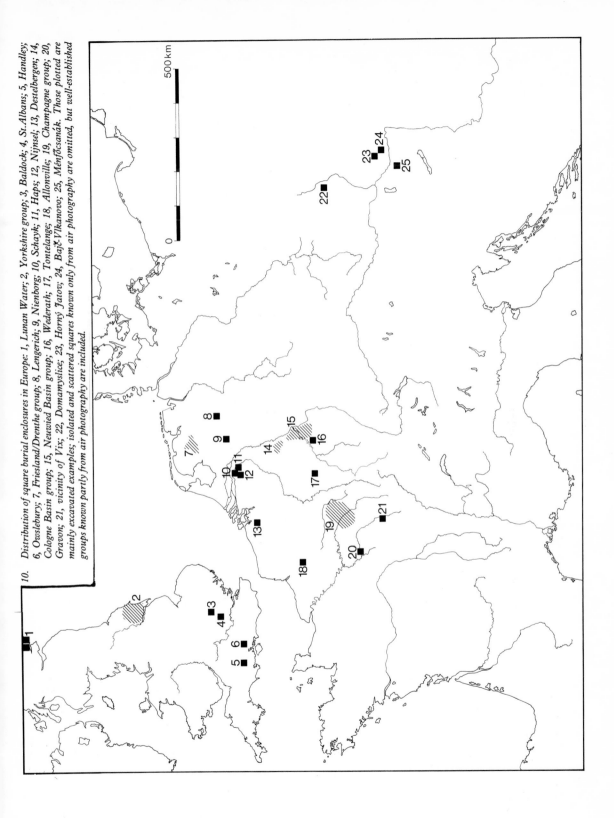

10. *Distribution of square burial enclosures in Europe: 1, Lunan Water; 2, Yorkshire group; 3, Baldock; 4, St.Albans; 5, Handley; 6, Owslebury; 7, Friesland/Drenthe group; 8, Lengerich; 9, Nienborg; 10, Schayk; 11, Haps; 12, Nijnsel; 13, Destelbergen; 14, Cologne Basin group; 15, Neuwied Basin group; 16, Wederath; 17, Tontelange; 18, Allonville; 19, Champagne group; 20, Gravon; 21, vicinity of Vix; 22, Domamyslice; 23, Horný Jatov; 24, Bajč-Vlkanovo; 25, Ménfőcsanák. Those plotted are mainly excavated examples; isolated and scattered squares known only from air photography are omitted, but well-established groups known partly from air photography are included.*

examples have been considerably increased by observation from the air (Decker & Scollar 1962; Wightman 1970) which has identified squares from 10m to 40m across, singly and in small groups, sometimes with a bank inside or outside the ditch, and sometimes with a central barrow. More than 100 such enclosures have been excavated in the La Tène III and Early Roman cemetery at Wederath (Kr. Bernkastel) (Haffner 1971) where small examples, 5m and less square, are common. The majority of excavated squares in the area seem, like Wederath, to start late in La Tène III and continue well into Roman times. There is little in the way of a local ancestry for the type, although there are two square enclosures (without burials) in an Early La Tène inhumation cemetery at Kärlich (Kr. Koblenz) (Röder 1948) whilst at Wallertheim (Kr. Alzey) there were squares enclosing La Tène III cremations in inhumation-shaped graves (Kessler 1930).

These Middle Rhineland features seem to resemble closely the La Tène III enclosures in Champagne — not only are they always associated with the cremation-rite, but they are often closely grouped, and even linked — with an enclosure ditched on three sides being tagged onto an earlier square (e.g. the excavated examples at Wederath, Haffner 1971, and the air photograph of Briedal, Kr. Zell, Decker & Scollar 1962: pl.xxiii, b, are very close to some in Champagne).

North of the River Ahr, in the Cologne Basin, slightly different enclosures have been recognised from the air (Scollar 1968). In contrast to the Moselle group, they include rectangular and trapezoidal shapes, and although they are presumed to be funerary, excavation has so far failed to produce burials or other internal features (Barfield 1965). These small square and rectangular enclosures (Grabgärten) of the Middle Rhine must not be confused with the larger enclosures (Viereckschanzen) like that at Holzhausen, near Munich, whose distribution is centred in southern Germany (Baden-Württemberg and Bavaria); the latter, sometimes associated with 'ritual pits' are not found with burials and have been interpreted as cult centres (Schwarz 1962).

In Moravia a La Tène I warrior-burial at Domamyslice was at the centre of a ditched enclosure almost 9m square (Čižmář 1973), and in south-western Slovakia La Tène II cemeteries at Horný Jatov and Bajč-Vlkanovo each had two burials central to similar enclosures (Benadik 1963:345-6). Ring-ditches of this size are found in the same area, but they too are rare (Čižmář 1973:622-3). South of the Danube, there are two square burial-enclosures in a cemetery at Ménfőcsanák, in north-eastern Hungary, one with a La Tène I warrior at the centre (Uzsoki 1970:41 and 50).

The areas discussed so far have square funerary enclosures associated with La Tène burials, but similar features have been found in the Low Countries beyond the limits of La Tène culture. In the cremation cemeteries north of the Rhine, in the northern part of the Netherlands, square enclosures have been found in contexts dating about the middle of the first millenium B.C., as at Ruinen (Drenthe, north Netherlands) where there is a mass of ditched enclosures and associated, but not central, cremations (Waterbolk 1962). A nearby and contemporary cemetery at Vledder (Ibid.) has rectangular formations of post-holes within square enclosures, as well as enclosures tagged onto others in a way resembling the La Tène III examples in Champagne and the Middle Rhine. Squares added to other squares and off-centre cremations seem to be features of these northern sites (Verwers 1972:34; Wilhelmi 1971; Bonenfant 1966) and despite their early dating they resemble La Tène III sites further south — especially Tontelange and Wederath, and perhaps also Bouy (Flouest & Stead, 1977:fig.13).

South of the Rhine, at Destelbergen, near Ghent, Belgium, in one of the Urnfield Culture cemeteries of East Flanders, there is a single square-ditched enclosure whose central cinerary urn has been dated Hallstatt C, whilst secondary cremations near the edge of the enclosure and in the filling of the ditch are Hallstatt D (de Laet 1966:14-15). Destelbergen differs from the other northern sites in that its square is isolated, with a central burial; it seems to be the only square in a true Urnfield Culture context, and it is an oddity because it is the sole example to have been found despite the excavation of a dozen cemeteries of that type in East Flanders. But it does suggest that square enclosures may yet be found in Urnfield contexts further south — particularly in Champagne, where they are so well represented throughout the La Tène period and where Urnfield cemeteries have so far been little explored. Chertier's recent work on the Urnfield sites of the Marais de Saint-Gond has identified square enclosures but none clearly earlier than La Tène (Chertier 1976:62). From this viewpoint his most intriguing site is Enclosure C at Broussy-le-Grand where an Urnfield circular enclosure was converted into two successive squares (Ibid: 88-92). Continuity between Urnfield and La Tène in Champagne is suggested by comparison of the enclosures at Aulnay-aux-Planches (Brisson & Hatt 1953) with those on the La Tène I sites at Manre and Aure, where not only the circles but perhaps also the long oval enclosure may be matched. At Aulnay-aux-Planches the long oval feature enclosed burials, unlike the shorter examples from the Ardennes La Tène I sites, but the burials need not be original; far away at Libenice in central Bohemia the burial in a somewhat similar enclosure may have been secondary (Rybová & Soudský 1962; Kruta 1975a: 97). Some of the cremation cemeteries in the Netherlands also have long rectangular enclosures, sometimes in the same cemeteries as squares (Lengerich, Wilhelmi 1971; Vledder, Waterbolk 1962).

These long oval enclosures in Hallstatt and La Tène cemeteries could have served a ritual but non-funerary purpose, and some of the Champagne enclosures with central arrangements of post-holes may also have been 'sanctuaries' rather than burial-sites. These post-holed 'sanctuaries' have been seen as the forerunners of both Romano-Celtic temples and Viereckschanzen (de Laet 1966); the thesis is attractive, but at least some of the post-hole features in Champagne had central burials (Flouest & Stead 1977), and the separation of Romano-Celtic temples and Viereckschanzen from cemeteries also suggests a somewhat different tradition.

However, the Yorkshire square barrows are not directly related to any of these sanctuaries, but they obviously belong to the same tradition as the continental funerary squares. It seems unlikely that the Yorkshire squares evolved from Urnfield proto-types either in Britain or abroad; the only possible association with cremations is at Skipwith, and those barrows cannot be dated. The earliest datable Yorkshire square barrow is La Tène I and it seems likely that it was a La Tène trait introduced at the same time, and from the same place, as the rite of cart-burial.

5. Barrow Groups, isolated barrows and flat-graves.

The burials of the Arras Culture are not all in large cemeteries: there are small groups of barrows, isolated barrows, and even some evidence for flat-graves. As far as the barrows are concerned, the variety can be seen most clearly from air photographs, where groups of three or four barrows, and isolated barrows, occur frequently — disting-uished by their square-plan ditches. The signifi-cance of the small concentrations as opposed to the large cemeteries remains to be seen: obviously large cemeteries must have grown from single burials via small groups, but there could be good reasons why other barrows are well-separated from the cemeteries. Garton/Wetwang Slack will provide useful information from this point of view, for in the excavation of a long stretch of the valley-floor two cemeteries have been uncovered as well as scattered burials between them (Brewster 1975: fig., p.106 —

the subsequently-excavated Wetwang cemetery is to the south of Wetwang Grange, adjoining 'disused railway'). The Garton Slack mirror came from one of a group of four square-barrows, and the cart-burial was in an isolated barrow.

The most significant barrow group yet excavated is that explored by Greenwell in 1867 at Cowlam (Greenwell 1877:208-13). He dug five barrows (his nos. L to LIV) of which four were classified as Early Iron Age, on the basis of grave-goods found with two of them, but the fifth was excluded. Barrow L was 22ft (7m) in diameter and 2ft (60cm) high. "At the centre, and placed on the natural surface, was the body of an aged woman, laid upon the left side with the head to the N.E., and the hands up to the face. On the wrist of the right arm was a bronze armlet, and near the chin a bronze fibula, with an iron pin. At the neck were seventy glass beads" (*Ibid*:208). At the centre of Barrow LI, 24ft (7.5m) diameter and 1ft (30cm) high, "on the natural surface, was the body of a woman in the middle period of life, laid upon the left side, with the head to N. and the hands up to the face. Upon the wrist of the right arm was a bronze armlet... The body... had been very much contracted, and only occupied, measuring from the ends of the toes to the back of the head, a space of 35in (89cm) (*Ibid*:210). Barrows LII and LIII were respectively 32ft (10m) and 42ft (13m) in diameter and each had at the centre on the old ground surface a crouched or contracted inhumation in a similar position. Barrow LIV, 50ft (15m) diameter, had an inhumation on the old ground surface, on its right side and with the skull to the south-south-west — perhaps because of the difference in orientation, Greenwell did not classify this mound as Iron Age.

Unfortunately Greenwell did not plot the posi-tions of his barrows, so when it came about that they were re-excavated, just over a century later, it was not possible to correlate the results exactly (Stead 1971; and p.99). Four of Greenwell's five barrows were completely re-excavated; no additional burials were found there, but the lack of central graves was confirmed, and in one case Greenwell's activities had left clear traces in the form of a series of parallel excavation-trenches. The re-excavation produced two important results — first, that the barrows had all been surrounded by square-plan ditches (Pl.6a), and second that there had been an Iron Age settle-ment on the site before the erection of the barrows. Greenwell had also noticed this domestic debris, in the form of sherds, flints, pits and trenches. In addition to the re-excavation of Greenwell's barrows, two other barrows in the group were recog-nised — each with square-plan ditch: the one was 9m across and lacked a burial — but the mound had been so flattened by ploughing that if there had been a burial on the old ground surface, as in Greenwell's barrows, it would not have survived. The other new barrow was rather smaller, 7m across, and at the centre the contracted inhumation of a child was found in a shallow grave.

In addition to the new barrows, random trial-trenching in the vicinity produced a couple of flat graves (p.99) which might well be of the same date. The Cowlam group, then, comprises six square barrows, possibly another, and two flat graves. It is worth noting its position — exposed on the top of the Wolds (158m high), in marked contrast to those cemeteries along valley-floors (Pl.6b); and the rite of burial on the old ground surface must be emphasised — only one barrow had a grave, and that was very shallow. Greenwell identified all five skeletons as female, and although his sexing of the skeletons may not be reliable, there is certainly not an obvious male burial in the group.

Another important La Tène barrow excavated in the nineteenth-century can perhaps be correlated with a recent excavation, in which case it too had a square-plan ditch. In 1972 T.G. Manby excavated a square ditched barrow at Grindale, 13.5 by 15m internally. It had been ploughed flat, but there remained a network of nineteenth-century trenches and a partially excavated grave in which the remains of a pig were untouched in one corner (A.E. 1972:39). It may be that this was the barrow in which Edward Tindall, of Bridlington, found a flattened-bow brooch and two penannular brooches in 1857 at Huntow. Tindall's excavation was reported to Thomas Wright, who committed it to print in all its obscurity: "The chalk rock had first been uncovered and hollowed out into the form of a bowl about eighteen inches (45cm) deep, and nine feet (2.7m) in diameter, for the reception of the deposit. After the latter had been placed in it, the bowl was filled in with fine mould, and above this was raised the tumulus, formed of large chalk stones, covered over, when finished, with a coating of rubble, and earthed up at the top with fine soil. The tumulus was about five feet (1.5m) high from the surface of the chalk. No traces of human remains were found in it; but there were a considerable quantity of bones of carnivorous and ruminating animals, fowls, &c., and three articles in bronze" (Wright 1861:23-4).

The nineteenth-century barrow-diggers might well have uncovered other La Tène burials, but in the absence of grave-goods there can be no certainty. Greenwell was well aware of this problem, as his comments on Cowlam show: "had the bodies occurred without the necklace, fibula, or armlets, I should not have hesitated the least about classing these four barrows with the other barrows in the immediate vicinity, which were of the time of stone, or more probably of bronze" (Greenwell 1877:212).

However, one of Mortimer's barrows, C.72 on Calais Wold, 25ft (7.6m) diameter and 1ft (30cm) high, certainly covered an Iron Age burial. The large grave — 16ft (4.9m) by 5½ft (1.7m) and 2ft (60cm) deep — held a skeleton with the skull to the north-north-west, crouched and on its left side, whilst at the feet were skeletons of a pig and two goats or sheep (Mortimer 1905:163). The size of the barrow, orientation of the skeleton, and comparison with the animal skeletons in Danes Graves Barrows 19 and 73 suggest a La Tène date, which has recently been confirmed by the discovery of a square-plan ditch in the course of field survey and air photography. Air photographs have shown that another four of Mortimer's barrows had originally been square (nos. 49, 117, and 125 in the Aldro Group, p.97; and no.59 in the Hanging Grimston Group, p.102).

Flat graves are more difficult to define. In the Burton Fleming cemetery a case has been made for a single flat-grave — the only north-south burial without a barrow ditch had subsequently been cut by another grave, which suggests that there had never been a covering mound. Two very tightly contracted skeletons in graves at Cowlam also lacked barrow ditches; at Garton Slack Brewster (1975:109-10) found flat-graves including one with a necklace of blue-glass beads; and Dent considers that there were some flat graves at Wetwang Slack. Thus there seems reasonable evidence for flat graves within the Arras Culture, and they can be identified if they have grave-goods or if they are in the vicinity of other La Tène burials — but only if there is reasonable certainty that a barrow was absent. Crouched or contracted burials unassociated or lacking grave-goods might well belong to earlier stages of prehistory.

Some Iron Age warrior-burials, clearly dated by their grave-goods, produced no evidence of barrows, although aerial photography has shown that two of them were in the immediate vicinity of square barrows. At Bugthorpe an iron sword in a decorated bronze scabbard was found "at a depth of 5 feet (1.5m) in draining a field" (Wood 1860). The very brief note which first records this discovery makes no reference to a grave, but a decade later one authority said that "a sword... and a fibula, had been previously found with an interment at Bugthorpe" (Thurnam 1871:475), whilst another recalled that "a body was discovered with which an iron sword in a bronze sheath and an enamelled bronze brooch were associated" (Greenwell 1877:50, note 1). The presence of comparable warrior-burials in the area supports the belief that the Bugthorpe sword had been found in a grave, and the square barrows now observed by H.G. Ramm in that area strengthen the argument — but at the same time raise the possibility that it was a barrow-burial rather than a flat-grave.

Shortly after the Bugthorpe discovery, and only about 6km away, a very similar grave was discovered at Grimthorpe. But despite the proximity of the two sites they are very different topographically — Bugthorpe in the flat Vale of York (found when draining) in marked contrast to Grimthorpe high on the western escarpment of the Wolds, with a view beyond York Minster to the Pennines. The Grimthorpe burial was found by chance, in a chalk-pit in 1868 (Mortimer 1869; and 1905:150-2). The skeleton, in a grave 4½ft (1.4m) by 2¾ft (85cm) and 4ft (1.2m) deep, was orientated north-south and crouched on its left side. It was accompanied by a shield, sword, spearhead and a number of bone pegs (Stead 1968: fig.77, for a hypothetical reconstruction of the plan). Three other burials found in the immediate vicinity lacked grave-goods, but two of them were superimposed — and the lower one had been slightly disturbed by the upper, which suggests that they were not contemporary. Secondary central burials in Arras Culture barrows are virtually unknown — so this is an argument in favour of a flat-grave. Furthermore, Mortimer specifically mentions the absence of any trace of a mound over the warrior-burials, and his trenching in the vicinity of the chalk-pit failed to locate any barrow ditch. But plough-damage on this site had been very marked indeed, even by Mortimer's day, for the bank and ditch of a hillfort had been levelled without trace (Ibid.). A crouched burial, on its left side and with the skull to the south-south-east was found in a grave in the filling of the hillfort ditch in 1961. It was 150m from Mortimer's burials, but might belong to the same period; certainly a barrow over this ditch-burial would be most unlikely.

A third burial of similar type, also from the western end of the Wolds, was found in 1902 during the excavation of a post-hole at North Grimston (Mortimer 1905:354-7). Two swords were removed on discovery, and then Mortimer was called in and the grave was thoroughly excavated. The skeleton had been extended, orientated south-north, and as well as the sword there were several rings, the remains of a shield, and the skeleton of a pig. There may have been more than one burial, for an iron spearhead "was found about thirty years before, near the same place" (Ibid:356). There was no evidence for a barrow on this site — like those at Bugthorpe and Grimthorpe, the North Grimston burial was found quite by chance — but again Ramm reports square barrows in the immediate vicinity.

Another chance find occurred at the opposite end of the Wolds in 1891, when a sword with a fine hilt was found with "some bones" in the kitchen garden at Thorpe Hall, Rudston (Allen 1906:269). There are no more details, but it could perhaps have been a burial

Warrior-burials also occur in the square barrow cemeteries, at Burton Fleming (p.14; Pl.4c) and at Wetwang Slack (p.16), but this is one class of burial which is not restricted to Yorkshire. An extended inhumation with short anthropoid sword was found at Shouldham, in Norfolk (Clarke & Hawkes 1955) and other La Tène III inhumations with swords have been recorded from St. Lawrence, Isle of Wight (Stead 1969); Owslebury, Hants. (Collis 1973:126-8); and Whitcombe, Dorset (Ibid:125-6). No British warrior-burial can be dated earlier than La Tène III.

A distinctive form of flat-grave burial which occurs certainly in the first century A.D., and might belong to the Arras Culture, has the grave excavated into the filling of an earlier ditch. How far this can be regarded as a specific burial rite is obscure — it could indicate no more than work-shy grave-diggers — but several burials do fall into this category. At Burton Fleming, Garton Slack and Wetwang Slack, secondary inhumations have been found in barrow ditches — particularly, at Burton Fleming, in the ditches of a distinctive type of rectangular barrow which lacked a central burial. At Grimthorpe, too, a burial has already been noted in the ditch of the hillfort, but not far removed from a small group of flat graves. Elsewhere there are burials in the ditches of settlements, apparently remote from other types of burial. At Rudston Roman villa three inhumations were found in graves in a single length of ditch — two of them had grave-goods in the form of brooches, one being a penannular brooch of a type found in pre-Roman contexts (Stead 1971:30, 39 and fig.7, no.4). Garton Slack (A.E. 1973:34 and Eastburn (Sheppard 1939:35) also produced burials in similar contexts. Barrows aligned with, and encroaching on, the ditches of settlements and drove-ways have been noted in several places on the Wolds — especially in the Burton Fleming and Wetwang Slack cemeteries; from here it is perhaps not a far cry to the inhumations actually in the filling of boundary ditches.

Most Arras Culture burials, whether under barrows or in flat graves, are crouched or contracted inhumations. Cremations are virtually unknown, although they may have existed at Skipwith where the 1849 excavators found "traces of burnt bones... in scattered and minute fragments" including part of a human skull, and Burton, a century earlier, was even more specific in mentioning calcined human bones (Stead 1961:49-50). Extended inhumations are exceptional, although in the Burton Fleming cemetery they form a distinctive group belonging to a late stage in the cemetery (p.14). Apart from Burton Fleming, extended burials are a great rarity

— there is a reference to some found in the 1816-18 excavations at Arras, but the skeleton in the Lady's Barrow is the only one to be well documented; the inhumation with the anthropoid sword, from North Grimston, was also extended; as was one burial at Garton Slack. Otherwise the rite of crouched burial is universal, and it goes back to the earliest stage of the Arras Culture, at Cowlam. But unlike the other aspects of the burial-rite — particularly square barrows and cart-burials — the crouched position does not seem to have close continental links.

La Tène cultures almost invariably employ the extended position, although here and there an odd crouched burial has been recorded. In Champagne, a crouched burial in the cemetery at Manre, Mont Troté (Rozoy 1970:45) belonged to the earliest phase (Hallstatt D) and is perhaps no more strange than the occasional cremation also found in La Tène I cemeteries. In the same area, a crouched burial at Aulnay-aux-Planches was found as a secondary in a ditch which surrounded a primary Hallstatt D cremation (Brisson & Hatt 1953:222, fig.55) and the same site produced another crouched burial (undated) within the 'cursus' (*Ibid*:216, fig.50). But these crouched burials are very definitely atypical in Champagne. The only continental La Tène province where such burials are more common is in Moravia and the Carpathians (Filip 1960:180) — but even there the crouched position is a minority rite in cemeteries of extended burials. At Bučovice, Moravia, in a small cemetery of 20 burials, five were crouched (Filip 1956:294, with cemetery plan fig.89, and skeleton fig.84, no.12), and that proportion does not seem to be exceeded elsewhere. The crouched burial-rite in Moravia is interpreted as a survival of an earlier rite in the area, and it can have little direct significance for Yorkshire.

If the rite of crouched burial is not to be regarded as an important trait, then it may have been a native practice of long standing. Greenwell took this view, for leaving aside the grave-goods he could see no difference between the Cowlam skeletons and those accompanied by Beakers and Food Vessels: he deduced that iron had been introduced without any change of population: "that no new people had come in with iron, but that acquaintance with and use of this metal were gradually developed amongst an originally bronze-using people" (Greenwell 1877:212). But Greenwell's inhumations with Beakers and Food Vessels were of the Early Bronze Age, and it seems that this burial-rite was at an end by 1400 B.C. (Burgess 1974:194) — a thousand years before Cowlam. For the Middle Bronze Age, Deverill-Rimbury groups practiced cremation-burial, but their distribution is limited and extends into Eastern Yorkshire only to the extent of a single site — Catfoss (*Ibid*:215, McInnes 1968), a flat urnfield with cremations in simple pots and no associated artefacts. No Deverill-Rimbury burial can be dated to the Late Bronze Age (Burgess 1974:218). The evidence for Late Bronze Age burials dated by metalwork has now been considered in great detail (Burgess 1976), and there are a few ill-documented instances of inhumation, but it is clear that the first half of the first millenium B.C. is devoid of a majority burial rite, in Yorkshire and in the south.

One of the most interesting of the burials which might belong to this period was found in a barrow at Aldro (Mortimer 1905:56-7, pl.xiv, figs.107 and 108; Challis & Harding 1975:42-3 and fig.20). Mortimer's Barrow 108, opened in 1868, was 27ft (8m) diameter and 8 to 10in (20 to 25cm) high, and it had had a wide berm because the surrounding ring ditch had a diameter of 48ft (14.5m). The central grave was described as a "circular hollow 2 feet (60cm) deep and 2½ feet (75cm) across the top". At the bottom of the grave was a heap of calcined bones accompanied by pieces of bronze, broken and distorted by heat. Some of the bronze fragments are ribbed and some are ornamented with settings resembling cylindrical bronze rivets — two of these still hold pellets of crystal or glass. There is also a cast bronze pommel, resembling a small 'horn-cap' in form. But until this Aldro collection has been studied in detail it would be unwise to hazard a guess as to its date or its significance.

Another possible burial of the period was found at Ebberston — but here the query is not with regard to the date of the objects, but to the nature of the deposit. The find, made in March, 1861, consisted of a bronze Hallstatt C sword and a winged chape, found "together with another sword and a quantity of human bones" (Bateman 1861; Howarth 1899:65 and 77; Cowan 1967:444, no.195; Sheffield Museum, reg. no. 93.436 and 463). The second sword is perhaps the one found "near Scarborough" and acquired in 1864 by Scarborough Museum (reg. no. 814.38; Cowan 1967:444, no.196). It is conceivable that the swords were found with burials, but the record is very inadequate.

Perhaps Mortimer's Barrow 33, in the Riggs Group (Mortimer 1905:175-6), also belongs to the first half of the first millenium B.C. It was opened in 1865 and seems to have produced four cremations — one unaccompanied, two others each with a simple undecorated pot, and the fourth with the base of a large urn. This low barrow, 40ft (12m) in diameter, was peculiar in having a slight bank outside the ditch, the whole monument measuring 84ft (25m) across, whilst on the south-east side there was a 6ft (1.8m) wide causeway across the ditch. Cremations have been found in a few other simple undecorated bucket-urns in the area (McInnes 1968:3).

A group of barrows on Ampleforth Moor also deserve mention here, but the results of the excavation were inconclusive (Wainwright & Longworth 1969). The nine small barrows, 24ft (7m) to 32ft (10m) diameter, had been previously robbed, but it was apparent that the burials had been either on the old ground surface or in shallow graves. No trace of a burial was recovered, although charcoal on the old ground surface provided C.14 dates of 537 and 582±90 b.c. In the nineteenth-century a previous excavator (Eastmead) was satisfied that he had "sufficient proof that bodies had been burnt there" but he found no pots (*Ibid*:293).

Such are the possibilities for burials in Eastern Yorkshire in the half millenium before Cowlam, and one significant fact is the absence of any trace of a crouched or contracted inhumation. Beyond that, it is a vague record of doubtful or undated burials. Perhaps this lack of burials represents a de-population — but it seems scarcely conceivable that an area so attractive to prehistoric man as the chalk Wolds should ever be deserted, or even under-populated. Alternatively, the people who lived there could have disposed of their dead in a way which has left no trace. Such a phenomenon has occurred throughout prehistory, and the people responsible for it have suffered in the eyes of archaeologists. Most La Tène cultures, fortunately, were flamboyant in their death.

One disposal rite which might have left some slight trace is exposure, particularly if bodies were exposed on or near settlements, and it has been argued that because fragments of human bone are frequently found on Iron Age settlements throughout southern England, exposure of bodies might have been a regular burial-rite (Ellison & Drewett 1971:190-2). In Yorkshire very few Iron Age settlements have been excavated, but it is worth noting that three of them — all dating before the influx of La Tène culture — have human bones scattered amongst domestic rubbish. Such finds have been observed at Grimthorpe (Stead 1968:190), Scarborough (Rutter 1959:37-41) and Staple Howe (Brewster 1963:137-8). But these human remains could be explained other than by exposure — they could be from disturbed burials of an earlier period, for instance. Cannibalism is another possibility to be considered, and although this must always be difficult to prove (Brothwell 1961), Dunning (1976:116-17) has argued strongly for an example at Salmonsbury (Glos.). The predominance of skull fragments in the small sample of human bones from Iron Age settlements is also worth noting, for skulls could have been retained for display.

South of the Humber Iron Age burials are unusual before the appearance, in the second half of the first century B.C., of cremation-burials of the Aylesford Culture. Before that, some flat-grave inhumation cemeteries are known, particularly in south-western England where skeletons in stone cists have been recorded at Harlyn Bay (Cornwall) (Crawford 1921:283-6) and Mount Batten, Plymouth (Devon) (Spence Bate 1866). In Dorset, too, there are inhumation cemeteries, but they seem to date from the years immediately before the Roman conquest, and are typified by the well-known war-cemetery at Maiden Castle (Wheeler 1943:351-6). A recent survey (Whimster 1977) has emphasised the number of odd isolated inhumations found on Iron Age settlements in southern England — usually deposited in pits which had been dug for other purposes, but occasionally buried in carefully-excavated graves. These burials could never be seen as the sole method of disposal of the dead — they must represent a minority rite — but Whimster's work has shown that a large percentage are crouched or contracted, and many of them are orientated north-south — the same as the normal rite in the Arras Culture. For example, a skeleton from Maiden Castle, illustrated by Wheeler 1943: pl.xlix, is indistinguishable from the Yorkshire burials even to the extent of having a pot in front of the face and a pig-humerus adjoining (cf. Pl.4b).

The reason for this widespread and specifically British rite of crouched burial has yet to be found. It could, of course, have spread to the rest of England from Yorkshire, for none of the southern burials can be shown to be earlier than Cowlam, but other aspects of the Yorkshire burial-rite — cart-burial and square barrows — did not extend further south. It is more likely that Yorkshire and the south shared a common tradition throughout the first half of the first millenium B.C. The majority disposal-rite at that time, and in the south for the centuries following, could have been the same and could in some way have involved the crouched or contracted position of the corpse. At Cowlam, of course, the burials were under barrows — but they were on the old ground surface and not in graves, and it could be that elsewhere the bodies were merely exposed, or covered with slight, superficial mounds.

It seems that even the earliest stage of the Arras Culture included a native as well as a continental element in the burial-rite. How the two aspects came together is unknown, as is the reason for the introduction of extended burials at a much later stage at Burton Fleming. Indeed it is ironical that the appearance of extended east-west burials — the usual continental La Tène rite — causes surprise in Yorkshire in the first century B.C. whereas if they had been dated to the fifth or fourth centuries B.C. they would have been accepted naturally as accompanying the first intrusive square barrows.

THE FINDS

(Abbreviations to museum collections on p.97).

1. Wheels

(i) **Arras A.1. The King's Barrow.**

(a) Fragments of one iron tyre, 38mm wide, and mounted for display at *c*. 870mm diameter. (Y.M. 936.1 to 13.48). Stillingfleet 1846:29 records the diameter as a trifle more than 2ft 11in (*c*. 890mm).

(b) Fragments of two nave-hoops, the more complete having a diameter of 125 to 130mm internally. They have been iron bands, D-section, with a casing of bronze which covered the rounded outer side and turned under both edges of the flat inner side. The bronze case is 14mm wide. (Y.M. 936.14 to 19.48; Fig.11, no.2).

(ii) **Arras A.2. The Charioteer's Barrow.**

(a) Slightly more than half of an iron tyre, together with smaller fragments; *c*. 790mm diameter and *c*. 35mm wide. On the inner face of the tyre corrosion products preserve traces of the wooden felloe, and in one place there is a clear rectangular impression — possibly a dowel — measuring 12mm wide and at least 33mm long; its impression is not central to the width of the tyre, being about 8mm from one edge and 15mm from the other. (Y.M. 935.1 to 16.48, labelled 'Hessleskew A'). Stillingfleet 1846:31 records that "oak was still attached to part of the tire of the wheels, and the nails which had been used as rivets, were entire". Davis & Thurnam 1865 repeat this observation and add that the wheels "appear each to have been furnished with as many as sixteen spokes, with spaces of about six inches (15cm) between them". There is no sign of nails in the surviving tyre fragments.

(b) Only small fragments of iron nave-hoop survive. Flat on the inside, rounded on top, they measure 18mm wide. (Y.M. 935.17 to 19.48, and one fragment 905.1 to 8.48; Fig.11, no.3). Stillingfleet 1846:31 gives the diameter as about 5in (13cm), whereas Greenwell 1906:282 puts it at 6in (15cm) and notes that it was attached by iron rivets.

(iii) **Arras A.3. The Lady's Barrow.**

(a) The iron tyres, 36 to 38mm wide, are broken and distorted; segments give diameters between 780mm and 900mm. (B.M. 77.10-16.1 and 2). Greenwell recorded the diameters on different occasions as *c*.2ft 8in (81cm) (1877:455), and 2ft 10in (86cm) (1906:285).

(b) The four nave-hoops survive, and have an internal diameter of between 124 and 130mm. They each comprise a circular iron ring only 7mm wide, with a wide bronze cover, 40 to 46mm wide. The ends of the bronze covers overlap by between 13 and 26mm and are there attached to the nave by two bronze nails, from 25 to 31mm long. The two nail-heads best preserved bear concentric-ring decora-

tion. The shafts of two nails are bent towards the point, showing that they had penetrated the thickness of the nave which was here *c*. 23mm. (B.M. 77.10-16.3 to 6; Fig.11, no.1; Greenwell 1906: fig.28).

(iv) **Beverley.**

(a) The two tyres are in fragments and considerably conglomerated, so that measurements are obscure; some fragments seem to be 36mm wide and others more than 40mm wide. (B.M. 75.10-5.1). Greenwell 1906:278 recorded the diameter as 2ft 4½in (72cm).

(b) One iron nave-hoop measures *c*.132mm diameter internally, and has a rectangular section 10mm wide and 7mm deep. There are fragments of two others, more corroded, of which one seems to have been thicker and more oval in section. (B.M. 75.10-5.2; Fig.11, no.4).

(v) **Cawthorn Camps.**

(a) Two iron tyres survive, mounted in plaster of paris on wooden boards; it is impossible to obtain a width measurement, but their diameters are *c*. 700mm and *c*. 700 to 710mm internally. In one place traces of the *inner* edge of the felloe survive in the form of iron-replacement. (Y.M.).

(b) Fragments of nave-hoops are mounted at the centre of each of the boards displaying the tyres. In the centre of one are small fragments of a wide bronze cover, *c*. 30mm wide, with a central cordon. There is no sign of an iron core (cf. the Lady's Barrow, Arras) but the fragments are small — the largest is only 50mm long — and they are mounted with the inner face downwards. In the centre of the other wheel various fragments of rings, etc., include one piece from a similar nave-hoop, 70mm long, completely covered with iron corrosion products. (Y.M.; Fig.11, no.5). Mortimer 1905:361 refers to the nave-hoops as being of iron plated with thin bronze.

(vi) **Danes Graves 43.**

(a) A complete iron tyre, mounted in plaster of paris, 720 to 760mm diameter and 35 to 38mm wide. (Y.M. 937.7.48). There is also less than half of a tyre *c*. 37mm wide and 780mm diameter mounted with fragments to a diameter of 740mm (Y.M. 937.1.48). Mortimer 1897:10 measured one wheel at 2ft 6¾in (78cm) and the other 2ft 5¼in (74cm) and suggested that they were not a pair (cf. also the different nave-hoops, below).

(b) An almost complete iron nave-hoop has an internal diameter *c*. 136mm, and seems to have been *c*. 11mm wide and 6mm thick. Another, of similar type, is more distorted. (Y.M. 937.3 and 9.48; Fig.11, no.7). There are also small fragments from two other nave-hoops of a different type, with curved section and 17mm wide (Y.M. 937.2 and

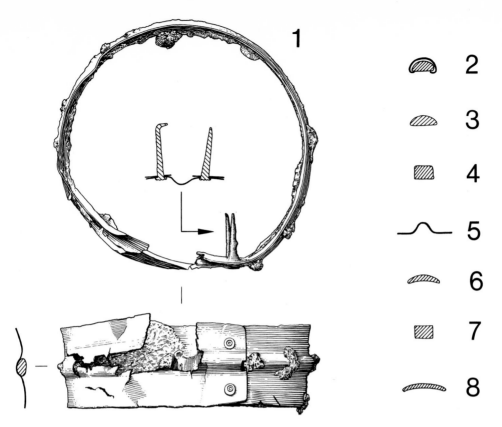

11. *Nave-hoops: 1, Lady's Barrow, Arras; 2, King's Barrow, Arras; 3, Charioteer's Barrow, Arras; 4, Beverley; 5, Cawthorn Camps; 6 and 7, Danes Graves; 8, Pexton Moor. Scale ½.*

8.48; Fig.11, no.6). Mortimer 1897:10 records the nave diameter as 5in (13cm) and Greenwell 1906:277 says 5½in (14cm).

(c) A badly corroded iron rod, now 90mm long, possibly part of a cleat — if so, much of the body survives, square in section, and part of one arm which is broad and thin (but in part flaked). There are wood traces on the arm, which support the identification as a cleat, and it is conceivable that this piece was used to join a single-piece felloe — certainly its position in the grave, just within the iron tyre, would be consistent with this explanation (Y.M. 937.4.48; Mortimer 1897:pl.i, no.12).

(vii) Garton Slack.

(a) The two wheels from Garton Slack were 860mm diameter and 44mm wide (Brewster 1971:290; H.M.).

(b) Three nave-hoops were of bronze, some 19mm wide with a central cordon, and between 125 and 130mm internal diameter. The fourth nave-hoop

was of iron and in its slightly distorted state measures 138 by 125mm diameter. (H.M.).

(viii) Pexton Moor.

(a) The tyre found in 1935 is in fragments and has been mounted for display at a diameter of between 800 and 820mm; it is about 40mm wide. (Y.M.). Kirk 1911:62 recorded the diameter of the 1911 tyre as 30in (76cm).

(b) One of the nave-hoops from the 1935 excavation has an internal diameter of about 120mm, is 23mm wide and curved in section; the other is similar but with an internal diameter nearer 130mm (Y.M.; Fig.11, no.8).

The wheels from the Yorkshire cart-burials were quite light, judging from their surviving metal fittings. All the tyres are distorted, but they vary considerably in diameter from *c.* 700mm at Cawthorn Camps to 890mm at the King's Barrow, Arras, and "nearly 3ft" (90cm) at Hunmanby. In width they measure between 35 and 40mm, but for

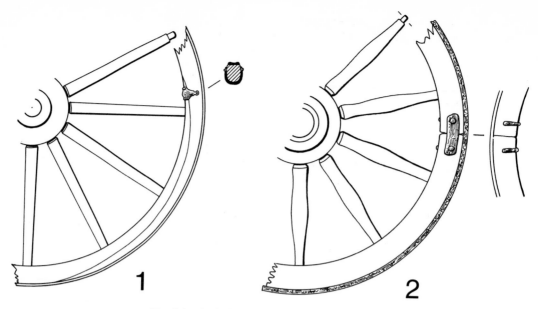

12.   *Joints for single-piece fellows: 1, Dejbjerg; 2, Newstead.*

those from Garton Slack which are 44mm; none is in a good state of preservation, thickness measurements vary according to flaking, and it is impossible to judge whether they were new or worn when placed in the grave. From Llyn Cerrig Bach, Anglesey, fragments of tyres from at least 20 wheels had an average width of 1½in (38mm) and varied in diameter from 2ft 6in (76cm) to 3ft (91cm), with a single exception which measured 4ft (1.2m) across (Fox 1946:11-13).

Comparison with the tyres from continental La Tène cart-burials reveals very similar measurements. In Champagne, the tyres from Beine, "Le Montequeux", and Châlons-sur-Marne were 800mm diameter (Coyon 1924; Lemoine 1905) and the rest fall between 840mm and 915mm. The tyres from the Middle Rhine graves include examples only 700mm in diameter (Günther 1934:8 and 13) but range up to 950mm (Haffner 1976:33). La Tène tyres on the continent in general seem to vary between 700 and 950mm with the exceptions of those found in the cart-burials at Nanterre (1.3m diameter and 50mm wide, Hubert 1900:411) and Attichy (1.1m to 1.2m diameter and 36 to 39mm wide, Duval & Blanchet 1974:404). The Nanterre tyres were also exceptional in having marked flanges on both faces, indicating little or no wear.

The surviving Yorkshire tyre fragments, in common with other examples from the British Iron Age, lack nails to secure them to the felloe (Fox 1946:11), and must have been attached merely by contraction, after having been fitted when hot. On the continent many Iron Age tyres had been nailed to the felloes — in Champagne five or six nails seem to have been usual and in the Middle Rhine 15 and more nails were used (Haffner 1976:29, 30) — but the tyring could have been carried out as in Britain, differing only in the finishing process. The modern practice is for a wheel to be fitted with a hot tyre, which is then cooled rapidly so that it contracts to clasp the felloe tightly and secure the wooden joints; the final stage is the fixing of two or three nails to prevent the tyre from being jerked aside (Sturt 1949:129; Jenkins 1961:75 and 78).

The Yorkshire evidence for the construction of felloes is negligible, but elsewhere entire wheels have been preserved on rare occasions, and it is apparent that two types of felloe construction were used in the Iron Age and Roman period in Britain. On the one hand, two wheels from an Antonine context at Newstead had single-piece felloes whose straight joint is held by a cleat; the eleven spokes have very short rounded tongues which penetrate only 20mm into the felloe (Fig.12, no.2; Curle 1911:292, pl.lxix, no.2; Piggott 1965:245, fig.137). A wheel found in a similar context at the Bar Hill,

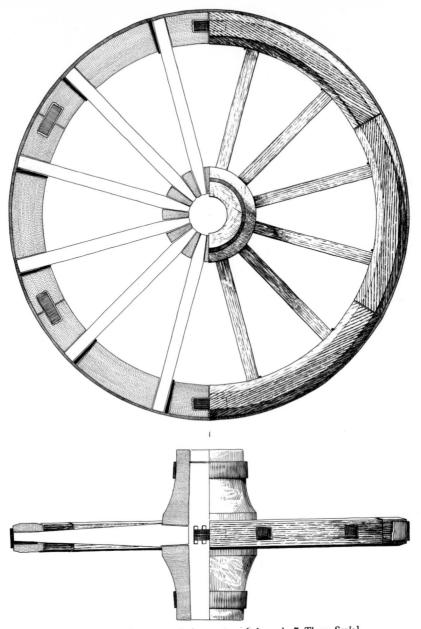

13. *The Holme Pierrepont wheel reconstructed; drawn by J. Thorn. Scale ⅛.*

(Dumbartonshire) also had a single-piece felloe with a straight joint — but apparently no iron cleat — and **eleven spokes (Macdonald & Park 1906:92 — 4, fig.34).** The undated wheel from Ryton, (Co. Durham) must also have had a single-piece felloe because of the odd number of spokes (nine) (Piggott 1949a); and this method of construction continued in use into Medieval times (Jenkins 1961:27 and 68). On the other hand, there are also Roman wheels from Newstead and the Bar Hill with multiple-felloes — composed of six segments dowelled together, in the way used by wheelwrights to the present day (Curle 1911:294; Macdonald & Park 1906:99, fig.33, no.4). Each length of felloe receives two spokes — so that there is always an even number of spokes, and the tongues (tenons) of the spokes pass entirely through the felloe. A wheel from Holme Pierrepont, (Notts.), apparently of Iron Age date, was constructed in this way and is exceptionally well-preserved (Fig.13; Musty & MacCormick 1973).

La Tène wheels from the continent are known only with single-piece felloes. There was a good example, with the wood surviving, from La Tène itself (Vouga 1923:92, fig.9) and the wheels on the Dejbjerg waggons were probably similar — their felloes, now fragmentary, had straightened in drying out but seem to have had a single scarf-joint which was secured by a bronze clamp (Fig.12, no.1; Klindt-Jensen 1949:89). The evidence of similar metal fittings from continental vehicle-burials also attests the popularity of the single-piece felloe. Thus the Late Hallstatt waggon found in a grave at Bell (Kr. Simmern) had an iron clamp nailed to the felloe which bore traces of the tapered joint (Rest 1948:137). Likewise the wheels from cart-burials in Champagne must have had single-piece felloes, for similar U-shaped clamps have been recorded from and wheel-holes of several graves (Stead 1965b:261, and fig.2).

But it has been shown that for a wheel 800-900mm diameter a single-piece felloe is feasible only if it is 40-50mm thick (Kossack 1971:144-6). Some Late Hallstatt wheels certainly had thicker felloes, so some form of multiple-felloe construction must have been employed, and there are metal fittings which provide hints of this construction. The study of remains from Hradenín (Kolin) and Grosseibstadt (Bavaria) (Ibid:149-55) suggests that the felloe was composed of two bands, one outside the other, and the outer band certainly was constructed in several segments. The construction of the inner band is not so clear, but as the spokes pass through both bands and leave traces on the inner side of the iron tyre is it probable that they too were made in segments. Unfortunately no wooden examples survive to give further details of the construction of these Hallstatt wheels, there is no hint of them throughout the La Tène period on the continent, but they emerge again in Roman times in a form very similar to the Holme Pierrepont wheel. An example from a well at Zugmantel, a Roman fort on the Upper German limes, has a felloe in six segments (Jacobi 1912:68-70, fig.29 and pl.xvi, 1) and was found with a wheel with single-piece felloe of the usual La Tène type (Ibid: fig.29 and pl.xvi, 2). The few surviving traces provide an incomplete story of the development of the wheel throughout the Iron Age, but the wheelwright had clearly acquired a very considerable skill and it is obvious that this was a field in which the Celts excelled — apparently the Romans learnt a lot from them, judging from the unusual number of

Latin words for waggon terminology which were borrowed from Celtic sources (Wild 1976:62).

However, to return to the Yorkshire graves, two pieces of evidence are worth noting, though neither is conclusive. On the one hand a mark in the corrosion-products on the inside of a tyre from the Charioteer's Barrow may represent a dowel — which would mean that the wheel employed a multiple felloe construction. On the other hand a possible cleat found near one of the Danes Graves tyres could have been used to link a single-piece felloe. Further evidence might come from detailed laboratory work, for the Pexton Moor tyre, and even more one of those from Cawthorn Camps, has considerable wood traces on the inside of the iron tyre.

Naves were made entirely of wood, but they were bound on each side by metal bands, which have been found in most of the Yorkshire cart-burials. Modern wheels have a cast-iron box inside the nave to take the wear of the revolving wheel and in the nineteenth century this usually took the form of a couple of bushes, one at either end (Jenkins 1961:80-1). Similar iron cylinders were used on one of the Newstead wheels (Piggott 1965: fig.137), but they are absent from the Yorkshire graves and Llyn Cerrig Bach, and there is no trace of them on surviving hubs from Holme Pierrepont and Glastonbury (Bulleid & Gray 1911:328 and 337-40).

Nave-hoops from the Yorkshire graves vary considerably in form, indeed no two examples are exactly the same (Fig.11). Iron ones range from the wide band, slightly curved in section (Pexton Moor, Danes Graves), via a narrower rather flatter band (Danes Graves, Charioteer's Barrow, Arras, and possibly Hunmanby), to a thicker band (Beverley, and the odd one from Garton Slack). The other two Arras graves are similar in having nave-hoops whose iron cores were wrapped with bronze, but whereas in the King's Barrow the bronze case is tucked under the iron, in the Lady's Barrow there is a wide bronze flange. The bronze nave-hoops from Cawthorn Camps resemble those from the Lady's Barrow and may also have had iron cores, but the narrower examples from Garton Slack certainly lacked the iron element.

Some of this range can be matched at Llyn Cerrig Bach (Fox 1946), where no.125, narrow and flat, resembles Danes Graves; no.39 is not unlike Beverley, although it is smaller; and no.37, of cordonned bronze, recalls the one from Cawthorn Camps. On the other hand, the full range of iron nave-hoops described above can be matched in La Tène I graves in Champagne, so these simple types had long lives. A more significant parallel, because the type is more elaborate, is that between the Cawthorn Camps and Nanterre bronze nave-hoops (Hubert 1900:411, fig.2).

2. Linch-pins

(i) Arras A.1. The King's Barrow.

A single linch-pin survives. It has an iron stem and bronze terminals. The stem is now broken and the two parts do not join, so its length is not known. Both terminals are in part covered with iron corrosion products and it seems likely that these obscure a perforation through the upper terminal. (Y.M. 901.2.48; Fig.14, no.1; Davis & Thurnam 1865: nos.11 and 12; Greenwell 1906:fig.21; Ward Perkins 1940:fig.1, no.5).

(ii) Middleton-on-the-Wolds.

A linch-pin with iron shank and bronze terminals, 135mm long. The upper terminal is surmounted by a large ring, whose edge is ridged and the two central ridges have zig-zag ornament, below which the terminal is perforated (in the plane of the ring, and the wheel) with a ridged border at either end. On the outside, on line with the perforation, is a circular motif of red glass, whilst the inside (shown on Fig.14, no.2) is undecorated and considerably worn. The foot is also markedly worn on the inside. (H.M.; Fig.14, no.2; Mortimer 1905:360, fig.1022; MacGregor 1976:no.135).

(iii) Danes Graves 43.

Two iron linch-pins. The one is 130mm long in the vertical plane (153mm overall maximum length) and has a squarish head 29 by 28mm; the curved shaft tapers from 12mm to 9mm diameter and terminates in a circular disc 14mm diameter. (Y.M. 937.6.48; Fig.14, no.3). The other linch-pin is similar, but damaged at both ends; it has been cleaned at some time and there is a perforation in the shaft below the head. (Y.M. 937.5.48).

(iv) Arras A.2. The Charioteer's Barrow.

Well-polished piece of antler, possibly used as a linch-pin (two were found, but only one survives). Its maximum length is 124mm and it tapers from a diameter of 22 by 18mm to a disc-terminal c. 11mm across. On the upper part is a band of lattice ornament and below, in the plane of the curve, a rectangular perforation 8 by 7mm. One side has been worn — noticeable particularly on the terminal disc and in the panel of lattice ornament. (Y.M. 903.1.48; Pl.8a; Fig.14, no.4; Davis & Thurnam 1865: no.8; Greenwell 1906: fig.25).

Metal linch-pins are not regularly found in the Yorkshire cart-burials — an observation emphasised by the absence of linch-pins in the carefully excavated Garton Slack grave-group. Amongst the older discoveries there are no surviving linch-pins, nor any record of them, from the reasonably recorded graves at Beverley and Pexton Moor; as well as the Lady's Barrow, Arras (though the grave-group may be incomplete) and Cawthorn Camps. No linch-pin survives from Hunmanby, and although Greenwell (1906:311) writes "two large

curved articles of iron are probably linch-pins", Sheppard (1907:483-4) records "two curved pieces of iron of doubtful use" in the grave, as well as "one or two curved pieces of iron" in the material which had fallen from the grave; in the absence of these iron pieces it is impossible to decide if they were linch-pins.

Metal linch-pins were included in the King's Barrow grave-group, in the Danes Grave cart-burial, and there is one from a possible cart-burial at Middleton-on-the-Wolds. These three sites had had linch-pins of different types. The one from the King's Barrow, an iron rod with bronze terminals, belongs to a popular British type (e.g. Bigbury, Kent, Ward Perkins 1940: fig.1, nos.1 and 2; Trevelgue, Cornwall, Ward Perkins 1941: pl.x; Wigginton Common, Tring, Herts., Ibid:pl,xi; Owslebury, Hants., Collis 1968:31, pl.xii) which was certainly in use in La Tène III (Llyn Cerrig Bach, Fox, 1946:78, pl.xv, no.42) and even into the second half of the first century A.D. (Stanwick, North Yorks., MacGregor 1962: fig.11, no.75). The Middleton linch-pin is an elaboration, with the upper terminal surmounted by a ring in a similar way to examples from the Stanwick hoard (Ibid: figs.10 and 11, nos.70 and 79). Simple rod linch-pins are found on the continent (Joffroy & Bretz-Mahler 1959: fig.6, no.1) and some are surmounted by rings (Bussy-le-Château, Marne, Stead 1965a: fig.16, no.1) but none are closely comparable to the British examples.

On the other hand, the linch-pins from Danes Graves, made entirely of iron and with long curved shanks and square heads, are extremely rare in Britain, but do occur abroad. The only comparable British piece known to the writer was found at Thornham, Norfolk (Norwich Castle Museum, 180.955; information from Miss B. Green). In Champagne similar linch-pins have been found in La Tène I cart-burials, e.g. at Prunay, Marne (Rowlett 1969:13 and fig.19) and Condé-sur-Marne (Stead 1965a: fig.16, no.4). More elaborate versions with bronze heads are found in later contexts ('Paris', Jacobsthal 1944: no.163; Nanterre, Hubert 1900:416, fig.1).

Apart from the metal linch-pins, one other object from a Yorkshire cart-burial might have served the same purpose, and that is the piece of decorated antler from the Charioteer's Barrow, Arras. Two such objects were found, but only one survives. The excavators associated them with the bronze case which has been interpreted as a pole-terminal, but they offered no identification for the antlers. Other writers have offered unconvincing identifications such as part of a horse-bit (but there were already two iron bits in the grave) and hand-holds at the

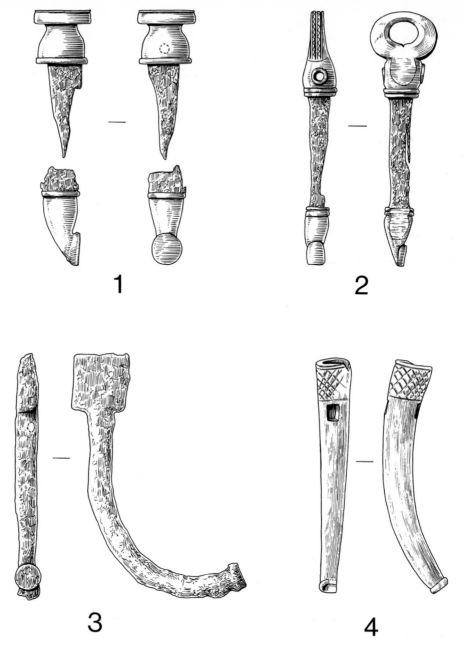

14. *Linch-pins: 1, King's Barrow, Arras; 2, Middleton-on-the-Wolds; 3, Danes Graves; 4, Charioteer's Barrow, Arras. Scale ½.*

back of the vehicle. But the surviving object does have something in common with a linch-pin: its general shape resembles the curved piece from Danes Graves; the decorated head, perforation, and knob on the foot are all features of linch-pins; and above all, there is marked wear on one side of the head. No metal linch-pin was found in the Charioteer's Barrow, and there seems no reason why a piece of antler should not have served this purpose. Indeed, linch-pins could have been made of even less durable material — Brewster 1971:291 has suggested that hard wood could have been used, and some such explanation seems necessary at Pexton Moor and Cawthorn Camps where the vehicles had been buried complete, with the wheels on the axle, but no linch-pin was found. In the Middle Rhine linch-pins are extremely rare (there is one, an isolated find from Niederweis, Jacobsthal 1944: no.161, comparable with those from 'Paris' and Nanterre) and there too their absence from vehicle-burials has led to the suggestion that they were made of wood (Haffner 1976:30).

3. Horse-bits

(i) Arras A.1. The King's Barrow.
A pair of horse-bits was found, but only the one survives. It has iron rings encased in bronze, whilst the three links are entirely of bronze. Three bronze pins with large heads (a fourth is missing) penetrate the bronze casing and iron rings at either side of the side-links. The side-links and rings are joined in a fixed position, at an angle of 152°, but with the two rings set in opposite directions; the overall length would have been 272mm, the rings are 80 by 82mm and 78 by 84mm diameter, the side-links 64mm long and the central link 73mm. (Y.M. 900.48; Fig.15, no.1; Stillingfleet 1846: fig. p.29; Davis & Thurnam 1865: no.10; Greenwell 1906: fig.22).

(ii) Arras A.3. The Lady's Barrow.
A pair of horse-bits. The rings are of iron encased in bronze; round the outside there is a slight ridge which expands into a lobe as it approaches the side-link. The rings are not exactly circular, nor are they equal in size: (10) is 71mm by 65mm and 68mm by 64mm, and (11) is 75mm by 70mm and 72mm by 71mm. The stops on the rings at either side of the side-links are bronze pins with quite large heads, 6mm across and 5mm high. The side-links are solid bronze, and are quite firmly fixed at an angle of about 145° to the rings. They are 55mm long, with well-worn circular perforations, 9mm by 12mm, and a slight cut centrally on each inner face. The central link is 49mm long and the perforations are worn. Overall lengths (i.e. present maximum lengths, they cannot be fully straightened) 236mm and 244mm. (B.M.77.10-16.10 and 11; Fig.16; Greenwell 1906: fig.29).

(iii) Garton Slack.
A pair of horse-bits of similar form, but made entirely of iron. The side-links and rings are corroded in a fixed position — set almost at right-angles to one another. The rings are on average 70mm diameter, the side-links between 52 and 58mm long and the central link c. 52mm long. (H.M.).

(iv) Beverley.
Two iron horse-bits, still in a conglomerate as excavated, and awaiting treatment. The rings seem to be very large c. 85 to 90mm diameter, but in their present state detailed measurements are not possible. (B.M. 75.10-5.3).

(v) Arras A.2. The Charioteer's Barrow.
Fragments of iron horse-bit(s) survive, but like those from Beverley treatment is needed before they can be studied. One iron ring, c. 70mm diameter, appears to have a long side-link attached (or possibly merely corroded onto it); the link is c. 85mm long and projects back into the ring where it terminates in a large disc c. 30mm diameter. (Y.M. 905.1-8.48).

(vi) Hunmanby.
A single bronze horse-bit, differing from the Arras type in that each side-link and ring are cast in one piece — both are now broken, both in the ring and link components. The rings are c. 72 and 75mm diameter, and the central link is 61mm long. (H.M.; Fig.15, no.2; Sheppard 1907:pl.).

(vii) Pexton Moor.
A badly corroded horse-bit. The rings are iron and one has the remains of a bronze casing: 62 to 70mm and 62 to 67mm diameter respectively. The side-links are also of iron, and appear to have been made in one piece with the rings — certainly there is no trace of a linking ring. The side-links are connected by a central circular iron ring, 27mm diameter. One side-link is covered with a bronze case 35mm long and 26mm diameter; the other is similarly cylindrical in shape but is a mass of iron with no trace of bronze. (Y.M.; Fig.15, no.3; Stead 1959:fig.1).

(viii) Danes Graves 43.
Parts of a horse-bit include a bronze cylinder 31mm long and 17 to 19mm diameter with an open joint along one side, set in plaster of paris; this feature resembles the cylinders on the Pexton Moor bit. Two iron rings are respectively 70 by 72mm and 77 by 82mm diameter; the ring-terminal of a side-link is attached to the bronze cylinder and linked with part of the central ring. (Y.M. 937.13, 15 and 18.48).

(ix) Cawthorn Camps.
The debris displayed at the centre of one of the iron tyres includes iron cylinders separated by a wooden packing from a central iron rod — these may well be the features observed on horse-bits from nearby Pexton Moor and from Danes Graves. (Y.M.).

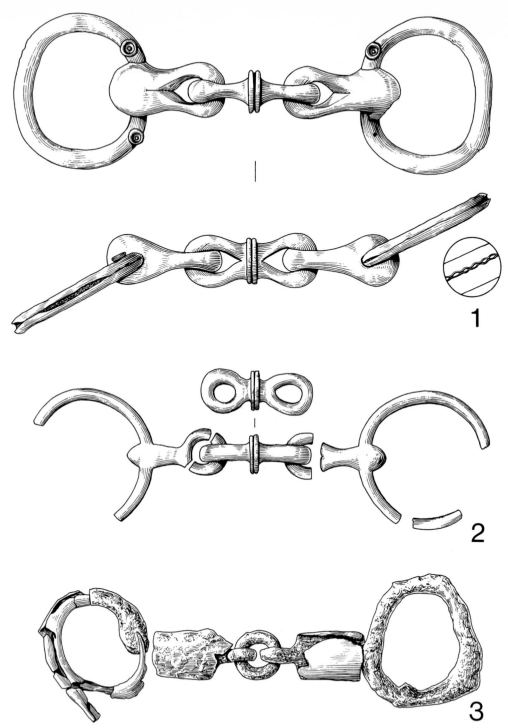

15.   *Horse-bits: 1, King's Barrow, Arras; 2, Hunmanby; 3, Pexton Moor. Scale ½.*

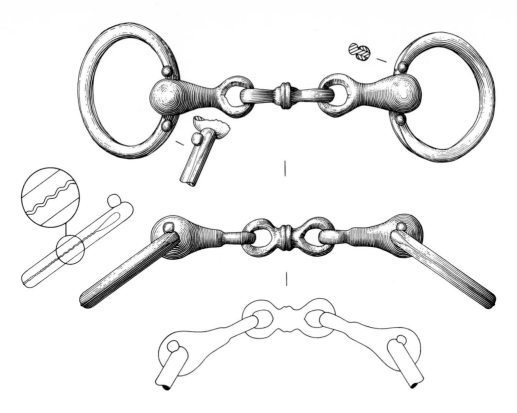

16.   Horse-bit from the Lady's Barrow, Arras. Scale ½.

The bits from the Lady's Barrow have rings and side-links firmly fixed at an angle of 145°, this can be no accident of corrosion, so the links must have been deliberately cast onto the rings in this position. The rings would have been so attached to go round the horse's cheek in the position necessary for use; the angle of use being clearly shown by the wear on the rings of the central link (Fig.16). The Garton Slack bits, entirely of iron, are also set at a rigid angle, and indeed so is that from the King's Barrow, which in its use of bronze and iron is closely comparable with the Lady's Barrow bits. But the rings on the King's Barrow bit would not fit comfortably round the horse's cheek — one of them would have projected outwards. It is obvious that the King's Barrow bit was the result of careless workmanship: a ring which had been formed in iron, encased in bronze and secured with bronze pegs was then set upside-down for the side-link to be cast on. There can be no doubt that the mistake was made at this stage because of the position of the surviving peg-head, and this is particularly interesting from a technological point of view because it suggests a sequence of manufacture different from that employed at Gussage All Saints. At Gussage, the rings were first attached to the side-links, and then the central link was cast on (Spratling, personal communication). But if this sequence had been adopted for the King's Barrow bit surely it would have been noticed that a ring had been attached upside-down. It seems more likely that the mistake was made in the final stage, which would thus have been the casting of one of the side-links onto a ring. It is also interesting from a ritual point of view: the bit could never have been used, for it would have been too uncomfortable (and predictably, in contrast to the Lady's Barrow bit, it shows no sign of wear), but it was regarded as good enough to suit the purposes of the dead 'King'.

The bronze and iron bits from the King's Barrow

and Lady's Barrow at Arras, and the iron examples from Garton Slack, belong to the same type, but the fragmentary iron bit from the Charioteer's Barrow is slightly different. Little can be said about this piece until it has received conservation treatment, but if the side-link does project back into the ring and terminate in a large disc, then it can be compared with examples from Hengistbury Head (Ward Perkins 1939:191 and pl.xvii, upper and middle) and Llyn Cerrig Bach (Fox 1946:81, no.51, and pl.xxiv) — both seem to have had decorative enamel bosses on their terminals.

The typology of British Iron Age horse-bits was first considered by Ward Perkins (1939) who drew attention to a fundamental division between two-link and three-link bits. Only the latter are found in the Arras Culture. Fox devised a typology of three-link bits (1946:30-1 and 82) subsequently modified by others (Clarke 1951:218-19; Barber & Megaw 1963), but it does not stand up to critical examination (Stead 1965a:41-2; Wainwright & Spratling 1973:123). The earliest form, typologically, is the one which has all components moving freely, and this is represented in an early (fifth century B.C.) context at Somme Tourbe, "La Gorge Meillet", (Marne) (Fourdrignier 1878: pl.iii). The Somme Tourbe bit is unique, and is considerably earlier than any other three-link bit from a datable context, but that is no reason to divorce it from the rest of the series. From this French prototype two main streams of development can be traced: the one, represented only in Ireland (Haworth 1971) has side-links with the two perforations in the same plane, as at Somme Tourbe; the other, found in England, has side-links whose perforations are in opposite planes. The Arras bits are some way removed from the assumed prototype, indeed they are more similar to those for which moulds have been found in the remains of a foundary at Gussage All Saints (Dorset), a deposit dated to the first century B.C. (Wainwright & Spratling 1973:121, 123 and pl.xxii, 1 to 3). The dating evidence for horse-bits epitomises the problems of British Iron Age chronology: contacts with the classical world provide one anchor in the fifth century B.C. and another four centuries or so later, leaving the Arras material floating vaguely between the two.

The Hunmanby bit is entirely of bronze, with the side-link and ring cast in one piece, in a straight line, and without pegs. Its ancestry could diverge from the main series of three-link horse-bits at an early stage, before that represented at Arras, although the most closely comparable bit, from Old Windsor (Barber & Megaw 1953) has residual peg-heads on the rings. The descendants of the Hunmanby type of bit are well known in the north, where some examples can be clearly dated to the first century

A.D. (MacGregor 1962:23, nos.37-50). From the area of the Arras Culture there is one example of this later series, found unassociated at Rise, in Holderness (Greenwell 1906: fig.23).

The horse-bit from Pexton Moor is also of three-link form, but its central link is a simple ring, quite different from the bits considered so far. Iron three-link bits with central ring have been found with three La Tène I cart-burials in Champagne (Prunay, "Les Commelles", Marne, Favret 1929:25 and fig.iv; Fère-en-Tardenois, "La Sablonnière", Aisne, Moreau 1894: pl.F; Ciry-Salsogne, "Les Grévières", Ibid. pl.140). None of these French examples has a casing over a side-link, as at Pexton Moor, but a two-link bit from London has iron rings in a comparable position (Wheeler, 1946:149, pl.lix, no.2) and they are very like 'cherry-rollers' on modern bits. The Danes Graves and Cawthorn Camps horse-bits may be compared with Pexton Moor on the grounds of the cylindrical covers for the side-links, but other features of these bits are obscure. The Pexton Moor type of horse-bit does not seem to have become popular for no other examples have been noted in Britain.

4. Terrets

(i) Hunmanby.
An undecorated bronze and iron terret. The iron has corroded, and very little survives, but it probably formed a fairly straight bar. The curved bronze part had been cast onto the iron and at the surviving terminals it is clear that the bronze was encasing the iron (it is also clear that just beyond the terminals the bronze is solid). 71mm across. (H.M.; Fig.17, no.1; Sheppard 1907:pl.).

(ii) Arras A.1. The King's Barrow.
Two bronze and iron terrets, each formed like the Hunmanby example and having very little surviving iron; but they differ from Hunmanby in having lip-ornament. The larger piece, 66mm across, has nine lip-mouldings including squashed versions at the terminals; the smaller piece, 62mm across, has seven lip-mouldings — the outermost mouldings forming the terminals. (Y.M. 902.1 and 2.48; Fig.17, nos.3 and 4; Davis & Thurnam 1865: no.13 — presumably represents the heavier piece, but shows it terminating in full lip-mouldings and with a complete iron cross-bar).

(iii) Arras A.3. The Lady's Barrow.
A single bronze and iron terret very similar to those from the King's Barrow, and made in the same way. It measures 58mm across and has 10 lip-mouldings, the terminal ones being abbreviated; the iron cross-bar survives intact. (B.M. 77.10-16.9; Fig.17, no.2; Greenwell 1906: fig.30).

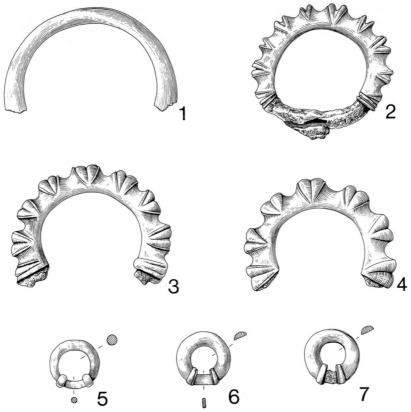

17. *Terrets: 1, Hunmanby; 2, Lady's Barrow, Arras; 3 and 4, King's Barrow, Arras. Harness loops: 5, Hunmanby; 6 and 7, King's Barrow, Arras. Scale ⅔.*

(iv) Garton Slack.

Five terrets were found, the two now on display are 41 and 51mm wide, and the excavator refers to four medium terrets and one larger. They have iron cross-bars and bronze bodies, and resemble the example from Hunmanby, but with the addition of a bead of ?coral on the top. (Brewster 1971:290; H.M.).

Harness rings:

(v) Danes Graves 43.

Two iron rings, with a bronze casing for much of their circumference; very light in weight, presumably because of the corrosion of the iron; badly corroded and set in plaster of paris. The one is 62mm diameter and the bronze covers all but a length of about 30mm; the other is 47mm diameter and about 20mm of the iron is uncovered. (Y.M. 937.11 and 12.48). Mortimer 1897:9 describes five

"hollow rings of bronze, resembling thin tubing" (his nos.2, 3, 6, 7 and 9) — the only items in his account which might be correlated with these pieces in the Yorkshire Museum. Two of Mortimer's 'hollow rings' were 2in (5cm), two were 2½ (6cm) and the fifth was 2¾in (7cm) in diameter.

(vi) Cawthorn Camps.

Of the objects displayed in the centre of one of the wheels there appear to be no D-shaped terrets, but there could well be harness-rings resembling those from Danes Graves. (Y.M.).

(vii) Beverley.

There is part of a smaller ring in the conglomerate with one of the horse-bits. (B.M. 75.10-5.3).

Harness loops:

(viii) Hunmanby.

A single small bronze ring, somewhat corroded and damaged, with two rounded mouldings separating a

51

length on which a leather strap would have pivotted. The piece is 22mm across, and completely rounded in section. (H.M.; Fig.17, no.5; Sheppard 1907:pl.).

(ix) Arras A.1. The King's Barrow.
A pair of similar harness loops, but they have stronger and more elongated mouldings, and are completely flat on the back. 22 and 23mm across. (Y.M. 902.3 and 4.48; Fig.17, nos.6 and 7; Davis & Thurnam 1865: no.14).

Terrets of D-shape have been regarded as characteristic of the Arras Culture, although they have been found in only four burials. Two survive from the King's Barrow and one from the Lady's Barrow at Arras; there is one from Hunmanby; and five from Garton Slack. Leeds (1933:121-2) deduced from the Stanwick hoard that a set of double-harness included five terrets; his conclusion was supported by the record of five being found in the King's Barrow, and is now fully confirmed by the discovery of five at Garton Slack. One terret in the set is always larger than the others; the four similar in size would have been positioned at either side of the horses' heads, where surviving wooden yokes have holes in appropriate positions for reins (Vouga 1923:pl.xxxv, 1 and 2; Piggott 1949b: fig.1). The fifth terret, the large one, could have been positioned on the pole, or centrally on the front of the bodywork. Two cart-burials, Hunmanby and the Lady's Barrow, produced only one terret each: both burials had been disturbed by quarrying before they were examined by archaeologists, so that it is possible that the grave-groups were incomplete; but it is unlikely that much would have escaped the attentions of such determined collectors as Greenwell and Sheppard, and it may be that these graves had only a single terret, corresponding, perhaps, with the larger terret from other harness-sets.

D-shaped terrets were found at three sites in the Arras Culture, and each site produced a different type. That from Hunmanby is the simplest, a plain unornamented bronze, lacking the iron cross-bar. It may well have had terminal bronze mouldings originally, in which case it would have resembled one of the terrets from Llyn Cerrig Bach (Fox 1946:79, no.44, pls.ii and xvi). The Garton Slack terrets differ from Hunmanby only in the addition of a bead of ornament on the top. With the further addition of similar ornament on the sides this type was to become a popular form, particularly in north Britain (MacGregor 1976:nos.64-109). The lipped terrets found at Arras can be readily matched in southern England, and when they occur in a datable context it seems to be La Tène III (Richmond 1968:40, fig.31, from hut 60; Bulleid & Gray 1911:230, pl.xliv, E.192; Wainwright & Spratling 1973:121).

The ancestry of the type is not easy to establish. It flourished in Britain in the first centuries B.C. and A.D., with several more varieties than those present in the Arras Culture, and on the continent La Tène III also saw the popularity of terrets. But the continental forms are quite different from the British, having complete rings surmounting broad central stems. The two principal types (Menke 1968) have been found in La Tène III oppida, and they also occur in late cart-burials in France at Nanterre, (Seine), (Hubert 1900:411-12, fig.10) and Armentières, (Aisne), (Mariën 1961: fig.68, no.8). Elaborate terrets are a feature of the group of late vehicle-burials in north-west France and Belgium (p.26), but these grave-groups were not scientifically excavated, so they may be incomplete and there is no record of the position of the terrets in the graves. At both Nanterre and Leval-Trahegnies three terrets survive from a presumed set of four; elsewhere La Tène III terrets occur singly or in pairs, but this is not particularly significant because the only burials are cremations, where incomplete collections of vehicle-remains and harness are to be expected.

La Tène I vehicle-burials did not have specialised forms of terret, but made use of simple rings. The best evidence comes from Champagne, where there are plans of carts laid out with harness in position: at both Somme Tourbe, "La Gorge Meillet" (Fourdrignier 1878: pl.i) and Châlons-sur-Marne (Lemoine 1905: pl.i) the plans show a line of four rings across the grave mid-way between the wheels and the horse-bits. As already noted, D-shaped terrets were found in only four of the Arras Culture cart-burials, and elsewhere it seems likely that simple rings served the purpose, as in Champagne. Such rings were found with the cart-burial at Danes Graves where iron rings partly covered with bronze were probably used as terrets. These pieces could have formed an intermediate stage between the bronze rings on the continent and the D-terrets used in Britain. There are simple rings from other Yorkshire cart-burials, but no proof that they were used as terrets.

The small harness loops from Hunmanby and the King's Barrow at Arras were associated with cart-burials so their identification as part of the harness seems clear. But this type could have had other purposes, and it is worth noting a couple of similar pieces in the coin-hoard (A.D. 74) from Honley, near Huddersfield (Richmond 1925:14 and figs.2 and 2a; MacGregor 1976: nos.52 and 53) where there were no other items of harness or vehicle-fittings. Unlike the larger versions this miniature D-terret can be matched on the continent, for there is a piece of similar size (25mm) and form (but hollowed round the edge to house inlay) amongst the harness and cart-fittings at Leval-Trahegnies (Mariën 1961:49, no.61).

5. Miscellaneous Cart and Harness Fittings

(i) **Bronze Case:** Arras A.2. The Charioteer's Barrow.

An open bronze case, maximum length 140mm. It is tubular towards one end, with a flared terminal, *c.*53mm diameter, ringed with nail-holes and now damaged. The main part is half-tubular and has nail-holes at the side and end. At the tubular end the joint, on the underside, is covered on the inside with a strip of iron-corrosion about 17mm wide. In the centre there is a rectangular perforation, 16 by 9mm, and adjoining it is the remains of an iron nail. (Y.M. 903.2.48; Fig.18, no.1; Davis & Thurnam 1865: no.9; Greenwell 1906: fig.26).

The purpose of the bronze case from the Charioteer's Barrow is a puzzle which several authorities have tackled without reaching a satisfactory conclusion. It seems generally agreed that it was the terminal of a length of wood, and the discussion centres on whether that wood was a cart-pole or a yoke.

The excavators seem to have identified the piece as a case for the antler 'linch-pin' (p.45), and Greenwell (1906:283) whilst noting that it was regarded "by others as the end of the pole of the chariot" was himself content to call it no more than a "bronze object". Fox (1949a) endorsed the pole-tip theory, and compared it with one of his finds from Llyn Cerrig Bach; but later he rather spoilt his case by comparing it with a pair of objects from Lough Gur (Fox 1950) which are more reasonably interpreted as terminals of a yoke (Piggott 1969:381).

The possibility that the Arras piece could belong to a yoke was considered by the present writer without conviction (Stead 1965a:35) and Piggott (1969) also toyed with the idea. The principal objection to this theory is that unlike the Lough Gur bronzes, there is only one piece from Arras, not a pair. It is conceivable that a second bronze case from Arras was disposed of elsewhere — for the Yorkshire Museum received less than a half-share of the finds from the 1815-17 excavations — but there is no mention of another in the excavators' records. As yoke-mounts the Lough Gur pieces have been compared with the 'chariot-horns' from Waldalgesheim (Piggott 1969; Jacobsthal 1944: no.156a) which had been reconstructed on the ends of a yoke by Mariën (1961:176, and fig.66). Mariën suggested a similar function for the 'chariot-horn' from Somme Tourbe, "La Bouvandeau", which had been compared with the Waldalgesheim pieces by Jacobsthal (1944: no.168), but only the one 'chariot-horn' was found there (Flouest 1885,102). If the bronze objects from Somme Tourbe and Arras were found singly then it is better to assign them to a unique position on any reconstruction, which tips the balance in favour of the cart-pole-terminal.

(ii) **Iron Case:** Garton Slack.

An iron case from the Garton Slack cart-burial has been interpreted as a cap for the end of the pole. (Brewster 1971:291; H.M.).

(iii) **Bronze Disc:** Arras A.2. The Charioteer's Barrow.

A circular bronze disc, dished in the centre and cordonned on the flange, 113mm diameter. It has a central iron nail whose head stands well-proud of the bronze. The disc has a separate bronze binding which is complete but in two parts: the two terminals of the binding are perforated through both faces (one terminal has two perforations) matching a pair of holes near the edge of the disc. The additional perforation of the binding might well have been too near the edge to hit the disc; and a further pair of perforations on the disc would have been rendered useless because one perforates the rim. (Y.M. 904. 1.48; Fig.18, no.4; Davis & Thurnam 1865: no.7; Greenwell 1906: fig.24).

As with the bronze case from this grave, there is no ready explanation of the function of the disc. Bronze and iron discs comparable in size to that from the Charioteer's Barrow have been found in several contexts in the European Iron Age — indeed, both Hallstatt (Kromer 1959:25, pl.7, no.11; pl.79, nos. 3 to 6, etc.) and La Tène (Vouga 1923: pl.xxxvii, no.3) have produced examples. The Charioteer's disc differs from others in two respects — it is concave in the centre, and it has a separate bronze binding round the rim. Nevertheless, it may be classified under the general heading of 'phalera', although the precise function of such pieces is a matter of controversy — indeed different pieces no doubt served different functions (Kimmig 1970; Snodgrass 1973). In western Europe they have been interpreted as horse-brasses, shield-bosses and ornaments on tunics or belts. The context of the Arras example, in a vehicle-burial associated with harness, would be consistent with the horse-brass interpretation, although there are no strap-loops on the underside of the disc. If it is to be interpreted instead as part of a shield it might appear odd that no weapons were found in the grave — although it would not be unique in such a situation, for shields without weapons have been recorded in other La Tène graves (Stanfordbury, Stead 1967:36; Snailwell, Lethbridge 1953:32).

Certainly the excavator regarded it as part of a shield, and his description implies that more than one disc (or boss) was found (Stillingfleet 1846:30) — one was adjoining the skull, which had been stained green by the contact. Stillingfleet also

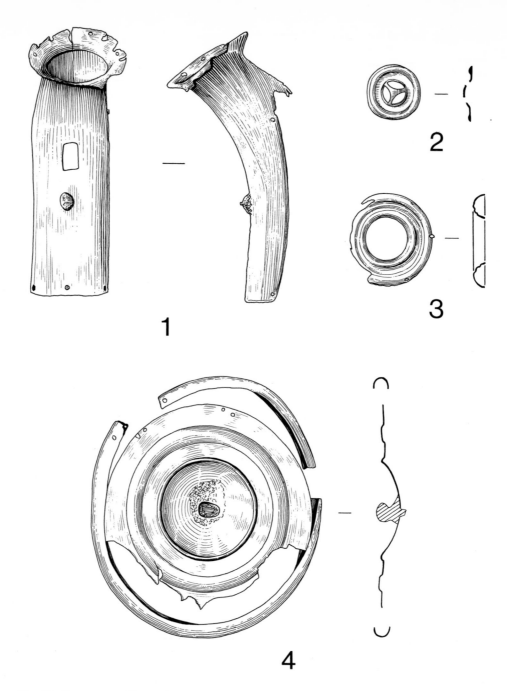

1

2

3

4

18. *Miscellaneous cart and harness fittings: 1, bronze case, Charioteer's Barrow, Arras; 2, bronze disc, Charioteer's Barrow, Arras; 3, bronze disc, Danes Graves; 4, bronze disc, Charioteer's Barrow, Arras. Scale ½.*

confirms that the disc had been attached to wood; but if it had belonged to a shield, then because of the dished centre and the position of the binding, it must have been mounted on a wooden disc subsequently attached to the shield, and it can hardly have been the central boss covering the hand-grip. But it could have ornamented a shield in a way like the terminal discs on the Battersea and Witham shields, or like the smaller Bugthorpe and Grimthorpe discs (p.59).

Otherwise the main wooden objects in the grave would have been the body of the vehicle, which could have been ornamented with one or more bronze discs, and the yoke. It is conceivable that the disc ornamented the same object as the curious bronze case — indeed, the flaring end of the case could have been expanding out to the borders of the disc. The yokes from La Tène do terminate in discs (Vouga 1923:95-6 and pl.xxxv) but they are less than half the size of the Arras disc.

(iii) Bronze Strap-links: Garton Slack.
A pair of bronze strap-links comprising a figure-of-eight design with a bar at each side (H.M.).

For the type see Bulleid & Gray 1911:228-9, pl.xliv, no.E.262; and they are listed by MacGregor 1976:56.

(iv) Bronze Caps and Ferrules:
a. Arras A.3. The Lady's Barrow.
Greenwell 1877:456 describes a bronze cap, now lost. He likens it to a box-lid, about 1in (25mm) diameter and slightly less in depth, with two long pins to fasten it to the wood. He suggests that it may have been the metal end of a whip.
b. Garton Slack.
Brewster (1971:290) describes a bronze pommel and bronze strips which he also interprets as parts of a whip.

(v) Miscellaneous objects: Danes Graves 43.
a. An iron ring, c.50mm diameter. Although found near the skull it was immediately adjoining the harness rings and is unlikely to have been a personal ornament. (Y.M. 937.17.48; Mortimer 1897: pl.i, a).
b. A circular disc of thin bronze, half-tubular in section, 49mm diameter and 13mm across, ornamented with three slight cordons. The ring is broken along the outer edge of one half, but along the surviving edge there are three perforations, of which the central one bears the remains of a short iron nail. (Y.M. 937.10.48; Fig.18, no.3; Mortimer 1897: pl.i, no.1).
c. "Two small button-shaped plates of thin bronze, slightly convex on one side and concave on the other" ¾in (2cm) and 1in (2.5cm) diameter respectively. "The larger one has a small hole through the centre, and on the convex side is a faintly-engraved representation of a wheel with four spokes" (Mortimer 1897:9-10). These objects have not survived.

(vi) Miscellaneous objects: Arras A.2, The Charioteer's Barrow.
a. Iron ring, 35mm diameter, with traces of a bronze cover (Y.M. 905. 1-8.48).
b. Part of a flat iron ring, 45mm diameter (Y.M. 905. 1-8.48).
c. Short iron strip, 72mm long and 10mm wide, with a nail through one end (Y.M. 905. 1-8.48).
d. Short length of bronze case, 37mm long, with two perforations in each face (Y.M. 904.5.48).
e. A bronze disc whose central dome has cut-out ornament. Flat on the under side, with traces of iron corrosion attached. (Y.M. 925.48; Fig.18, no.2; Greenwell 1906: fig.27). Although included in the Charioteer's Barrow group by Greenwell (Ibid.: 283-4) it is not mentioned by Stillingfleet and is registered separately in the Yorkshire Museum.

6. Shields

(i) Grimthorpe
a. A domed bronze cap, slightly elongated oval in shape, with a central nail in situ and holes for four other nails, two at the ends and two centrally on the sides. The cap, which would have ornamented the centre of the boss, is decorated with a punched and engraved design which creates a central circle divided into quarters. The cap is 109mm long and 84mm wide. (B.M.1876.2-8.1; Fig.19, no.1; Mortimer 1905: frontispiece; Stead 1968: fig 12, no.1).
b. Two flat crescentic-shaped bronze plates, which would have adorned the shield at either side of the central cap. The outer band is decorated by a series of punched L-shaped motifs. The plates have been nailed to the body of the shield, but none of the nails are in position now. Both plates had cracked while in use, and had been nailed again along the lines of the cracks. It seems that the piece was fastened with different types of nail, presumably at different times. There are small and large circular holes, and also some rectangular holes with associated iron-staining. The plaques are 312mm long. (B.M.1876.2-8.1; Fig.19, no.1; Mortimer 1905: frontispiece; Stead 1968: fig.12, nos.2 and 3).
c. Two lengths of half-tubular sheet-bronze, rounded at the one end and open at the other. These pieces, respectively 280 and 290mm long, covered lengths of the spine of the shield. There is a small panel of ornament, similar to that on the bronze cap, towards the open end of each piece. The spine-covers have each been attached by two rivets, one at either end, and one surviving at a rounded end is 17mm long. The surviving rivet has a large, well-rounded head on the inside of the shield.

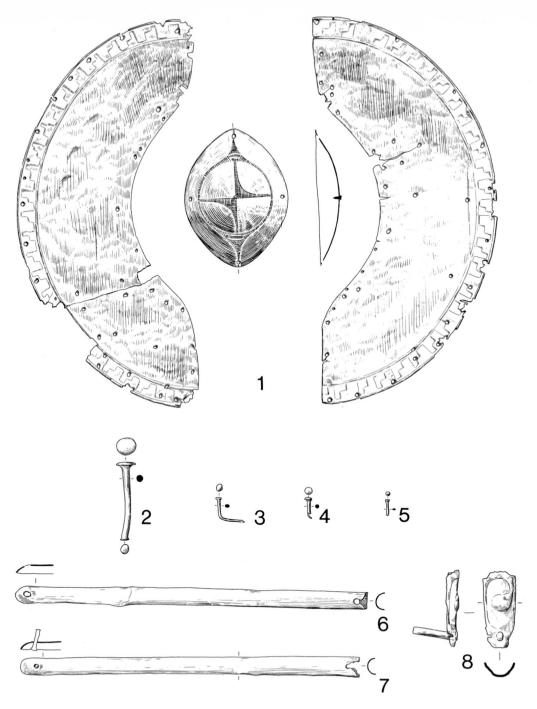

19.   *Shield fittings: 1-7, Grimthorpe; 8, North Grimston. 1, 6 and 7, Scale ⅓; 2-5 and 8, Scale ⅔.*

(B.M. 1876.2-8.2; Fig.19, nos.6 and 7; Mortimer 1905: frontispiece, shows all rivets in position; Stead 1968: fig.12, nos.4 and 5).

d. Another rivet, similar to the one in the spine-cover but 30mm long. It seems likely that this would have been at the open end of the spine-cover, where it would have had to be longer because of the increase in thickness of the spine towards the central boss. (B.M.1876.2-8.6; Fig.19, no.2; Stead 1968: fig.12, no.6).

e. Three short bronze pins; two broken, now 6mm and 8mm long; the third is complete, but bent, and 18mm long. Possibly used to secure the bronze plates to the shield. (B.M.1876.2-8.7 and 8; Fig.19, nos.3 to 5; Stead 1968: fig.12, nos.7 to 9).

(ii) Eastburn

Half-tubular length of sheet-bronze, very similar to those from Grimthorpe. It is 301mm long and curved in section — open at one end, where it is 17mm wide and about 6mm high, and closed at the other end where it has narrowed to 13mm wide about 3mm from the end. It has been attached by two bronze rivets, again very similar to those from Grimthorpe, each about 3mm diameter with slightly enlarged flattened heads. The one rivet is centred about 8mm from the open end and is about 29mm long; the other is centred 14mm from the closed end and is about 20mm long. (H.M.3032.42; Sheppard 1939: pl.i, no.3).

There is also a length of bronze shield-binding from the site — possibly from the same shield, but the Eastburn finds were not recorded in grave-groups. It is associated with three bronze clips which would have attached it to the wood, and has been mounted and restored for display. The binding is straight, and 307mm long: the two outermost clips are centred 300mm apart, and the middle one is only 2mm away from being central to them. The clips are held by rivets about 10mm long and they appear to have been attached to wood about 7mm thick. (H.M.3033.42; Sheppard 1939: pl.i, no.4).

(iii) North Grimston

The rounded terminal of a spine-cover, very similar to those from Grimthorpe and Eastburn, except that this one has a fragment of repoussé ornament. It has been attached by a rivet, about 3mm diameter and 18mm long, centred 5mm from the end. There are five other fragments of half-tubular bronze from the grave — one 58mm long and 12mm wide is fairly flat and may also have been part of a spine cover; the others could have been from the binding of the edge of a shield. (H.M.3005.42; Fig.19, no.8; Mortimer 1905: fig.1019).

(iv) Hunmanby.

Sheppard 1907:483-4, refers to a wooden shield with bronze binding and thin plates of bronze ornamenting the upper surface. Among the finds surviving are four short lengths of half-tubular bronze — the longest is 43mm — and they vary from 6 to 8mm across; they seem quite narrow for shield-binding, but in view of Sheppard's description they cannot be discounted (H.M. 3017.42). Several other pieces of bronze survive, including one which is slightly ridged. A large fragment, about 75 by 80mm, has one original edge, with an engraved line and a rivet adjoining; from the edge the piece curves upwards and inwards — similar to the curve on an umbo but rather higher — more like that of a helmet. (H.M. 3018.42).

(v) Burton Fleming.

The iron fittings of a shield were found in 1975 — comprising a curious figure-of-eight umbo and some iron binding. These pieces are still undergoing conservation and study.

(vi) Wetwang Slack.

A fragment of iron binding was found in the same grave as the sword.

Apart from the Burton Fleming example, and the Hunmanby and Wetwang Slack fragments which defy classification, the shields belong to the same type, which is best represented at Grimthorpe. It must have been an oval or rectangular shield with a long central spine swollen in the middle to form a boss. Wooden shields of this type are well known from La Tène (Vouga 1923:59-62) and from Hjortspring (Rosenberg 1937:48-61 and 106-9), and metal fittings have been found frequently in continental graves. But those fittings are usually of iron, and they comprise umbos to cross the central boss and edge-bindings. On continental shields the ends of the spine were usually left uncovered, and bronze was very rarely used. But in Britain the situation was quite different — on this type of shield the whole length of the spine was often covered and sometimes elaborated into a major decorative feature; iron was used only rarely.

Continental shields with bronze-covered spines seem to be extremely rare, but an example from Etrechy, Marne, has a single long narrow cover for the boss and the full length of the spine (Stead 1968: 176 and fig.17, no.5). Such a shield could have been ancestral to the Grimthorpe type, and other British shields (Ibid.; fig.18). The Etrechy shield is La Tène I (cf. the associated plaques, Jacobsthal 1944: no.376, whose decoration compares with objects in Early La Tène graves in the Rhineland, e.g. Ibid.: nos.26 and 34).

The following discs are not obviously parts of shields, but a case can be made for their identification as shield-fittings and they fit better here than elsewhere in the text:

(i) Grimthorpe.

A bronze disc 48mm diameter (almost the same as the smaller disc from Bugthorpe, below) with lobed

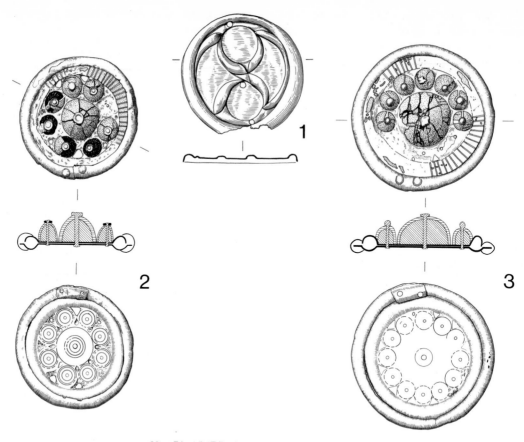

20. Discs: 1, Grimthorpe; 2 and 3, Bugthorpe. Scale ⅔.

repoussé ornament in a central circle with an asymmetric border. There are three nail-holes in a line across the disc, and on the underside a slight stain in the patina along the same line. (B.M. 76. 2-8. 3; Pl.8b; Fig.20, no.1; Mortimer 1905: frontispiece; Stead 1968: fig.13, no.1).

(ii) and (iii) **Bugthorpe.**

Two bronze discs with red glass ornament on the upper face. B.M. 1905.7-17.4 is 58mm diameter and consists of a bronze disc with a concentric channel *c*. 5mm wide set about 5mm from the edge. In the channel is a ring of red glass which seems to be partitioned by a closely-spaced series of thin bronze plates — giving the surviving surface a ribbed effect. At the centre of the disc, on the upper surface, is a large red glass dome (21mm across) secured by a central bronze rivet. The surface of the dome is cracked, but details of its construction are obscure. Between the central dome and the ring of red glass there have been 12 smaller red glass domes (7 to 8mm diameter) of which seven survive. The smaller domes are pinned in the same way as the central dome, and one of them appears to be a replacement

— it is made of glass with a slightly more orange tint, and its bronze pin has a more elaborate head. The positions of the domes are reflected by inscribed circles on the underside. The disc has a separate bronze binding whose joint is secured by two rivets which share a common rectangular washer on the underside.

B.M. 1905.7-17.5 is similar, but smaller, 49mm diameter. Its central dome is 16mm diameter and is surrounded by eight smaller domes (7 to 8mm diameter) of which seven survive. It seems that the domes on this piece were constructed in a slightly different way, and they have a dark grey matrix. (Fig.20, nos.2 and 3; Greenwell 1906: fig.125 illustrates the larger disc, omitting the position of one of the domes; for an analysis of the glass see Hughes 1972: 102)

As the construction of the Bugthorpe discs is by no means obvious, they were submitted to the British Museum Research Laboratory for technical examination. The following report has been prepared by P. T. Craddock and M. S. Tite:

58

"The following description of how the discs were constructed is mainly based on visual examination under the binocular microscope, and from radiographs. In addition, qualitative surface analysis of some of the components was carried out by X-ray fluorescence spectrometer.

The circular base plates of the discs are both of unleaded bronze and are approximately 0.5mm in thickness. The raised annular decoration of the base is quite pronounced, and this suggests they were cast, not hammered. No negative of this work appears on the opposite face, thus repoussé is ruled out. Examination of the groups of circles surrounding the stud holes on the back plates suggest they were on the original casting, not chased on afterwards, as none of the characteristic marks left by such work can be observed. The radiograph of the large disc reveals a large oval hole in the base plate, (once concealed by the studs, and now obscured by corrosion); this is almost certainly a casting flaw and is confirmation that the bases are cast, not hammered up.

From the radiographs it can be seen that there are a series of circular holes in the edge of both base plates. These holes are now covered by the rough rims that surround the edges. The holes on the edge of the large disc lie in two irregularly spaced groups of several holes each. The holes are of similar size to the rivet holes, but it is most unlikely that they orginally held studs similar to those surviving inside, as there is insufficient space between the holes and the ring of enamel. The very irregular spacing of the holes mitigates against this interpretation as well. More probably they were holes made to facilitate securing the disc to some backing of cloth, leather or wood. The openwork base of the smaller disc has a regularly spaced group of eight gaps formed between the central stud and the ring of smaller studs surrounding it. These gaps have a distinctive dart shape, formed of a circle with 'V' extension (see radiograph). A further 16 of these distinctive shapes although fragmentary can be seen on the radiograph repeated at regular intervals around the edge of the back plate, once again now covered by the attached rim. The original edge of the back plate as seen on the radiograph is very rough and has already been cut back; thus there is a very distinct possibility that the original disc had an outer ring of sixteen studs of which the only evidence is now the openwork edges of the circles on the base plate. Both discs were modified by having a rim attached. This consists of a sheet of unleaded bronze bent around the edge in a rough semicircle and held at the join by two bronze rivets passing through the sleeve.

The studs are held to the base by rivets, and in the case of the smaller disc the heads have washers. In both cases the studs are made up of glass arranged upon a bed of putty. Qualitative analysis showed this to contain mainly calcium, iron and silicon. This suggests the putty backing originally consisted of a mixture of calcite and sand held together by wax. Such backings were common in the Roman and Migration period (Arrhenius 1971:216-19).

As well as the studs, the two discs each have an annulus of red enamel held in an iron cellular structure. It is not certain how the iron was originally held to the base. Although the use of separate rivetting can be ruled out, it is probable that the iron was originally not just a ring but a circular plate extending beneath the studs, and was held by their rivets. Unfortunately, the iron is totally corroded, and no definite trace of such a plate exists now. It is, however, interesting to note that the red glass of the stud stops short of the base plate by about a millimetre suggesting that the corroded material now there may have once been a continuous iron plate. Otherwise the enamelled ring would have just been glued to the base plate which seems rather flimsy, especially when compared with the elaborate rivetting of the studs."

The Grimthorpe disc has long been regarded as a shield ornament (Smith 1905:104-5), although precisely where it was fitted on the shield is a matter of conjecture. Similar decorative features are known on some continental La Tène shields, as well as on sculptural representations of shields (Stead 1968:176-8; Moucha 1974, shows decorative plaques of different shapes on a La Tène I shield).

The Bugthorpe discs are more a problem, for although they were found with a warrior-burial within about 6km of Grimthorpe there is no record of a shield having been found. In two nineteenth-century accounts (Thurnam 1871:475; Greenwell 1877:50, note 1) it was assumed that the discs were brooches, but no springs or pins survive. However, there is a striking parallel from Bohemia, where a warrior grave at Sulejovice, dating from the end of La Tène I, produced a couple of iron discs each with central inlay dome surrounded by radiating beads and bordered by a ribbed ring of inlay (Moucha 1969:597-8, pl.iii). The Sulejovice discs, slightly smaller than those from Bugthorpe (30mm diameter) were found on the body of the warrior at either side of the remains of an iron umbo and hand-hold. Their identification as shield ornaments is further supported by another find from Czechoslovakia, for a nineteenth-century excavation of a warrior-burial at Letky, near Prague, produced a grave-group including a sword, spearhead, shield-remains and three discs. Two of the Letky discs are more comparable in size to the Yorkshire ones (46mm diameter) and the third is only 25mm (*Ibid.*: 606-7). In publishing these Czechoslovak discoveries Moucha also drew attention to another

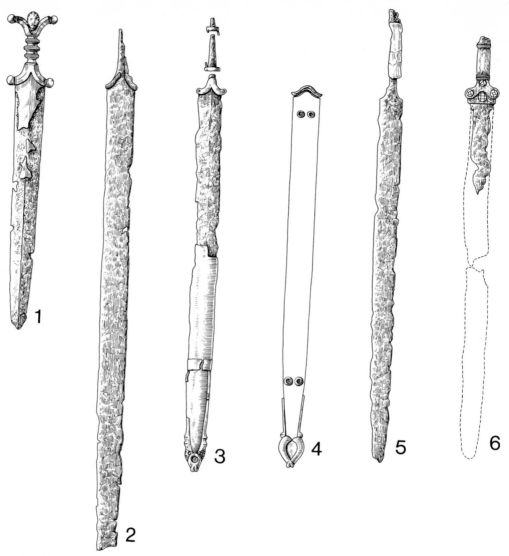

21. *Swords and scabbards: 1 and 2, North Grimston; 3, Grimthorpe; 4, Bugthorpe; 5, Eastburn; 6, Thorpe. Scale* ⅛.

pair of decorated discs, possibly similar in function, found in Champagne (*Ibid.*: 606, fig.6).

The Grimthorpe disc can undoubtedly be accepted as a shield ornament, and on the analogy of the Czechoslovakian finds it seems likely that the Bugthorpe discs also ornamented a shield — although precisely how they were fitted to the shield is not obvious. It may be that the argument can be taken a stage further to involve the disc from the Charioteer's Barrow, Arras, which shares with Bugthorpe the feature of a separate bronze binding — but the Arras disc is much larger (113mm) and it has been classified above as a phaleron (p.53).

7. Swords and Scabbards

(i) **Bugthorpe.**

An iron sword in a bronze and iron scabbard. It has a bronze hilt-end, deeply grooved at the front, but the rest of the hilt and even the tang is now lacking. The blade must have measured about 570mm; it is *c.* 40mm wide and narrows only slightly for 450mm — it is 37mm wide at the top of the chape. There seems to be no midrib — and certainly there is no central ridge in the bronze scabbard-plate.

The scabbard measures 608mm in full, and consists of a bronze front-plate whose edges have been wrapped over the edges of an iron back (most of the back is now lost), down to the level of the chape which then binds the two plates. The front plate is superbly decorated: below a top panel with a circular motif and a pair of studs, there is a flowing design covering the full length and width of the scabbard-plate. The design is no doubt chased rather than engraved, but the surface is considerably eroded. The chape has been 146mm long, but the upper part is now missing. The chape-end is a heavy bronze moulding terminating in a lip-motif surmounted on each face by a heart-shaped perforation. At either side of the perforation, on the front face only, are relief lobe-motifs with a hatched background. The chape-end is capped by a moulding on either side; no bridge survives to link the chape-sides, but there is a fragment of cut-out ornament at the bottom on the back. A pair of studs fitted to the bronze scabbard-plate mark the top of the chape, and match the very similar pair just below the mouth of the scabbard.

A couple of bronze studs were found at the same time and they doubtless decorated the hilt. At the front their heads match the four studs on the scabbard, but these loose studs each have two circular heads (the back ones undecorated) linked by a bronze shank. They measure 20-22mm long and the heads are 14mm diameter.

(B.M. 1905.7-17. 1, the sword and scabbard, Pl.10a, Fig.21, no.4; 2 and 3, the two studs, Fig.22, no.3; Piggott 1950: fig.2, no.5, and pl. iii; Fox 1958: pl.53, c).

(ii) Grimthorpe.

An iron sword in a bronze and iron scabbard. The tang is now broken, and in three parts which do not join, but the entire piece must have measured at least 720mm. The blade is 41mm wide at the top, and has a slight midrib; it has been about 590mm long, maintaining the top width to about 440mm and thereafter tapering — the blade cannot be measured more closely because of the scabbard. At the top of the blade is a highly arched bronze hilt-end terminating in transverse projecting rods at either end. The top of the hilt-end extends up the shaft of the tang — so the perforation through which the iron tang passes measures only 13mm across (cf. the Bugthorpe example whose hilt-end fits lower on the shoulder and has an elongated perforation *c.* 30mm across). The tang is fitted with two thick iron washers — the lower one some 24 by 28mm and the upper about 23 by 25mm — which seem to have been linked by iron strips which would have formed a frame for the hilt.

The scabbard has a bronze plate at the front and an iron back — the edge of the bronze being wrapped over the iron; Mortimer's illustrations shows the full bronze plate, but only the lower part now survives. The bronze plate has a central ridge which clearly reflects the midrib of the sword. The chape is of bronze, and its upper terminals are quite crudely wrapped with a strip of bronze 17mm deep. The back of the chape is bridged by two bronze bands with cut-out designs and hatched ornament quite similar to that on the central cap of the shield. The heavy chape-end is of cast bronze with mouldings on the side and at the tip, and a large circular perforation in each face. On the front there are three sockets at each side of, and above, the large perforation, and Mortimer recorded that they were "set with small rubies, which were all absent but one". The description fits a small bead (4.5mm diameter) with a bronze pin (4.5mm long) through the centre (Fig.22, no.2a) now separate from the sword, and there can be little doubt that the chape was originally decorated with six such beads. The surviving bead has been examined by Dr G. F. Claringbull, Keeper of Mineralogy at the British Museum (Natural History), who reports: "it is almost certain that the material is *Corallium rubrum,* the red coral of the Mediterranean. For certain identification the material would have to be sectioned and this obviously is out of the question".

Two small bronze studs may well have decorated the hilt, as suggested above for similar pieces from Bugthorpe. Unlike the Bugthorpe studs, those from Grimthorpe only have the one head, 11.5mm diameter, on a quite short shank, 9mm long. The heads are ornamented in so far as they have a raised centre and border with a concentric channel between — conceivably the channel originally held inlay-ornament.

(B.M. 76. 2-8. 10, sword and scabbard, Pl.10b, Fig.21, no.3, Fig.22, no.2; 9, coral bead, Fig.22, no.2a; 4 and 5, bronze studs, Fig.22, nos.4 and 5; Mortimer 1869: pl.xxii, and 1905: frontispiece; Piggott 1950: fig.7, no.1).

(iii) North Grimston.

Short iron sword with a fine bronze hilt figuring a human head. Its total length is 509mm, and it measures 390mm along the blade. The blade is 48mm wide at the top, and has a marked midrib; it tapers gradually to 42mm at 265mm from the hilt, then more sharply until it is 26mm wide about 20mm from the tip, and in the final 20mm it comes in sharply to a point.

(H.M.; Front cover, Fig.21, no.1, Fig.22, no.1; Mortimer 1905: figs 1019 and 1019a; Clarke & Hawkes 1955: pl.xxvii, no.4).

(iv) North Grimston.

A long iron sword, lacking the end of the blade and part of the tang. The total length is now 831mm of which the blade, measuring from the outer edge of the shoulder, is 740mm. The blade, which has no midrib, is 47mm wide at the top and still 45mm wide some 500mm from the shoulder; beyond that it

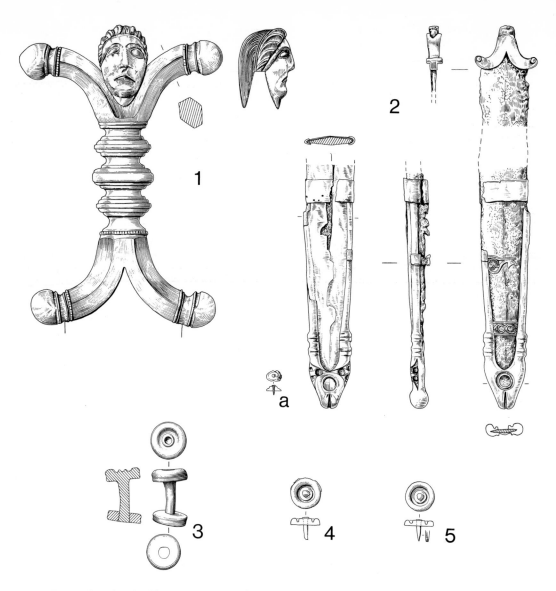

22.   *Details of swords and scabbards: 1, North Grimston; 2, 4 and 5, Grimthorpe; 3, Bugthorpe. 1, 2a, 3-5, Scale ⅔; 2, Scale ⅓.*

appears to taper, but is badly preserved. It seems certainly to taper from 600mm from the shoulder, for the final 140mm as it now survives (perhaps 180mm originally). At the top of the blade is a highly arched iron hilt-end.

Two iron rings from the grave-group may have belonged to a sword-chain. One, fragmentary, has been about 35mm diameter, whilst the other, about 40mm diameter, has an attachment from which another ring was suspended.
(H.M. 3002.42; Fig.21, no.2; Mortimer 1905: fig.1019).

(v) Thorpe, Rudston.

An iron sword with a fine decorated hilt. The blade, 40mm wide at the top, is in very poor condition and now only 146mm long — although when discovered it was complete, but in two parts, and measured 1ft 10⅝in (574mm) (Allen 1906:269, fig.1). The bronze hilt-end is arched above and flat below, inset with panels of red, yellow and blue glass on the front and sides, and above it a bone handle covers the iron tang. The bone is in two portions, separated by ribbed iron washers 8mm deep; the lower part surmounts the hilt-end and is ornamented front and

back with circular bronze studs inlaid with coloured glass, whereas the upper part is a cylindrical bone tube 22mm diameter capped by another deep washer from the top of which the iron tang protrudes. The surviving length of the hilt is 106mm.
(Y.M. 938.48; Pl.9; Fig.21, no.6; Allen 1906: fig.1 and in coloured frontispiece; Piggott 1950: fig.10, no.3; MacGregor 1976: no.157).

(vi) Eastburn.
A fairly small iron sword, 720mm total length, lacking the tip of the blade, but with the tang apparently complete (and with traces of a ? wooden hilt). The blade measures 580mm, has well-preserved sloping shoulders and possibly a slight midrib. The blade is 37mm wide at the top, and still 35mm wide some 440mm from the shoulder — beyond which it tapers towards the broken point. The blade is in bad condition, particularly in the lower part. (H.M.; Fig.21, no.5; Sheppard 1939: pl.iv, bottom).

(vii) Burton Fleming.
Ten swords have so far been found at Burton Fleming; they have been lifted in polyurethane foam, most are still encased and all are in the course of conservation treatment, so any detailed comment would be premature. However, a radiograph of one sword (FN.BP) is published here (Pl.8c) because of the light which it throws on the hilts of the Bugthorpe and Grimthorpe swords, and some approximate measurements are worth recording. Two exceptional weapons are a very short sword or dagger with a narrow blade 230mm long and 30mm wide; and a longer piece with a straight scabbard-mouth and tapering blade 520mm long and 50mm wide at the top. Otherwise the swords seem to have been of similar type, with some arched hilt-ends surviving, and with blades which begin to taper only near the end. The blades vary considerably in size and the following are some approximate measurements: 610mm long, 48mm wide at the top; 590mm, 45mm; 495mm, 45mm; 450mm, 36mm (two examples); 415, 40mm.

(viii) Wetwang Slack.
The sole sword, found with a north-south crouched burial, has an arched hilt-end and a blade 470mm long and 38mm wide at the top.

One of the Arras Culture swords fits very readily into a continental La Tène context, and that is the short sword with bronze anthropoid hilt, from North Grimston. It is fascinating as the only representation of a human face from the area of the Arras Culture — hence its selection here as the Front cover — and as a fine example of the bronze-smith's art. It belongs to a class of weapon known throughout the La Tène world (Clarke and Hawkes 1955), and is particularly close to an example from Châtenay-Mâcheron (Haute-Marne) which was also found with a long sword in an inhumation grave (*Ibid.*: 223, and pl.xxvii, no.3, where it is shown with the North Grimston sword, no.4). As the North Grimston sword betrays none of the departures from the continental norm which British metalworkers seemed quick to develop, it could have been an import. Another French example, with a slightly more classical face, was found in an apparent grave-group at Châtillon-sur-Indre (Indre), (*Ibid.*: 223, and fig.6, no.2) where associations included Roman amphorae and bronzes — amongst them a Kelheim jug with Silenus head at the base of the handle which might well be pre-Caesarian.

The associated North Grimston long sword would not occasion surprise if found on the continent, although it has few diagnostic features. The arched hilt-end and the shape of the blade would be at home in a La Tène II context, and its length falls just within the range of Middle La Tène swords from La Tène measured by de Navarro (1972:342, 344). But the other swords listed above are much shorter than the range of La Tène II Swiss swords, and more comparable in length with La Tène I examples (*Ibid.*: 38-40). Certainly they are far removed from the typical continental La Tène III sword, long and heavy and with a rounded end, which is occasionally found in Britain (Piggott 1950: fig.10, no.6).

However, the East Yorkshire swords, despite their short lengths, are not La Tène I weapons although diagnostic features other than blade measurements are few. Where hilt-ends survive they are arched, and of La Tène II derivation, apart from the straight hilt-end from Thorpe Hall which is influenced by La Tène III forms.

Sword-scabbards should offer very much more scope for comparison, but only if they are made of metal, or have metal fittings. The Burton Fleming, Wetwang Slack and Eastburn scabbards, assuming that those swords were indeed in scabbards, would have been of leather or wood which has left nothing for the typologist to work on. Not one of the swords or scabbards listed above was associated with a suspension-loop; both Bugthorpe and Grimthorpe had metal scabbards but that part where the suspension-loop would have been attached has not survived.

The Bugthorpe and Grimthorpe scabbards, with bronze front plates and fittings and iron backs, are unusual in a European context, where metal scabbards were predominantly of iron, but in Britain the use of bronze is relatively common. The bronze plate from Bugthorpe is decorated overall and this is most unusual — only one other English scabbard has decoration along its full length, and that is an isolated plate from the River Trent at Sutton (Notts.) whose incised ornament alternating with 'laddering' has been seen as showing the influence of the Hungarian 'sword-style' as well as the work of north Swiss armourers (de Navarro 1966:148-50; 1972:310).

Chape-ends give scope for ornamentation, and for typological comparisons, but there are only the two, on the metal scabbards (radiographs suggest that there may be a metal chape-end on one of the Burton Fleming scabbards as well). The pedigree of the Bugthorpe chape-end is fairly clear, for a heart-shape surmounted by mouldings was a popular continental La Tène II form (*Ibid.*: fig.12) which gave rise to a series of British pieces (Piggott 1950: fig.3). The Grimthorpe chape-end is further removed, for the two sides merge together and a sharply-defined central circle provides an eye for a very fishy head.

None of the other Yorkshire swords seem to be earlier than La Tène III. Eastburn has produced La Tène III objects (pp.77 and 86) but nothing particularly early; the Burton Fleming swords accompany what seems to be a late series of burials (p.14); and the Thorpe sword — a weapon of comparable size — has a La Tène III hilt-end and studs set with multi-coloured glass. There can be no doubt that this Yorkshire series is La Tène III, and that in the north of England, unlike the south and the continent, long swords gave way to short swords — a development culminating in Piggott's Brigantian swords, and implying a different approach to warfare.

An interesting detail of the Yorkshire swords is the way in which the hilt was decorated. It must have been usual for the hilts to have been made of wood, but the Thorpe Hall sword, fortunately, had a hilt of bone — and it has survived, together with its arrangement of enamelled studs. One of the Burton Fleming swords had bronze fittings on a presumed wooden hilt — it was lifted with surrounding earth by means of polyurethane foam and a radiograph shows the bronze fittings more or less in position (Pl.8c). At Burton Fleming and Thorpe Hall the hilt had had an arrangement of three studs — one central over the hilt-end and the others in the wings of the hilt, surmounting the sides of the hilt-end (one of these side studs was removed from the Burton Fleming sword in the course of excavation, before the radiograph was taken). Bronze studs from the Bugthorpe and Grimthorpe graves (Fig.22, nos.3 to 5) must, on analogy, have occupied similar positions. Furthermore, the Burton Fleming radiograph shows bronze strips, which must have formed a decorative framework for the central part of the hilt; from Grimthorpe there are traces of comparable iron fittings (Fig.21, no.3).

8. Spearheads

(i) **Eastburn.**
A damaged iron socketed spearhead, quite small and delicate; now 110mm long. (H.M.; Sheppard 1939: pl.i, no.2).

(ii) **Grimthorpe.**
Fragment of an iron spearhead, now 61mm long. (B.M. 76.2-8.11; Mortimer 1905: frontispiece; Stead 1968: fig.13, no.4).

(iii) **Burton Fleming.**
Spearheads were found as grave-goods with eight skeletons, and three others had been buried with spearheads embedded in their bodies.

There is little point in considering the two broken spearheads from Eastburn and Grimthorpe in any more detail: discussion must await the publication of the Burton Fleming burials.

9. Brooches

(a) **Arched Bow:**
(i) Cowlam, L.
Bronze brooch, 49mm long. High arched bow and a foot terminating in a flat disc with central dot (not a rivet-hole, because it does not perforate the disc) — apparently the foot has not been further ornamented. The large spring, with external chord, has the appearance of a four-coil spring: to the left of the bow are two coils, the outer one broken and repaired recently (hence the odd illustration given by Greenwell, in which the two parts have been wrongly joined), whereas to the right of the bow there are one and a half coils — possibly an original feature, see below. Greenwell (1877:209) records an iron pin, "inserted into a piece of wood placed within the coil constituting the spring", whose tip survives in the catch-plate. (B.M. 79.12-9.535; Fig.23, no.1; Greenwell 1877: fig.111 and 1906: fig.4; Fox 1958: pl.2d).

The high bow, large four-coiled spring, and especially the high rounded return of the foot are characteristics of so-called 'Marzabotto' brooches (they take their name from what is at best a very atypical specimen, Kruta-Poppi 1975:348) — one of the distinctive artefacts in the earliest burials at Münsingen (Hodson 1968:15). Early associations are well-documented — including an example with an Etruscan beaked flagon at Somme-Tourbe, "La Gorge-Meillet" (Marne) (Fourdrignier 1878: pl.viii). Other 'Marzabotto' brooches are known from England (Hodson 1964:137), and there is no reason why they should be later than their continental analogies, which suggests a date early in the fourth century B.C. (*Ibid.*). However, one aspect

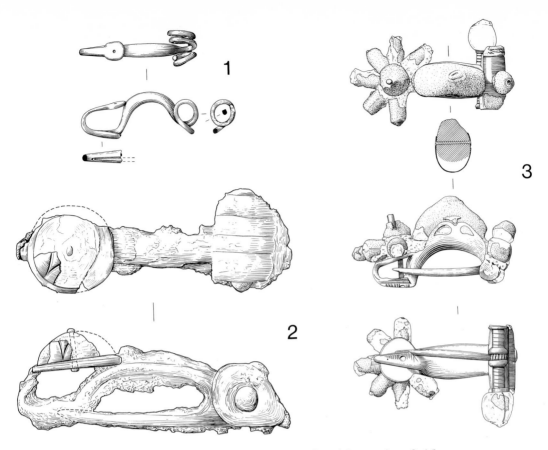

23. *Brooches: 1, Cowlam; 2, Burton Fleming; 3, Queen's Barrow, Arras. Scale ⅔.*

of the Cowlam brooch provokes a rather more cautious approach. It is not a perfect specimen — lacking the pin and part of the spring — indeed it is possible that the pin was pivotted, and not sprung. The point at which the 'spring' now ends corresponds to the point where the skeuomorphic springs of other native British brooches terminate — to be completed by a separate coil in one with the pin, the whole linked by a rivet through the 'spring' (Hodson 1971: especially pl.xiv, a). On the Hammersmith examples illustrated by Hodson the two terminals of the coils taper neatly so that the junction is disguised; the corresponding terminal on the Cowlam brooch also tapers slightly, and the patina suggests that this is an original feature. Although the Cowlam pin does not survive, it was mentioned, but not illustrated, by Greenwell (1877:208) — "a bronze fibula with an iron pin". An iron pin is not likely to have been an original

feature of this brooch, although other British bronze brooches with iron pins have been found (Ham Hill, Somerset, Gray 1912:121; Cold Kitchen Hill, Wilts., Fox 1927: fig.23b). Brooches of the Hammersmith type (Hodson 1971:54) would be liable to lose their pins if the central rivet became dislodged, broken or corroded. If the pin was lost while the brooch was still in use, it would have been a simple matter to fit a replacement. Far from being an import, the Cowlam brooch *could* have been a crudely repaired version of a British variety of a continental brooch. At least one other 'Marzabotto' brooch was British-made and operated without a spring mechanism, for an example probably from Lakenheath (B.M. 1927.12-12.8) pivots on a large bronze cylinder-rivet. Although typologically the Cowlam brooch is still the earliest in Yorkshire, its value as a firm chronological peg is somewhat reduced (and see now p.94).

(ii) Arras A.4. The Queen's Barrow.
Bronze brooch, 66mm long, with massive inlay ornament of pinkish-white coral. The bronze bow is hollow with two petals of cut-out ornament on each side, and between them a bronze rivet which crosses the bow, piercing the inlay ornament. On the circular foot-disc is a star-shaped pattern of inlay, whose rays (originally seven but now six) are attached by ?iron pins. The centre-piece has a bronze rivet which passes through the foot, crosses the foot-space and terminates on the underside of the catch-plate. At the head, the pin, whose ring-head is ribbed, pivots on an iron bar held by four bronze tags; between the two side-tags the iron bar has ribbed bronze covers — skeuomorphic of a bronze spring. The central iron bar extends to pin a large bead of coral inlay at each end (only one bead survives). The long 'spring' is covered by a length of inlay in turn surmounted by a central bead attached by a bronze pin. Much of the ornament at this end of the brooch has a smooth brownish cover — possibly due to iron-staining (Greenwell 1906:297, note a). (Y.M. 907.48; Fig.23, no.3; Davis & Thurnam 1865: nos.18a and b; Greenwell 1906: fig.43; Fox 1958: pl.9, c and d).

(iii) Burton Fleming.
A large iron brooch, c. 115mm long, with a large disc-foot, c.35mm diameter, bearing a reddish bead attached by an iron rivet. The mechanism of the brooch is obscure, and radiographs have failed to elucidate it. At either end of the 'spring' there have been reddish beads — only one survives and it measures 23mm across — which were presumably linked by a central iron rivet of which there is no trace on the radiographs. (Fig.23, no.2; Stead 1971:36, fig.6, no.3).

(Other arched-bow brooches from Burton Fleming and Wetwang Slack await publication, including a bronze example from Wetwang with La Tène II construction).

The Queen's Barrow brooch finds its best parallel in one from Harborough Cave (Derbyshire) (Leeds 1933: fig.17) which also has a star-pattern of inlay on the foot (the Harborough star has had 16 rays) and a bow hollowed for a large inlay ornament (which is calcite but certainly not coral). No other British brooch has this star pattern, but there are several with large ornamental discs, including the one from Burton Fleming, as well as Trevone (Cornwall) (Dudley & Jope 1965: 19-20, fig.7, left) and Maiden Castle (Dorset) (Fox 1927:79-81, fig.25). Not one of these British brooches employs the spring mechanism. The form of bow and foot has an ancestry which can be traced on the continent, particularly in Switzerland, where brooches with such coral-ornamented discs have been named after the site at Münsingen (Jacobsthal 1944:129). The British brooches most closely resemble the more flamboyant Swiss examples (e.g. from Münsingen tombs 156 and 149 — the latter including a brooch of Middle La Tène construction, Hodson 1968:139 and 142). The Swiss brooches all employ the spring mechanism, but it is interesting to note a Moravian brooch, from Mistřín (Filip 1956:103 fig.32, 1) whose bronze foot clearly imitates the elaborate coral-ornamented Swiss brooches, and whose pin is hinged, like the British examples.

(b) **Long Flat Bow:**
(i) Huntow.
Bronze, 82mm long as it survives (part of the external chord missing). It has had a four-coil spring and external chord, but only two coils and the start of the chord survive, so in view of the comments about the Cowlam brooch it cannot be proved to have had a true spring. The 17mm diameter foot-disc, which is preceded by a heart-shaped moulding, is clasped by a collar onto the end of the bow. (A.M. 1927:877; Fig.24, no.1; Wright 1861: figs.1 and 2; Watson 1947: pl.xxvii, no.3).

(ii) Sawdon.
Bronze, 89mm long. It has a three-coil mock-spring with tubular rivet. The circular foot-disc is perforated for an ornamental bead and attached to the end of the bow by a collar. The bow has finely-engraved ornament, including two tightly-wound spirals. (S.M. 1.47.1; Fig.24, no.2; Watson 1947: figs.1 and 2, and pl.xxvii, no.1).

(iii) Burton Fleming.
Bronze, 77mm long. Has a three-coil mock-spring with central solid bronze rivet terminating in beads of pinkish ornament. The small foot-disc is in the form of a shallow cup (or possibly flat, surmounted by a shallow cup) and there are two rivet-holes where the inlay would have been attached. The foot is clasped to the bow with a collar. (Fig.29, no.1; Stead 1977: fig.4, no.1).

(iv) Burton Fleming.
Iron, 78mm long. Appears to have a similar three-coil mock-spring; foot-disc, but no indication of a collar. (Fig.24, no.4; Stead 1971:35, fig.5, no.4).

(v) Danes Graves 19.
Iron, 90mm long. Badly corroded, and now lacking the foot and much of the catch-plate. It seems to have a three-coil mock-spring. (B.M. 79.12-9. 2073; Greenwell 1865: fig.1. — shows the foot and catch-plate; Watson 1947: pl.xxvii, no.6; Stead 1965a: fig.26, no.1).

(vi) Danes Graves 59.
Iron, at least 75mm long — it is not clear whether or not there are true joins at two breaks. There is a three-coil mock-spring, comprising three solid discs with a solid central rivet. A disc on the foot, but no trace of a collar. (Y.M. 930.3.48; Greenwell 1906: fig.15 — inaccurate; Stead 1965a: fig.26, no.2).

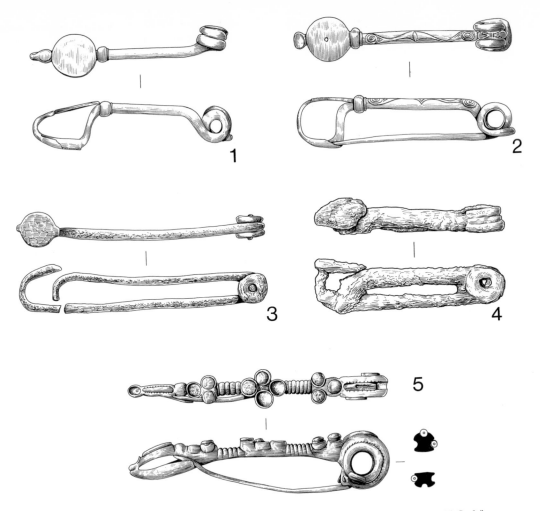

24. *Brooches: 1, Huntow; 2, Sawdon; 3, Danes Graves 94; 4, Burton Fleming; 5, Danes Graves 95. Scale ⅔.*

(vii) Danes Graves 94.
Iron, *c.*105mm long. Three-coil mock-spring with a solid rivet, as no.vi. There is a disc on the foot with a slight projection beyond, but no sign of a collar. Possibly a bead of inlay on the foot, but it is obscured by iron corrosion. (H.M. 3024.42; Fig.24, no.3; Mortimer 1911:41, fig.4; Stead 1965a: fig.26, no.3).

(Among the unpublished Burton Fleming brooches are 18 of this type, including four whose mock-springs have solid discs and soild rivets. Most of these brooches have clear circular discs on the foot, and the remainder are certainly flattened and expanded at the foot. There is only one brooch of this type from Wetwang Slack).

(viii) Danes Graves 95.
Bronze, 108mm long. It has a curious shape, with a long low bow and sharply reverted foot. The foot, bow and head are covered with small panels of inlay ornament, and between them the bow is ribbed. The pin is hinged, with the hinge held by two tags below the head. The inlay ornament on this brooch was studied by A. A. Moss (in Hawkes 1946) who identified three different materials: "white stone, of the nature of tufa or travertine", "presumably shell, possibly *dentalium*" and "a resin, possibly amber". The perforated beads in the head of this brooch seem to be similar to those on the Danes Graves pin which have been identified as coral (p.87) but the long bead of inlay on the foot has a different

appearance. (H.M.; Fig.24, no.5; Mortimer 1911:42, fig.5; Hawkes 1946: pl.xxvi, fig. p.187).

Most, perhaps all, flattened bow brooches from the Arras Culture graves have a three-coil mock-spring mechanism — a subject recently researched by Josephine Ridgeway, who has co-operated in the study of the Burton Fleming brooches, and whose findings are incorporated in the present discussion. These brooches are constructed in two parts, linked by a rivet: the one part consists of the bow and the central ring of the 'spring'; the other part is the pin, the two outer rings of the 'spring' and the external chord. The three rings are linked usually by a hollow cylinder-rivet (Fig.25, no.1) but occasionally they are discs rather than rings and the linking rivet is solid (Fig.25, no.2). Nearly all these brooches have clear circular foot-discs, and on the bronze examples (the iron specimens are usually too corroded) there is always a clear collar of La Tène II construction.

The form of the mock-spring is distinctively British, and even the long flattened bow is not usually found abroad. There are iron brooches with longish and quite flat bows, particularly from Bohemia, Moravia, and even from Champagne, in contexts of La Tène II or late in La Tène I, but invariably they have some form of globular feature on the foot, instead of the disc (Weinzierl 1899: pl.iv, no.24; Filip 1956:113, fig.34; Quatreville 1973:36, fig.15, no.4). Long flat brooches with this mock-spring mechanism and a globular feature on the foot have been found in southern England (e.g. Swallowcliffe, Wilts., Fox 1927: fig.23d; see also p.94).

The brooch from Danes Graves 95 is rather different from the others discussed here, although it has a long flattish bow. The hinged pin can be matched on the involuted brooch for Danes Graves Barrow 57; the ribbed bow may be compared with flattened bow brooches, particularly in the south of England (e.g. Ham Hill, Somerset, Gray 1910:55, pl., no.8; Swallowcliffe, Wilts., Fox 1927: fig.23d), but the form of the foot puts it into a class by itself. This is the only Arras Culture fibula yet published which obviously does not have a circular foot-disc, (see p.73, comments on Arras A.6; and also now p.94).

(c) Involuted Bow
(i) Danes Graves 48.
Bronze, 36mm long. The short bow has a 'stop' at the head and a moulding adjoining the tiny foot-disc. There is more moulding at the end of the brooch, and on the underside of the catch-plate. The foot-disc is perforated and cross-hatched on the upper surface to secure an ornament which has not survived. A three-coil mock-spring mechanism, with the central coil ribbed and the three coils linked by a

cylinder-rivet. (B.M. 1918.7-10.1; Fig.26, no.4; Greenwell 1906: fig.14).

(ii) Eastburn.
Iron, two fragments which do not join. The head has the same three-coil mock-spring mechanism, with a hollow bronze cylinder-rivet. The foot, lacking the catch-plate, has a flat disc surmounted by a large bead c.19mm diameter attached by a central bronze pin with decorated head (or a washer — a flat disc ornamented with an incised triangle with a central dot which is the projecting stem of the pin). No trace of a collar. (H.M. 3028.42; Fig.26, no.2; Sheppard 1939: pl.i, no.1)

(iii) Garton Slack.
Iron, 43mm long. It has a three-coil mock-spring and a very wide flat foot. There are fragments of two other brooches with similar feet, in the same collection. (Grantham Collection; Challis & Harding 1975: fig.32, nos.4 and 5).

(iv) Danes Graves 89.
Iron, 40mm long. Presumably a mock-spring, but no radiograph available. (Y.M.)

(v) Danes Graves 93.
Iron, 46mm long. As no.iv.

(vi) Danes Graves 43.
Iron, a fragment of the head with a bronze cylinder-rivet, and the foot. (Y.M. 937.14 and 16.48; Greenwell 1906:277 gives a description of a complete brooch, with inlay).

(vii) Eastburn.
Two beads of inlay, probably from the foot of an involuted brooch (cf. an unpublished brooch from Wetwang Slack). (H.M.; Fig.26, no.3; Sheppard 1939: pl.i, 1).

(viii) Eastburn.
Iron, c.74mm long. Lacking the foot, and with no hint of a collar. It has a mock-spring with three solid discs linked by a solid rivet, and there is no 'stop' at the end of the bow. The central disc is ribbed on the edge. (H.M. 3029.42; Fig.26, no.7; Sheppard 1939: pl.i, 1).

(ix) Garton Slack.
Iron, 67mm long. Has a mock-spring with solid discs. (Grantham Collection; Challis & Harding 1975: fig.32, no.6).

(x) Burton Fleming.
Bronze, 48mm long. It has moulding on the end and on the catch-plate, a foot-disc cross-hatched and pinned for an ornamental bead, and a 'stop' at the head of the bow — all features which can be matched on the brooch (no.i, above) from Danes Graves Barrow 48. But the Burton Fleming brooch differs in having a thick ring at the head, in place of the three-coil mock-spring, and the underside of the ring has been cut away to house a simple hinged pin. The ornament on the foot has been identified as a quartz clay fabric whose surface has been glazed.

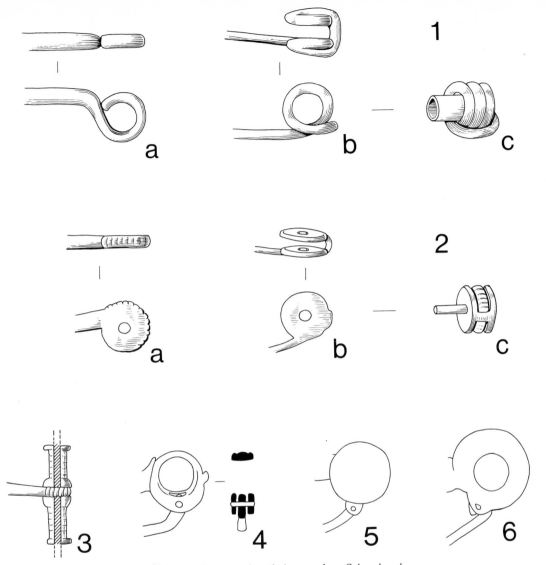

25. *Sketches to illustrate spring-substitutes on Arras Culture brooches.*

(Fig.26, no.5; Stead 1971:36, fig.6, no.4 and 1977: fig.4, no.2).

(16 iron involuted brooches from Burton Fleming employ the above three fastening mechanisms — the three-coil and solid disc mock-springs, and the hinged pin housed in a cutting under the head. There are 21 iron involuted brooches from Wetwang Slack.)

(xi) Danes Graves 57.

Bronze, 65mm long. Moulded on the underside of the bow and on the catch-plate, this brooch has also been shaped to be virtually covered with inlay — much of which survives (p.87). Not only is there a large ornamental foot-disc, but the whole of the bow is covered with a similar material (now lacking a slice towards the centre) and on each side of the head is a circular disc, the two pinned through with bronze. In addition, there have been panels of inlay in the space between and over the head-discs, and on the foot of the brooch, below the end of the foot-

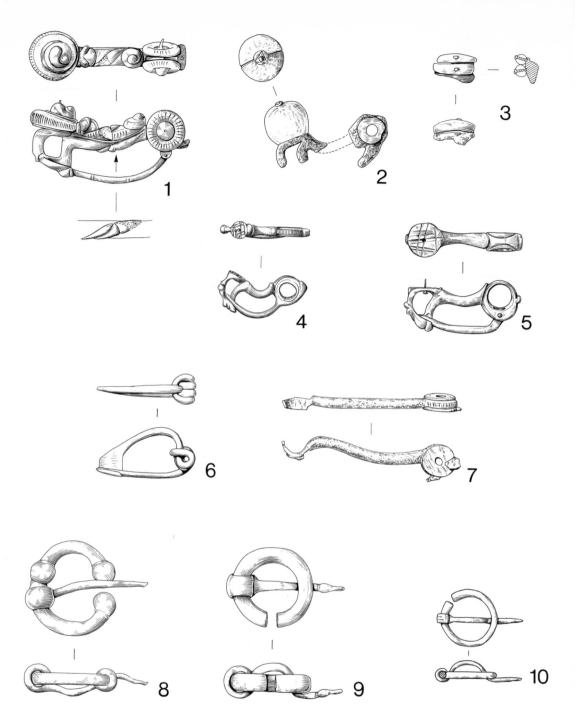

26.　Brooches: 1, Danes Graves 57; 2 and 3, Eastburn; 4, Danes Graves 48; 5 and 6, Burton Fleming; 7, Eastburn; 8, Sawdon; 9, Huntow; 10, Burton Fleming. Scale ⅔.

disc. The pin hinges on a short iron bar which is fixed through a pair of tags suspended below the head. (Y.M. 930.2.48; Fig.26, no.1; Greenwell 1906: fig.13; Fox 1958: pl.9, e and f).

The step from the flattened bow brooch to the form with involuted bow is not great — a long wirey bow might easily get distorted into a down-curved shape. Burton Fleming has produced a couple of brooches with slightly down-curved bows, and there is a more exaggerated version from Trevone (Cornwall) (Dudley & Jope 1965:19, fig.7, right). The foregoing, with the flattened bow brooches, have three-coil mock-springs with external chords, and on the involuted brooches there is often an additional feature — a 'stop' at the head of the bow which would come into contact with the external chord when the pin was fully open. Most of the Yorkshire brooches seem to have the pin attached to one of the outer rings of the mock-spring — the two outer rings then being linked by the external chord (Fig.25, no.1b); but elsewhere there is a variety with the pin forming the link between the rings (e.g. Beckley, Oxon., Evans 1915) and it is conceivable that some of the iron brooches from Burton Fleming are of this type. Another variety, whose mock-spring has solid discs instead of rings and a solid central rivet, is well attested from Yorkshire (nos.vi and vii, above, and several from Burton Fleming) in the involuted as well as the flattened bow form (Fig.25, no.2).

Apart from the brooches with mock-spring mechanisms, there is a group with simple hinged pins. The spring, however, had been such a major decorative element that a skeuomorphic version still survived, with the hinge slotted into the bottom of it (Fig.25, no.4). This version was employed on several iron brooches from Burton Fleming, but the development represented by the brooch from Barrow 57 at Danes Graves (Fig.25, no.5) — where the hinge is suspended on tags below the head — is unmatched on an involuted brooch, although it is a feature of the curious brooch from Danes Graves Barrow 95 (Fig.25, no.6) as well as of some arched bow brooches such as Harborough Cave (Leeds 1933: fig.17) and Maiden Castle (Fox 1927:79-81, and fig.25).

All Arras Culture brooches belong to native British varieties. In origin the forms have continental ancestry, but there are no imports here, and the native element is particularly marked in the various means employed to avoid the spring mechanism. This use of pivot devices can be traced back to the very start of La Tène, if not to Late Hallstatt times (Hodson 1971:53), but the British tradition was clearly influenced by contact with the continental sequence at several points: the 'Marzabotto' brooches, the Münsingen brooches,

and brooches of La Tène II construction. In Britain these brooches are by no means restricted to Yorkshire, where they are well-represented principally because of the number of burials excavated; very similar brooches are found throughout southern England (Fig.35). But unlike southern England, Yorkshire was not affected by the arrival of the La Tène III brooch: Burton Fleming is the only cemetery to have produced a brooch of La Tène III construction and that was only the one specimen (Fig.26, no.6). It is conceivable that the native tradition of flattened bow and involuted brooches was not replaced until the arrival of Roman types, circa A.D. 50, shortly before the Roman conquest of Yorkshire (Stead 1971:32, 39-40).

(d) Penannular Brooches:
(i) Huntow.

A pair, bronze, 33mm diameter and with heavy rings 6.5mm thick. There is a simple break, 3 to 4mm wide, with the terminals in no way emphasised. The pins are highly arched — like the bow of a 'Marzabotto' brooch; they are 47mm long and have rings 13mm diameter and 9mm wide, threaded onto the main ring of the brooch — and they could easily slip off. The pin terminates in a simple 'bird-head' moulding. (A.M. 1927.878a and b; Fig.26, no.9; Wright 1861: fig.3; Watson 1947: pl.xxvii, nos.4 and 5).

(ii) Burton Fleming.

Bronze, 23mm diameter. The terminals are slightly expanded, and the pin, 36mm long, is quite highly arched. (Fig.26, no.10; Stead 1971: fig.7, no.1).

(iii) Sawdon.

Bronze, 38mm diameter. A heavy brooch, in this way resembling those from Huntow, but it has marked globular terminals and a similar globular moulding on the body. The pin is highly arched. (S.M. 1.47.2; Fig.26, no.8; Watson 1947: pl.xxvii, no.2).

(iv) Arras W.45.

Iron, c.30mm diameter. Circular terminals, visible on radiographs, are obscured by corrosion. The pin is now broken, but might have been arched. (Cambridge University Museum of Archaeology and Ethnology; Stead 1971: fig.7, no.2).

(v) Danes Graves 88.

Iron, c.24mm diameter. Only half survives, and neither the form of the terminals nor the shape of the pin is clear. (Y.M.).

(vi) Danes Graves 55.

Now lost. Iron, and according to Greenwell it was 1in (25mm) diameter and had a slightly arched pin 1½in (38mm) long. (Greenwell 1906:269, fig.16).

The Huntow brooch is the simplest in this series, because its terminals are not emphasised — which must have been a major disadvantage because it

27.　Bracelets: 1, Cowlam; 2 and 3, Arras W.24; 4 and 5, Arras A.4; 6, Cowlam; 7, Arras W.43; 8, Arras A.9. Scale ⅔.

allowed the pin to slip off. On the Burton Fleming brooch, a much smaller specimen, this deficiency was corrected by expanding the terminals and at Sawdon and Arras the development was taken further by making ornamental features of the terminals — as globes at Sawdon, and apparently as flat discs at Arras (perhaps like the brooch from Kilham, Stead 1971: fig.7, no.3). These Yorkshire examples seem to be as early as any pennanular brooch in Britain, and belong to types A and Aa of the sequence traced by Fowler 1960.

The origin of British penannular has given rise to considerable speculation, for although they occur on the continent in contexts as early as or earlier than the British examples, they are rarely found amongst the La Tène cultures which inspired most British metalwork (Fowler 1960; Alexander 1964). The argument for an independent British development is convincing, but there is no need to seek an independent discovery of the type in Britain. Examples do occur in continental La Tène contexts — there are a couple from Trugny and Pernant (Aisne) towards the north-western edge of the distribution of La Tène burials in Champagne (Rowlett 1966: fig.1; Lobjois 1969:72, pls.38 — fig.57, and 89 — fig.131). These French brooches have straight pins and simple unemphasised terminals — and it is interesting to note that the Pernant example was the only brooch from a fairly large cemetery. Given the aversion of British jewellers to the spring mechanism of the traditional fibula, it would have taken the sight of only a single penannular brooch for the possibilities of this alternative to be appreciated — such a brooch could have been French, or even Spanish — for there was contact with Iberia by way of south-west England.

(e) **Unclassified Brooches, now lost.**
(i) Arras A.6.
Bronze, with inlay ornament. Greenwell's description makes some sense when compared with a brooch from Wetwang Slack, as yet unpublished. (Greenwell 1906:301).
(ii) Danes Graves 46, 56, 68, 73 and 75.
Iron brooches.

10. Bracelets

(The measurements are external, with the width first and then the depth — viewed when flat with the opening at the front, as illustrated).
(i) **Cowlam L.**
Bronze, 59 by 57mm. The body has been thickened in five places and on four of these features there has been relief ornament, apparently cast, now very worn. The bracelet closes with a mortise-and-tenon fastening. The mortise-hole is in one of the swellings — a corroded example which may not have been decorated; numbering clockwise from there,

features 2, 4 and 5 have similar decoration and no.3 — which is opposite the fastening — appears to have had a different motif. The motifs are symmetrical, balanced on either side of each protuberance, but they are too worn for their details to be distinguished. (B.M. 79.12-9.534; Fig.27, no.1; Greenwell 1877: fig.110 and 1906: fig:3).
(ii) **Arras W.24.**
Bronze, 61 by 58mm. Employs the same fastening device, and has a circular bezel with a reddish stone which in part retains a polished surface. (Y.M. 921.2.48 and 927.2.48; Fig.27, no.2).
(iii) **Arras W.24.**
Bronze, 63 by 58mm. Similar to no.ii, but has angled ribbing on the edges of the body (perhaps also on the outer side originally, but it is well-worn), and an additional setting at the back of the bracelet. Both bezels are now empty. (Y.M. 921.1.48; Fig.27, no.3; Davis & Thurnam 1865: no.2; Thurnam 1871: 474-5, fig.174, shows a stone in one bezel (the back one on my illustration) of "red vitreous enamel" likened to another from Arras, presumably the other one from W.24, above).
(iv) **Arras A.4.**
Bronze, 63mm. It has a similar fastening, but a twisted body and a deep setting which is now empty. (Y.M. 908.48; Fig.27, no.4; Davis & Thurnam 1865: no.3; Greenwell 1906: fig.47).
(v) **Burton Fleming.**
Bronze, 60mm. Similar fastening, with a pair of settings side by side, both at the front and at the back. Each setting retains whitish inlay (Fig.29, no.2; Stead 1977: fig.4, no.3).
(vi) **Arras A.13.**
Now lost. Greenwell quoting from Stillingfleet's notes describes a pair of bracelets with settings which are likely to be of the general type of nos.ii2 to v. (Greenwell 1906:301).
(vii) **Arras A.4.**
Bronze, 61 by 58mm. It may well have had a similar fastening, but both ends are now firmly fixed in a globular feature which has three settings for inlay ornament — two of these sockets retain traces of a white substance. (Y.M. 909.48; Fig.27, no.5; Greenwell 1906: fig.49).
(viii) **Cowlam LI.**
Bronze, 61 by 56mm. A fine knobbed bracelet with excellent patina. It is ornamented with 36 knobs quite widely separated, and the body of the bracelet in between is ornamented with closely-spaced grooves. (B.M. 79.12-9.539; Fig.27, no.6; Greenwell 1877: fig.113 and 1906: fig.2; Fox 1958:pl.2a).
(ix) **Arras W.43.**
Bronze, 70 by 69mm. A fine knobbed bracelet, excellent patina, with quite closely-spaced knobs separated by fine grooves. (Y.M. 919.1.48; Fig.27, no.7 Davis & Thurnam 1865: no.4 — presumably

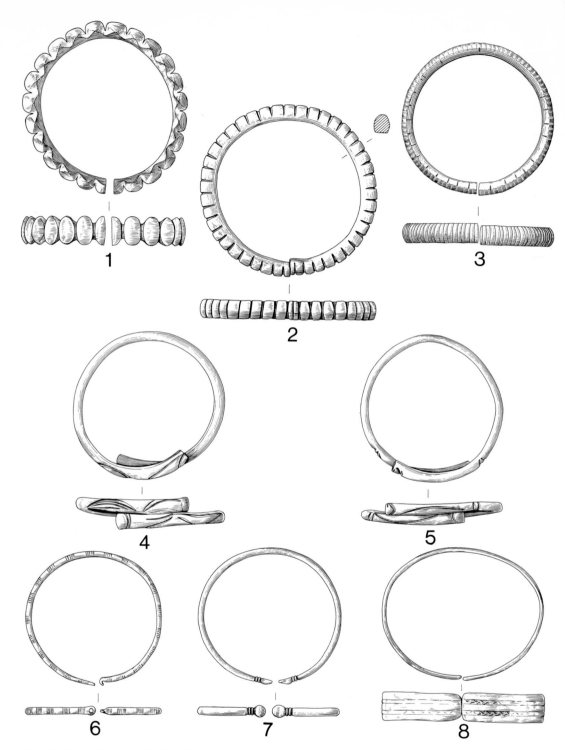

28. *Bracelets: 1, Raisthorpe; 2, Arras W.43; 3, Arras A.10; 4 and 5, Burton Fleming; 6, Arras A.8; 7, Arras A.11; 8, Eastburn. Scale ⅔.*

this bracelet, but it is shown with too many knobs; Thurnam 1871:474, fig.175; Fox 1958:pl.11b).

(x) Arras A.9.
Bronze, 64mm diameter. A knobbed bracelet, open, with the opening in the centre of a knob. There are 23 knobs, each separated by three fine grooves, and the bracelet shows little sign of wear. (B.M. 80.8-2.137; Fig.27, no.8; Greenwell 1906: fig.53; Fox 1958: pl.2c).

(xi) Arras W.43.
Bronze, 73 by 68mm. A heavy ribbed bracelet, flattened on one edge and rounded on the other. (Y.M. 919.2.48; Fig.28, no.2).

(xii) Arras A.10.
Bronze, 62 by 60mm. An open ribbed bracelet, notched along one edge, with the notches marking out groups of three ribs. (B.M. 80.8-2.138; Fig.28, no.3; Greenwell 1906: fig.54; Fox 1958: pl.2b).

(xiii) Danes Graves 81.
Now lost. Bronze, with 13 globular knobs, widely spaced. Greenwell 1906: fig.52 shows what appears to be a hinge, but he describes this feature as the fastening, secured by an iron pin (*Ibid:*300, note a).

(xiv) Arras A.13.
Now lost. Greenwell 1906:300, note a, refers to a bracelet similar to no.xiii.

(xv) Burton Fleming.
Bronze, a pair, 63 by 59mm and 58 by 59mm. The terminals overlap by 30 and 32mm respectively, and each terminal is decorated with deep incised ornament for just over the length of the overlap. The ornament on the two bracelets is similar, but not exactly the same. (Fig.28, nos.4 and 5; Stead 1977:fig.4, no.4).

(xvi) Danes Graves 2.
Bronze, 62 by 55mm. A finely-ribbed bracelet with overlapping terminals; one of the terminals is badly bent, but the overlap would have been between 50 and 60mm. (A.M. 1836.78; Thurnam 1859:83; Greenwell 1906:fig.19).

(xvii) Arras A.12.
Now lost. A bronze anklet with overlapping ends and globular terminals. (Oliver 1829:fig.7; Davis & Thurnam 1865:no.5).

(xviii) Arras A.12.
Now lost. A bronze bracelet with overlapping tapering terminals: not from the same skeleton as the anklet, above, although the account implies that they were found in the same grave. (Oliver 1829:4, fig.7).

(xix) Arras A.8.
Bronze, 56 by 53mm when closed. A small bracelet with hook and eye fastening, and decorated with groups of finely-incised lines. (Y.M. 927.1.48; Fig.28, no.6).

(xx) Arras A.11.
Bronze, 59 by 55mm. Small flat disc-terminals, each bordered by two cordons. (Y.M. 910.1 and 2.48; Fig.28, no.7).

(xxi) Eastburn.
Bronze, 67 by 54mm. It has deep flat sides quite crudely decorated with two very slightly raised bands which have apparently been knicked at either side to give the effect of a scroll. Worn, and in part obscured by corrosion. (H.M. 3031.42; Fig.28, no.8; Sheppard 1939: pl.i).

(xxii) Danes Graves 46.
Now lost. A possible bronze bracelet, seen as no more than a stain on the bone. (Greenwell 1906:305-6).

(xxiii) and (xxiv) Danes Graves 46 and 56.
Now lost. A couple of iron bracelets, apparently of the same type, "made of thin wire and quite plain". (*Ibid:*271 and 305).

(xxv) Burton Fleming.
Shale or jet, 84mm. A fine deep bracelet, rounded on the outside and with beaded edges. Another bracelet of similar type was found at the same site. (Fig.29, no.3; Stead 1971: fig.5, no.3).

(xxvi) Danes Graves 2.
Now lost. A shale or jet bracelet. (Thurnam 1859:83; Greenwell 1906:272).

(xxvii) Wetwang Slack.
There are 13 bracelets, 7 of iron and 6 of bronze. Four of the bronze bracelets have mortice-and-tenon fastening device.

(xxviii) Garton Slack.
An iron bracelet and one of sheet bronze, in the Grantham Collection.

There are few parallels in the rest of Britain for this collection of bracelets, and one explanation is the very few Iron Age inhumations to be encountered outside Yorkshire. The bracelet with mortice-and-tenon fastening is unknown in the rest of Britain, although the bezels may be compared with a pair of crude bracelets from Coygan Camp, Carmarthenshire (Wainwright 1967:83, fig.21, nos.1 and 2). On the continent the type seems to be absent from the Middle Rhine and rare in Champagne (Bretz-Mahler 1971:65, pl.73) — where torcs employ that fastening device — but it is found further south and south-east, from Burgundy to Bohemia. Such bracelets are frequent in the huge votive hoard at Dux (Kruta 1971: pl.23; 26, nos. 2-4; and 27, no.3) and are also found in the large cemetery at Jenišův Újezd (Weinzierl 1899: pl.vi, no.27), both La Tène I sites in Bohemia. From Libenice, in central Bohemia, there are three bracelets of this type in a grave-group with a Münsingen brooch, and one of them compares very closely with an unpublished bracelet from Wetwang Slack (Rybová & Soudský 1962: pl.xiv, with that closely comparable to the Yorkshire bracelet also shown on pl.xx). The same fastening device is found

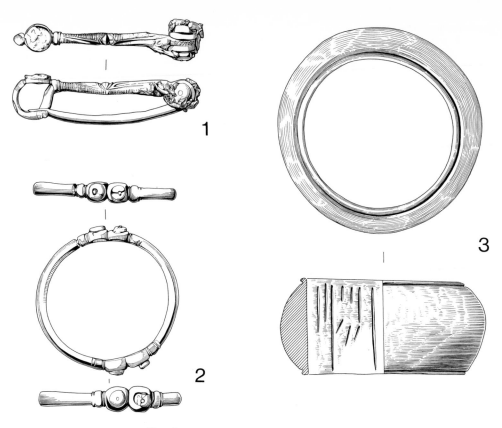

29. *Grave-goods from Burton Fleming. Scale $\frac{2}{3}$.*

on bracelets from sites in Moravia (Filip 1956: fig.103 and pl.liv, 7), but none of the Czechoslovakian sites seem to have a mortice-and-tenon fastening associated with a bezel. The same is true of Switzerland, where mortice-and-tenon bracelets are found in La Tène I contexts (e.g. Münsingen, graves 9, 32 and 84, Hodson 1968: pls. 6, 15 and 38) but never with bezels — although other Swiss bracelets do have this type of ornament. (e.g. Jacobsthal 1944: nos.255 and 6). In Burgundy, there is a bracelet from Lantilly (Côte d'Or) — one of four with mortice-and-tenon fastenings found in the same barrow — which has a bezel (Corot 1905: pl.iii, no.6); the fastening is further away from the bezel than at Arras, but it is a close parallel for the Yorkshire bracelets.

The Cowlam variety, ornamented with a series of five swellings, may also be compared with a bracelet from Lantilly *(Ibid.,* pl.iii, no.5) and there is another comparable piece from Yvonand (Vaud) which was associated, as was the Cowlam bracelet, with a 'Marzabotto' brooch (Viollier 1916: pl.22, no.122, and the brooch, pl.2, no.39). The decoration on the swellings of the Cowlam bracelet cannot be paralleled because they are far too worn to be clearly distinguished: a bracelet from Tiengen (Baden-Württemburg) (Giessler & Kraft 1941: fig.12, A, 1 and 4) with simple symmetrical designs on three swellings is perhaps comparable, and the designs on a bracelet from Obříství in Bohemia may be even closer (Kruta 1975b:70, 164, and fig.64, no.2) — but neither of these bracelets has a mortice-and-tenon fastening.

Bracelets with a series of well-defined knobs or bosses merge, via ill-defined bosses, into those decorated with slight vertical ribs. A loose find from Raisthorpe (Fig.28, no.1) is extremely close to nos.ix and x, above, but the site is well within the Arras Culture distribution and it is conceivable that the bracelet came from a burial. Another Yorkshire example, belonging to the same general class, was found unassociated in a hedge-bank not far from the Early Iron Age settlement on Castle Hill, Scarborough (Smith 1934). Half of a knobbed bracelet from South Ferriby, South Humberside, (May 1976:125, fig.66, no.5) has a hinge and may be comparable to the lost bracelet from Danes Graves 81; there are other fragments of this type from the cemetery at Mount Batten, Plymouth, Devon (Fox 1958: pl.31, nos.21-3). Part of a bracelet from Cold Kitchen Hill (Wilts.) with widely-spaced knobs (Cunnington & Goddard 1934:127, fig.21) also seems to be comparable with the Danes Graves Barrow 81 bracelet.

Ribbed bracelets, not common in Britain, include one with overlapping terminals from Crosby Garrett (Cumbria) (Greenwell 1877:386-7; Challis & Harding 1975:177, and fig.8, no.14), and part of a crude version from Hengistbury Head (Bushe-Fox 1915: pl.xxx, no.15).

On the continent, ribbed and more particularly knobbed bracelets are found in profusion, especially from Burgundy and Switzerland through to Czechoslovakia. Some of the closest continental parallels to the Yorkshire knobbed bracelets are from Hallstatt (Kromer 1959: pl.236, nos.5 and 7; pl.246, no.3) — a site which has produced a great variety of both knobbed and ribbed bracelets.

The Eastburn bracelet, flat and comparatively deep in section, is perhaps more distinctive, for on the basis of parallels in southern England it seems to be a La Tène III piece. The only complete bracelet found at Glastonbury (Bulleid & Gray 1911:217, pl.xlii, E.44) is of similar type, although with a hook-and-eye fastening, and another fragment (*Ibid*: E.12) may be from a similar bracelet. There is also a fine example from Borough Green, Wrotham (Kent) (Fox 1958: pl.26, d), found in a cremation-burial along with a pair of brooches and three bracelets, and dating from the second half of the first century B.C. (Warhurst 1953).

The deep shale or jet bracelets from Burton Fleming were doubtless made locally, for the industry was flourishing before La Tène times, and bracelets have been recorded from several Early Iron Age settlements in the area (Staple Howe, Brewster 1953:118-21, fig.66; Grimthorpe, Stead 1968:166, fig.10, nos.1 to 3; Cowlam, Greenwell 1877:209). The source of the jet would have been the Whitby area, where it could have been collected from the beach; a parallel industry was based on Kimmeridge, Dorset.

11. Swan's Neck Pins

(i) **Danes Graves 41.**

A bronze pin, 126mm long, with a ring-head in the form of a four-spoked wheel. The edge and both sides of the ring-head are grooved to receive inlay, whose surviving fragments are short cylinders of coral which have been perforated centrally along the length. The perforations in the coral can serve no function in their present context, so it seems likely that the inlay had been re-used and was originally part of a necklace. The 'wheel' has a central setting for inlay, on both sides, and each spoke has a similar setting on both sides; these beads may be coral, but they cannot be identified with certainty (p.87). A larger white bead has been attached by a bronze pin to the curved neck of the pin. (Y.M. 930.1.48; Fig.30, no.3; Greenwell 1906: fig.17; Fox 1958: pl.9b).

(ii) **Sawdon.**

A large bronze pin, 208mm long, with three bosses spaced equidistantly round the ring-head. A small pin-like projection on the curved neck may have been intended to take a bead of inlay, as on the Danes Graves piece. (Y.M. 939.48; Fig.30, no.2; Dunning 1934: fig.4, no.10).

(iii) **Garton Slack.**

A small pin, 71mm long, with cup-shaped head hollowed to take a large bead of inlay which has not survived. The outside of the head is decorated in relief with six eye-like motifs arranged in a zig-zag band. (Grantham Collection; Fig.30, no.1; Stead 1971: 36, fig.6, no.2).

(iv) **Burton Fleming.**

Only one small ring-headed pin has been found.

(v) **Wetwang Slack.**

Two short iron ring-headed pins (Dent, personal letter).

Fine cast-bronze swan's neck pins are a rarity in the Yorkshire La Tène repertoire but like most of the other metalwork the type can be matched in southern England. There is a very fine example with coral inlay ornament from the Thames at Hammersmith (Greenwell 1906: fig.18) and other simpler forms, including examples made of wire. One of the latter was found on a domestic site at Kilham, associated with an iron penannular brooch (Stead 1971:36, fig.6, no.1). Fine cast varieties are also found in Ireland, where features of the Yorkshire pins can be closely paralleled: an example of unknown provenance (Dunning 1934: pl.i, no.6) has a wheel-head (only three spokes) hollowed round the outside and a setting for inlay on the neck, like the Danes Graves pin; whereas the main features of the Sawdon pin appear on another Irish example (*Ibid*: pl.i, no.3). The similarity between the head of the Sawdon pin and the penannular brooch found in the same parish (Fig.26, no.8) is also worth noting.

The pins from Danes Graves and Garton Slack are noteworthy in having been found in graves, and both were discovered behind the skull (Mortimer 1897:2-3; Stead 1971:36), a position rare, but not unknown, for a brooch. This suggests a function different from that of a brooch, so rather than having been used to secure a cloak, these long-shanked pins might have been hair- or hat-pins.

The type is best regarded as a British development from an Urnfield source, as Dunning (1934) suggested, and Hodson (1964b) has selected it as a type-fossil of his native Woodbury Culture. On the continent pins are extremely rare after Urnfield

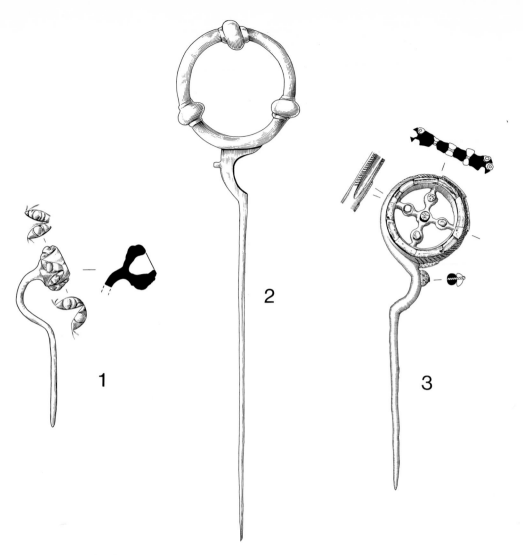

30.   Swan's neck pins: 1, Garton Slack; 2, Sawdon; 3, Danes Graves 41. Scale ⅔.

times: a cast bronze pin from Pont-Faverger, Marne (Dupuis 1940:65-6, fig.5) which lacks the swan's neck kink but would otherwise fit reasonably amongst the British series, is quite exceptional in a continental La Tène context.

12. Torcs, Necklaces and Beads

(i) **Arras W.57.**
a. A small blue glass bead. (Y.M. 922.2.48).
b. A jet bead, now lost. (Greenwell 1906:303).

(ii) **Arras A.4. The Queen's Barrow.**
This necklace is said to have had about 100 glass beads (Stillingfleet 1846:28) of which 67 survive in the collections of the Yorkshire and British Museums:
a. The 54 beads in the Yorkshire Museum (911.1-18.48, 912.1-14.48, 913.1-4.48, 917.1-18.48) are displayed as one necklace, and may be classified in five types:
(i)   19 blue beads each with three impressed white annulets (many now lack the white inlay).

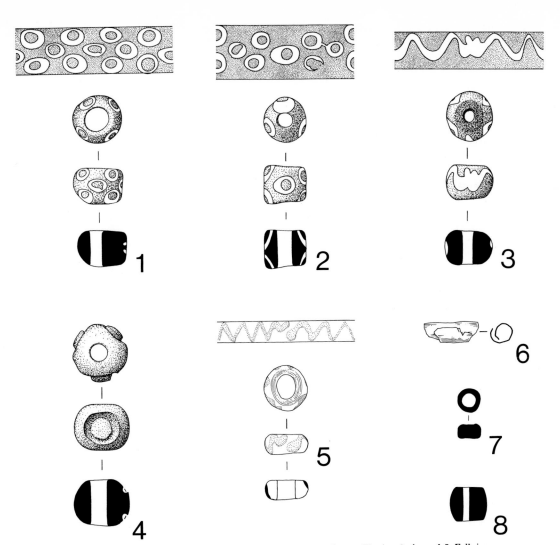

31. *Beads: 1-5, Queen's Barrow, Arras; 6, Danes Graves 90; 7, Burton Fleming; 8, Arras A.5. Full size.*

(ii) 2 blue beads with 15 impressed white annulets, and one with 12.

(iii) 14 blue beads with stratified eyes — a white ring with a blue centre; 9 have 12 eyes and 5 have 9.

(iv) 4 blue beads with white scrolls.

(v) 14 translucent beads, with a greenish tinge, decorated with white or yellow scrolls.

b. B.M. 73.12-19.176-9. From the Thurnam Collection, purchased from his widow (Thurnam 1871:497, note a — "a few were presented to me by the Rev. E.W. Stillingfleet"): 3 of type (i), 1 of type (iii) with 12 eyes, 1 of type (v).

c. B.M. 80.8-2. 142-4. Franks Collection: 1 of type (i), 1 of type (iii) with 9 eyes, 1 of type (iv).

d. B.M. 91.3-27. 1-4. Purchased from a Mr Edkins, of Bristol (cf. Thurnam 1871:497, note a): 2 of type (i), 2 of type (iii) with 9 eyes each.

e. B.M. 92.4-21. 78. Franks Collection: 1 of type (i).

Totals:	Collections:	a	b	c	d	e	Total
type	(i)	19	3	1	2	1	26
	(ii) 15 annulets	2	-	-	-	-	2
	12 annulets	1	-	-	-	-	1
	(iii) 12 eyes	9	1	-	-	-	10
	9 eyes	5	-	1	2	-	8
	(iv)	4	-	1	-	-	5
	(v)	14	1	-	-	-	15
							67

Illustrations: Fig.31, nos.1 and 2 (type iii), 3 (type

79

iv), 4 (type i), 5 (type v); Greenwell 1906: fig.42 (repeated in Fox 1958: pl.8a) shows 40 beads: front row 7 type (i), 3 type (ii); middle row 14 type (iii), 2 type (iv); back row 14 type (v); Davis & Thurnam 1865: nos. 15 (type iii), 16 (type i), and 17 (type v); Thurnam 1871: figs.189 (type i), 190 (type ii) and 191 (type iii).

(iii) Arras A.5.

a. A bronze torc, said to have been 5½in (14cm) diameter; now lost, and never illustrated. (Oliver 1829:4, note 7; Greenwell 1906:275, note a, and 301).

b. Nine small jet beads. (Y.M. 928.1-9.48; Fig.31, no.8). These beads, found in one of the Hessleskew barrows, were assumed by Greenwell (1906:301) to be those associated with the bronze torc.

(iv) Burton Fleming.

Only three small blue glass beads have been found. (Fig.31, no.7).

(v) Cowlam, Barrow L.

Of the 70 beads found in this necklace (Greenwell 1877:208) 60 survive — some of them in very poor condition. All the beads are blue, one has had 12 impressed white annulets (but the white glass is now missing) and the others are ornamented with white scrolls. (B.M. 79.12-9.536; Greenwell 1877: fig.112, illustrates the bead with impressed annulets).

(vi) Danes Graves 5.

Two multicoloured glass beads said to have been found at Danes Graves c. 1848 are likely to be post-Roman, in which case the provenance is suspect; two amber beads were registered at the same time with the same particulars. B.M. 76.2-12.10. Greenwell 1906:300 records only one glass bead from Danes Graves, below, Barrow 81.

(vii) Garton Slack, Grantham Collection.

A blue glass bead ornamented with white spirals. (p.102).

(viii) Garton Slack, 1970.

A necklace of 35 blue glass beads (Brewster 1975:110).

(ix) Danes Graves 81.

a. A small plain blue glass bead, now lost. (Greenwell 1906:300).

b. Two tubular bronze beads, c. ¼in (6mm) long, now lost. (Ibid.).

(x) Danes Graves 90.

A pair of short tubes of thin sheet bronze, simply wrapped with an overlap of c. 5mm. 14mm long and 7mm diameter; 15mm long, 5mm diameter. (Y.M.; Fig.31, no.6).

(xi) Wetwang Slack.

Five necklaces comprising in all 245 beads.

The torc from Arras is unique in Yorkshire, and indeed bronze torcs of any kind are most unusual in a British Iron Age context. But the Arras torc is now lost, and was never illustrated. On the continent

torcs were popular amongst many La Tène cultures, especially in Champagne, but elsewhere they could be comparatively rare. On the Swiss plain, at Münsingen, and on the southern side of the Alps, in the Ticino cemeteries, torcs were not worn but occasional bead necklaces are found instead (Hodson 1968: pls.5, 8, 12, 29, 64; Wyss 1974: 117, fig.10), and it is to this tradition that the Arras Culture seems to bear some affinity.

But in the Arras Culture only five necklaces of any considerable size have been found, three with plain blue beads from the recent excavations at Garton and Wetwang Slack, and one each with decorated beads from Cowlam and Arras found in the last century. Of the 70 beads from Cowlam all but one were of the same type, but the 100 beads from the Queen's Barrow, Arras, were more varied and have been used here as the basis for a classification of the Yorkshire La Tène beads.

Type i, with three impressed white annulets on a blue bead is known only from the Queen's Barrow necklace, where there are 26 examples out of the surviving 67 beads. Type ii, with 12 or 15 annulets similarly impressed is represented by three beads from the same necklace and one from Cowlam. Beads of these types are virtually absent from the rest of England — a recent comprehensive survey lists only two other specimens, neither of which is adequately recorded (Guido 1978: Class 1, type I). Thurnam had one of these beads analysed (Buckman 1851:352, no.1) which showed that lead was absent and that the blue colour was due to copper oxide.

Type iii beads are similar in appearance, but the decorative elements are differently constructed. Instead of white annulets inset in channelled rings, these beads have complete discs of white glass set in circular hollows with each surmounted by a central blue dot — the type is known as the stratified eye bead. In Yorkshire this bead is found only in the Queen's Barrow necklace, from which 18 examples survive, but elsewhere in England examples have been recorded from Swallowcliffe, Wilts. (Beck, in Clay 1925:88-9, pl.vii, F.1), Maiden Castle, Dorset (Wheeler 1943:292, fig.98, no.10), Meare, Somerset (Gray & Cotton 1966:292, pl.liv, G.8 and G.65), and elsewhere (Guido 1978: Class 1, type II).

Only five beads of type iv, blue bordered by a continuous white scroll, were found in the Arras necklace, but all but one of the Cowlam beads were of this type and there is an isolated example from Garton Slack. Beads with these general characteristics occur in a variety of Iron Age and Roman contexts in Britain (Guido 1978: Group 5A), whilst the other type of bead from Arras, type v, a greenish translucent bead with white or yellow scroll (Ibid: Group 5C), seems more unusual.

Early La Tène beads have been neglected by recent research on the continent, particularly in

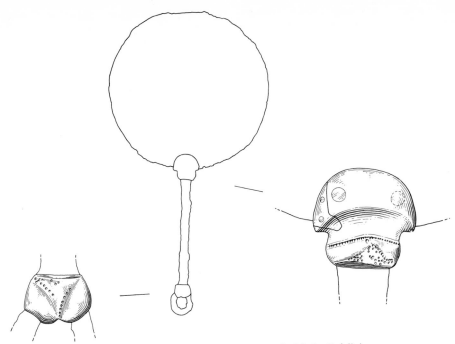

32. Mirror from the Lady's Barrow, Arras. Scale ¼, details full size.

Western Europe, and in the absence of a comprehensive survey of the material it is futile to seek significant parallels abroad. But it is worth mentioning that beads closely similar to the Yorkshire types iii and iv do occur on the continent (e.g. Bretz-Mahler 1971: pl.78, no.2; examples from Champagne in the Morel Collection, British Museum; Hodson 1968: pl.5; Gozzadini 1870: pl.15; Reinecke 1911:62 and 64, pl.14, nos.218 and 229; Haffner 1976: pl.58, no.6d, and pl.120, no.15; Moosleitner, Pauli & Penninger 1974: 143-52). A detailed analytical survey would be necessary to show whether the Yorkshire beads were imported or of local manufacture. In Champagne, bead-necklaces are uncommon, but beads occur on bracelets, torcs and pendants; even where bead-necklaces are found on the continent, as in Switzerland, the beads are often made of amber rather than glass.

Apart from the large bead necklaces, small undecorated blue glass beads have been found individually and in small numbers in the graves at Wetwang Slack, Burton Fleming, Arras W.57 and Danes Graves 81. Such beads could have been used as pendants, perhaps even suspended from ears (Stead 1971:35), and on occasions they have been found with beads of other materials. Small tubular bronze beads of the type from two graves at Danes

Graves do not seem to have been found elsewhere, although more elaborate tubular bronze beads are known abroad (e.g. Hallstatt, Kromer 1959: pl.61, no.15); and small jet beads are recorded only from Arras (W.57 and A.5). There is also part of a Bronze Age jet necklace from Arras (p.8; Stillingfleet 1846:27; Davis & Thurnam 1865: no.1; Y.M. 929.1-4.48) very similar to one from Middleton-on-the-Wolds in the Mortimer Collection (Mortimer 1905:353-4, fig.1017). The rarity of amber beads from the Yorkshire La Tène barrows is worth noting (there is only one, from Wetwang Slack), particularly when they were so popular in bead necklaces abroad.

13. Mirrors

(i) **Arras A.3. The Lady's Barrow.**

An iron mirror, 170 to 175mm diameter, with a handle 157mm long. The handle is square in section, and terminates in a ring some 25mm external diameter; it has two bronze fittings, one at the junction of the ring and the handle and the other at the top of the handle. The lower bronze is a tripartite form, with mouldings which encircle either end of the ring and unite to leave a triangular shape adjoining the handle at either side. The triangular shape has traces of punched infilling on one side — it may well have been so covered on both sides and subsequently worn. The upper bronze has a similar moulding over the handle — the triangles having punched infilling on both sides — surmounted by a lunate shape with traces of two bronze rivets which must perforate the iron mirror-plate. It would seem that handle and plate were made separately and were linked by this upper bronze mount. On one face the upper bronze mount has been curiously repaired — with a piece inserted and attached by two rivets. (B.M. 77.10-16.8; **Fig.32**;Greenwell 1906:fig.31; Dunning 1928: fig.3; Fox 1958: pl.7a).

(ii) Garton Slack.

Iron, with a plate 6½in (165mm) diameter and a handle 5½in (140mm) long. The handle consists of a simple bar with a ring at either end; there is a bronze mounting at the junction of each ring with the bar (apparently quite similar to the lower moulding on the Arras A.3 mirror), and a bronze moulding in the centre of the handle. (A.E. 1970:13 and pl.ii; Brewster 1975:110 and fig. on p.109).

(iii) Arras A.7.

Iron; now lost. Greenwell 1906:294, note a, quotes from Stillingfleet's notes: "The diameter of the circular part is about 7¼ inches (18cm). The length of the handle, including the perforation (a ring at the end of the handle and another where it joins the mirror), 5½inches (14cm). The iron is much corroded. The outer diameter of the two perforations 1½ inches (4cm), the inner diameter about ¾ inch (2cm)".

The three mirrors seem to be very similar in type, and in particular that from Garton Slack makes sense of Stillingfleet's description of the lost mirror from Arras A.7. Both the Arras Lady's Barrow and Garton Slack mirrors were found with skeletons identified by anatomists as female, but no ornaments or other personal grave-goods were found. The Arras A.7 and Garton Slack mirrors were unassociated, and that with the Lady's Barrow cart-burial cannot be closely dated.

La Tène mirrors are well-known in Britain — a few were made in iron, but the majority are of bronze. The most comparable piece to the Yorkshire mirrors is probably that found with an inhumation on Lambay Island, Co. Dublin: the plate and handle had come apart when excavated (MacAlister 1929:244, pl.xxv, no.2) and since then both parts seem to have disappeared completely (Rynne 1976:238); Dunning 1928 (published 1930) in a discussion on mirrors commented cautiously "in its present corroded condition the (Lambay Island) mirror is here included with all reserve". The published illustration shows the mirror-handle as a simple iron bar with no additional features. It seems possible that the mirror was found in the same grave as a sword and shield — a grave which might date from the second half of the first century A.D. (Rynne 1976). No other complete iron mirror has been found in Britain, but there is a handle from Carlingwark, in a hoard which contained Roman as well as native elements (Piggott 1952:30 and fig.8, C.3). Glastonbury produced an iron handle (which did not survive excavation) on a bronze mirror (Bulleid & Gray 1911:223, pl.xlii, E.100), whilst at Ballymoney (Co. Antrim) an iron mirror-plate had a bronze handle (Jope 1954:94). There is also a fragment from an iron mirror-plate found at Maiden Castle (Dorset) (Wheeler 1943:272, fig.89, no.2).

Features of the Yorkshire mirror-handles can be matched on bronze specimens, although the bronze handles are shorter and have much larger rings. The Arras A.7 and Garton Slack handles, with rings at either end, may be compared with the fine bronze handle with animal-head ornament from Ingleton (West Yorkshire) (Fox 1949b:27, fig.2), whereas the Arras Lady's Barrow handle resembles a bronze handle from Stamford Hill (Mount Batten) Plymouth, (Devon) (Spence Bate 1866:502, pl.xxx, no.2: this handle does not belong to the mirror-plate, *Ibid.*, no.1, as some reconstructions assume — they were found in different graves). These mirror-handles have been classified as 'bar handles', distinguished from 'loop handles' (Fox 1949b) which might well develop from them (via Billericay I and Bridport, Fox 1949b: fig.5) and they stand at the head of a series of bronze mirrors with fine decorated backs. The few associations for decorated bronze mirrors suggest a late date for the type — certainly post-Caesarian — and it has been suggested that they were a product of post-Caesarian contact with Rome (Spratling 1970:13-15). But the mirrors are not of Roman type, and although some of the handles may have been influenced by Roman patera handles (*Ibid*:11-13) it seems reasonable to acknowledge a native ancestry. Mirrors are so rare in La Tène Europe and so comparatively popular in Britain that an unbroken tradition of their use, and a continuous typology of form, seems likely. The Yorkshire mirrors cannot be dated, but they are likely to be pre-Caesarian, and although they are ultimately of classical derivation, their inspiration may well be Greek rather than Roman.

There are few La Tène mirrors on the continent, but sufficient to provide a context for the Arras finds. In Western Europe, north of the Alps, there are three mirrors in Early La Tène contexts — two, from Reinheim (Keller 1965) and Hochheim am Main (Main-Taunus-Kreis) (Wurm 1972) are made entirely of bronze and have anthropomorphic

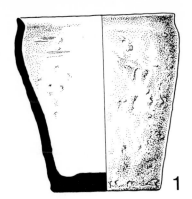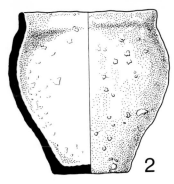

33. Pottery from Burton Fleming. Scale ⅓.

handles whose heads and raised arms are attached to the mirror-plate. Such mirrors may be compared with **Greek models** (*Ibid:* pl.31). The third continental piece is from a secondary burial in a large barrow, La Motte St. Valentin (Courcelles-en-Montagne, Haute-Marne) whose central grave held a large bronze stamnos, a Greek pot, and an iron sword (Déchelette 1913:101-51). This mirror has a bronze plate, whilst the handle, which was made of something organic and perishable but with bronze fittings, appears to have been a simple bar comparable with that from the Lady's Barrow, Arras. The upper bronze fitting, with 'arms' extending from the stem, could conceivably have been derived from a handle of Reinheim type. In some ways an even closer parallel is provided by the bronze mirror from Chotín, in Slovakia, whose long simple bar handle meets the mirror-plate with a curved or lunate shape. It was found in a large La Tène cemetery, but was regarded as a find of Scythian character (Dušek 1954:314 and fig.145; Filip 1956:281 and fig.83, no.12). Scythian mirrors, which were placed in graves with both men and women (Talbot Rice 1957:143) were usually copied from Greek prototypes (Minns 1913:65-6), but the simple bar-handle cannot be readily matched.

14. Pottery

(i) **Arras A.19.**
The excavators did not record any pottery from Arras, although a few sherds were registered in the Yorkshire Museum along with the rest of the Stillingfleet Collection, and as they were all thought to have been from the one pot they are more likely to have been with a burial than residual domestic material. (Y.M. 924.1-8.48, not yet located; Stead 1965a:103).

(ii) **Burton Fleming.**
So far 34 pots have been discovered at Burton Fleming, and Fig.33 shows fairly typical examples.

(iii) **Danes Graves.**
None of the pots found before 1881 has survived, although there are drawings of the pots from Barrows 6 and 7 in the British Museum. The following are listed under barrow numbers:

30. H.M. 3037 (but an Eastburn pot has the same number). "Body D 1881". (Mortimer 1899: pl.xlii).

31. H.M. 3038. "No.1 July 1897".

53. B.M. 1918.12-11.1. "1898 vii". (Greenwell 1906: fig.9, top left; Brewster 1963: fig.83, no.2; Challis & Harding 1975: fig.31, no.2).

54. B.M. 1918.12-11.2. "1898 viii". (Greenwell 1906: fig.9, bottom centre; Brewster 1963: fig.83, no.4; Challis & Harding 1975: fig.31, no.3). .

65. B.M. 1918.12-11.5. "1898 xxi". The base and body only, lacking the rim. (Greenwell 1906: fig.9, top right; Brewster 1963: fig.83, no.5).

70. B.M. 1918.12-11.3. "1898 xxvi". (Greenwell 1906: fig.9, bottom left; Brewster 1963: fig.83, no.3; Challis & Harding 1975: fig.31, no.1).

79. Perhaps H.M. 3021, "xxxviii 1898" — there was no barrow 38 in the 1898 excavations, and it would have to read 'xxxvi' to be correlated with my Barrow 79 (see also below, B.M. 1918.12-11.4).

91. H.M. 3022 and 3025, both labelled "xviii 1899", are considerably restored and may have been constructed out of the sherds of one pot. (Brewster 1963: fig.84, no.2; Challis & Harding 1975: fig.31, no.5).

93. a. H.M. 3042. "xx Body 1".
    b. H.M. 3019. "20.02. 1899". (Mortimer 1911: fig.3).

99. H.M. 3020. "Body 1 1909".

— Also, the base of a pot, B.M. 1918.12-11.4 "1898 ii", but no pot was recorded from the second barrow excavated in 1898 (Mortimer 1911: 32). It is conceivable that this was the base recorded from Barrow xxxvi, 1898 (my Barrow 79, above) — if so, the British Museum would have received all the 1898 pots, and if the numbering of the 37 barrows were reversed, no. xxxvi would be the second. (Greenwell 1906: fig.9, bottom right; Brewster 1963: fig.83, no.1; Challis & Harding 1975: fig.31, no.4).

(iv) Eastburn.

Three pots (H.M. 3036; 3037 — but see Danes Graves 30, above; 3043; Challis & Harding 1975: fig.31, nos.7-9) and the base of another (all four illustrated, Sheppard 1939: pl.iii, nos.1-4).

(v) Wetwang Slack.

Only 4 pots have been found.

There is little point in considering these simple jars in great detail — they belong to a ceramic tradition which must have included other forms, but clearly more variety is not going to be obtained from the burials. Although the crude jars of the Arras Culture have been contrasted unfavourably with the fine wares found in contemporary burials in Champagne, it is worth noting that not all continental La Tène cultures sent their dead to the other world with fine ceramics. In some areas pottery played virtually no part in the funeral ritual — Münsingen, for instance, despite a rich array of metal grave-goods produced only a couple of pots, and one of those is not unlike the jars from Danes Graves (Hodson 1968: pl.13, no.690).

15. Miscellaneous Objects

a. PENDANTS
(i) Arras W.57.
a. Bronze model of a looped socketed axe, with a moulding round the socket, 26mm long. (Y.M. 922.1.48; Fig.34, no.3; Stillingfleet 1846: 27, fig.; Davis & Thurnam 1865: no.6; Greenwell 1906: fig.57). Manning & Saunders 1972:281 consider that because of its La Tène context it is unlikely to have been a copy of a bronze axe, and they argue for the use of iron socketed axes throughout the Iron Age. Small bronze pendants, particularly in human and animal form, are found in Hallstatt and La Tène contexts on the continent (Déchelette 1914: figs.565-8) but pendants in the form of tools and weapons are not common. These pendants must be distinguished from the votive models current in Roman times. That the Arras axe was indeed a pendant is suggested by Stillingfleet's record (1846:27) that a pin connected it with a glass bead. Greenwell (1906:303) assumed that the 'pin' was a fragmentary ring mounted on the same card as the axe and a bead in the Yorkshire Museum.

b. A bronze ornament in the form of four circular pellets linked in a square formation, $\frac{5}{8}$in (16mm) across. Now lost. (Greenwell 1906:303, note a).

(ii) Arras A.4. The Queen's Barrow.
A circular bronze disc, 50mm diameter, with a projecting perforated tag for suspension. At the back, below the perforation is a triangular plaque attached by three rivets — presumably this attached the disc to a leather strap whose bottom edge can be distinguished in the patina, almost on line with the bottom of the triangular plaque. On the front there is a central domed stone — sandstone, probably from the Jurassic of North Yorkshire (Woodland, in Stead 1965a:64), surrounded by three rings of 'coral' segments — the inlay apparently attached by means of a black resinous substance. (Y.M. 906.48; Fig.34, no.1; Davis & Thurnam 1865: no.19; Greenwell 1906: fig.46; Fox 1958: pl.9a).

(iii) Arras A.5.
A bronze ornament in the form of a wheel with four spokes, now lost but recorded as 1in (25mm) diameter (Greenwell 1906:301 and note c). Wheel ornaments are well-known in La Tène times, particularly in votive contexts but occasionally in graves (Déchelette 1914: figs.560-2).

b. TOILET SETS
(i) Arras A.4. The Queen's Barrow.
a. A corroded length of bronze, 54mm long, suspended from a bronze ring 20-22mm diameter. It expands slightly towards the terminal, which is broken, but there is a hint of forking which would suggest its identification as a nail-cleaner rather than an ear-scoop. (Y.M. 916.1.48; Fig.34, no.4; Davis & Thurnam 1865: no.20; Greenwell 1906: fig.50).
b. A broken object comprising two strips of bronze 55mm long, ornamented with encircling engraved lines and linked by a bronze band. No doubt a pair of tweezers, as Greenwell (1906:299) suggested. (Y.M. 916.2.48; Fig.34, no.5).

(ii) Danes Graves 90.
A corroded iron object, c. 41mm long, which includes a ring with overlapping terminals (15-17mm diameter) and an iron rod. Possibly a toilet-set. (Y.M.).

(iii) Wetwang Slack.
Three pairs of tweezers, two of iron and one of bronze.

Toilets sets are not uncommon in La Tène contexts on the continent, and they sometimes have three components, tweezers, nail-cleaners and ear-scoop (Déchelette 1914:1271-2, especially fig.548, no.1). They are not necessarily associated with females, for in one La Tène province they occur exclusively in men's graves (Haffner 1976:29).

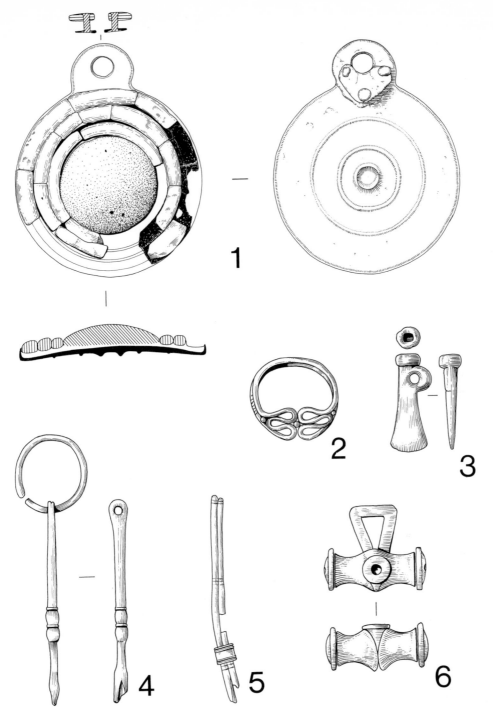

34. *Miscellaneous objects: 1, pendant, Queen's Barrow, Arras; 2, finger-ring, Queen's Barrow, Arras (after Greenwell 1906: fig.51) 3, axe-pendant, Arras W.57; 4 and 5, toilet set, Queen's Barrow, Arras; 6, toggle, Eastburn. Full size.*

c. TOGGLE

Eastburn

A bronze toggle 28mm long: the main body has a central circular moulding now hollow but perhaps once inlayed, and at either end is a bead of inlay with a central bronze pin. (H.M.; Fig.34, no.6; Sheppard 1939: pl.i, no.6).

A fairly close parallel from Hod Hill (Richmond 1968: 40, fig.31, pit 51a) was associated with Iron Age pottery, and quite similar pieces from both Glastonbury (Bulleid & Gray 1911:220, fig.44, E.92 and E.251) and Meare (Gray & Bulleid 1953:215, pl.xlvi, E.26 and E.125) suggest a La Tène III date for this piece. For later developments of the type see Wild 1970.

d. FINGER-RINGS

(i) Arras A.4. The Queen's Barrow.

The gold finger-ring from the Queen's Barrow has, unfortunately, not survived and even Greenwell had to rely on a scale drawing among the Stillingfleet papers for his illustration (Fig.34, no.2, after Greenwell 1906: fig.51). Judging from that illustration the ring had a central pellet supported on each side by three openwork interlocking lobes each with another pellet beyond; the central part of the body of the ring had been ribbed or notched.

Gold rings are found in La Tène graves on the continent, but only rarely (Keller 1965: pl.12, no.5; Jacobsthal 1944:124-6) and the openwork lobe-motifs may be compared with those arranged vertically on the gold ring from Münsingen (*Ibid*: no.77; Hodson 1968: pl.8, no.721).

(ii) Arras A.15.

A bronze finger-ring whose body has been crudely and faintly knobbed. Its terminals overlap slightly (less than 1mm) and it measures 22mm diameter. (Y.M. 920.48).

(iii) Garton Slack.

A bronze finger-ring with overlapping terminals. (Grantham Collection; Challis & Harding 1975: fig.32, no.7).

e. OTHER SMALL BRONZE RINGS

(i) Arras W.85

A heavy ring, 24mm diameter. (Y.M. 926.48).

(ii) Arras A.4. The Queen's Barrow.

A heavy ring, 21mm diameter. (Y.M. 914.48; Greenwell 1906: fig.48).

(iii) Arras W.17

Two small rings, 18mm and 15mm diameter. (Y.M. 918.1 and 2.48).

(iv) Arras A.16.

Small ring, 13mm diameter, with a ring of punched circles on either side. (B.M. 80.8-2.139; Greenwell 1906: fig.55).

(v) Arras W.57.

Ring 21mm diameter, with slightly overlapping terminals; probably found with the model axe and glass bead, and may perhaps have linked them. (In two parts, Y.M. 922.4 and 5.48).

(vi) Arras A.6.

A ring, possibly an ear-ring, now lost; Greenwell 1906:301.

f. AMBER AND JET RINGS

(i) Arras A.4. The Queen's Barrow.

A large amber ring, 38mm diameter. (Y.M. 915.48).

(ii) Arras W.57.

Piece of amber, from a ring. (Y.M. 922.3.48).

(iii) Arras A.14.

Jet ring, 29mm diameter. (B.M. 80.8-2.141).

g. SPINDLE WHORLS

(i) Arras A.18.

A large perforated piece of chalk, possibly a spindle-whorl, 37mm deep and 40mm diameter. (Y.M. 923.48; Greenwell 1906: fig.56).

(ii) Danes Graves 62.

A chalk spindle-whorl, now lost. (Greenwell 1906: fig.20).

(iii) Burton Fleming.

Three spindle-whorls have been found.

h. BONE PEGS

Grimthorpe.

The grave of the warrior produced 16 pointed and perforated bone pegs (only 13 survive), mainly cut from the cannon-bones of sheep (B.M. 76.2-8.13 to 25; Mortimer 1905: frontispiece; Stead 1968: fig.16).

They were found along the length of the grave, both above and below the skeleton, which led the excavator, Wilson, to suggest that they had been "used to secure some covering or wrapper round the doubled-up body" (Mortimer 1905:151). Mortimer's suggestion that their original purpose might have been lance-heads has been followed by some subsequent writers; but the type is common on Iron Age settlements and its primary use might well have been as a simple toggle or pin as Wilson suggested.

j. BRONZE RIVET

Arras A.17.

A heavy bronze rivet, 12mm long, with a large head, 27mm diameter; it passes through a small piece of sheet lead 40 by 28mm and was presumably used as a repair for something. (B.M. 80.8-2.140).

16. Inlay Ornament

Inlays of coral, glass, and other materials were frequently used on personal ornaments of bronze and iron. On the continent one of the organic gems — coral — was favoured in Late Hallstatt and Early La Tène times, and its popularity spread to

Yorkshire where it was used along with other organic materials such as shell and amber, imitation gemstones of glass, as well as pieces of sandstone and other rocks. No thorough survey of the inlays on Yorkshire brooches has been undertaken, but on various occasions archaeologists have called on scientists from different fields to identify individual specimens, and those identifications are worth collating. The most important recent work in this field has been carried out by Dr B.R. Rosen, British Museum (Natural History), a palaeontologist who specialises in coral and who has positively identified precious coral (*Corallium rubrum*) on a number of British and European objects of the La Tène period.

Coral has been described as a scaffolding upon the surface of which the boneless coral polyps live as a colony (Webster 1970:455). The original polyp of a new colony attaches itself to a rock and secretes calcium carbonate around the point of attachment to form the nucleus of the coral structure. The new colony is then populated by self-germination of the polyp, with the original base extending into a column upon which secondary polyps form and from which some lateral polyps give rise to branches, so that a fully developed coral has the appearance of a miniature tree. *Corallium rubrum* has a limited distribution and the most important fisheries are round the shores of the Western Mediterranean (*Ibid*: 456-7). In classical times coral from the Mediterranean was famous, for although it was known to occur in the Red Sea and the Persian Gulf, "the most highly-esteemed of all is that produced in the vicinity of the islands called Stoechades, in the Gallic Gulf (the Hyeres Islands, off the coast of Provence), and near the Aeolian Islands and the town of Drepana in the Sea of Sicily" (Pliny, *Nat.Hist.*, xxxii, 11). In Pliny's day coral was exported to India, but earlier "the Gauls were in the habit of adorning their swords, shields, and helmets with it" (*Ibid.*).

Rosen is satisfied that of the Yorkshire pieces the ornament on the Queen's Barrow brooch (Fig.23, no.3) is entirely of coral — and such a huge amount of precious coral would, if translated into modern terms, be most costly; the white rings on the Queen's Barrow pendant (Fig.34, no.1) and the similar pieces on the Danes Graves pin (Fig.30, no.3) are also coral, whilst a tightly involuted brooch from Wetwang Slack has a length of coral on which an off-shooting branch is very clearly visible. The bracelet from Burton Fleming (Fig.29, no.2) a comparable bracelet and a bronze brooch from Wetwang Slack were also examined by Rosen, but here the white beads were possibly, but not certainly, coral. The only other Yorkshire item to have been identified as coral ("almost certain") is

the small bead from the Grimthorpe scabbard (Fig.22, no.2a) (Claringbull, in Stead 1968:170).

Most coral found in graves both in Britain and in Europe is now white, although sometimes it has a lustrous pinkish surface; the explanation for the loss in archaeological contexts of the original red colour is unknown — but the cause of its natural colour is not fully understood either (Webster 1970:458).

Small, and often eroded, beads of white inlay have proved more difficult to identify. On the Danes Graves pin it was suggested that some beads were shaped fragments of chalk (Woodland, in Stead 1965a:64), whilst similar beads on the Danes Graves 95 brooch (Fig.24, no.5) were thought to be "white stone, of the nature of tufa or travertine" (Moss, in Hawkes 1946:187). Tubular white beads on an Eastburn brooch (Fig.26, no.3) resemble in arrangement those on a brooch from Wetwang Slack which are certainly coral — and they may also be compared with the thin tubes on the Arras pendant and the Danes Graves pin (the latter are perforated, which suggests re-use from a necklace). The elongated beads on the Danes Graves 95 brooch are "presumably shell, possibly *dentalium*" (*Ibid*:189) — although those in the head of the brooch are perforated and closely resemble the beads on Danes Graves pin.

Amber in the form of inlay occurs only on the one ornament — there are three beads on the Danes Graves 95 brooch (*Ibid*:188) — but there are a couple of amber rings, presumably pendants, from Arras.

Suitable stones were also used, and even quite finely carved. The central stone on the Arras pendant is a piece of sandstone, probably from the Jurassic of North Yorkshire, which has been shaped and coated with a red colour (Woodland, in Stead 1965a:64). The same rock was used for the Danes Graves 57 brooch (Fig.26, no.1), and although the stone was obviously carefully selected, it was equally clearly carved: again the surface had been coloured red. On a bracelet from Arras (Fig.27, no.2) the bezel held a fragment of polished red porphyr (?) (possibly of Cheviot origin) which might well have been derived from the beach or from local glacial drift deposits (*Ibid.*). Preliminary examination of some of the Burton Fleming inlays in the Ancient Monuments Laboratory suggests that natural red chalk was used, and in some instances a clay paste with haematite as the red colorant.

The popularity of the red colour is interesting — not only did they use red coral, amber, red chalk and a red pebble, but they also reddened the surface of sandstone and added a red colorant to a clay paste. This colouring is further emphasised by the other group of inlays to be considered — inlays of red glass. A sample of red glass inlays from British Iron Age and early Roman contexts has recently been studied by Hughes (1972), and amongst them the ornament on the discs from Bugthorpe has been analysed. This glass is of the alkali-lead-silica type, whose opaque red colour, sometimes referred to as 'sealing-wax red', is given by crystals of cuprous oxide. The glass was used in small lumps which were probably broken off larger 'cakes' and which, when softened by heating, were pressed into position on the metal object. Hughes considers that the 'cakes' of raw glass would have been traded from glassmaking centres — probably in the Eastern Mediterranean, in Egypt or Syria (*Ibid*:105). Apart from the Bugthorpe discs, opaque red glass has also been identified on a brooch from Eastburn (Fig.26, no.2) (Hallimond, in Sheppard 1939:38), and on the horse-bit from Rise, in Holderness (Hughes 1972:102; for the object see Greenwell 1906:fig.23) where blue glass was also used. The coloured inlays on the hilt of the Thorpe sword are still more varied — red, blue and yellow — but they have not yet been subjected to scientific examination.

The great interest of the inlays is that unlike any other aspect of the Arras Culture they point indubitably to trade with the continent. Red coral, and subsequently red glass, was traded from the Mediterranean to Britain where it was used to decorate native British artefacts. The use of coral by the Celts was known to classical writers, and archaeology has produced hundreds of examples of coral on continental La Tène objects, so the extension of this trade to Britain is not, at first sight, surprising. But detailed survey of the continental examples has suggested that the objects decorated with coral do not survive La Tène I (Champion 1976:36), and it has been argued that thereafter trade in coral was diverted to India (this was certainly the case in the first century A.D., when "owing to the value set upon it as an article of exportation, it has become so extremely rare, that it is seldom to be seen even in the regions that produce it" Pliny, *Nat.Hist.*, xxxii, 11). In Yorkshire few of the coral-ornamented artefacts can be dated before the very end of La Tène I, and some — such as the Grimthorpe scabbard and the tightly-involuted brooch from Wetwang Slack — must certainly be later. It is true that there is some evidence for the re-use of coral — beads on two objects from Danes Graves had originally been strung in necklaces, but it would be perverse to explain away all the Yorkshire coral as re-used material, and the huge quantities employed on the Queen's Barrow brooch (La Tène I/II transition) show that coral was definitely reaching Britain at a time when its trade is said to be waning on the continent.

DISCUSSION

The material described in this book meets the requirements of an archaeological culture: an assemblage of archaeological types regularly associated in a limited area. The only short-coming lies in the limited range of material available, which comes exclusively from burials, although many of the burials have accompanying artefacts. The lack of domestic remains, however, is a serious handicap to the achievement of a balanced study of the culture. In the predecessor of this work space was devoted to a discussion of settlements (Stead 1965a:70-77) but as far as the main floruit of the Arras Culture was concerned, the evidence was negative and there seems little point in repeating it. Some settlements in Eastern Yorkshire are known for the 500 years or so before the start of the La Tène period, and there are others which belong to the decades before the Roman conquest of Yorkshire in A.D. 71, but domestic material which can be assigned to the second half of the first millenium B.C. is scanty in the extreme. A site at Kilham, which produced an iron penannular brooch and a bronze swan's-neck pin (Stead 1971:28, fig.7, no.3 and fig.6, no.1; Challis & Harding 1975, figs.24-6) may belong here, for the brooch is not unlike one from Arras (Stead 1971:38, fig.6, no.2) and more elaborate forms of the pin have been found with burials (p.77). But the Kilham site has not been extensively excavated, nor fully published (for some of the pottery, see Challis & Harding 1975: fig.24-6). No other settlement in Eastern Yorkshire has produced Arras Culture artefacts, and a campaign of excavations is now needed to date the many settlements known from aerial photography.

But although the emphasis on burials leaves a distorted picture, it does provide information about fundamental aspects of society — in particular about the definition of communities and their origins. In burial practices tradition plays an important role, for funerals are conservative ceremonies in which the wishes of the deceased are respected, and the dead go to meet their ancestors in the time-honoured way. Hence the distribution of distinctive burial practices can be used to define communities with shared traditions, and the Arras Culture provides a particularly clear demonstration. The rite of cart-burial is limited to Eastern Yorkshire, and has been the foundation of the argument, although there are very few cart-burials — less than a dozen — and a distribution-map of so few examples lacks precision (Fig.7). But the other distinctive burial-rite, the use of a square barrow, can be used to amplify that distribution. The square barrow is now common in the area, and most can be spotted readily from the air: intensive air survey has provided a convincing distribution which may be modified slightly by future work, but whose boundaries seem to be firmly established (Fig.9). The limits to the east and south are definite and obvious, the waters of the North Sea and the Humber (obvious to all but modern politicians); to the west the River Ouse now appears with almost equal clarity — for air photographers have paid attention to both the west and east sides of the Vale of York, which share the same soil conditions, yet no square barrow has been found west of the Ouse; only to the north is the boundary not a waterway, and there the distribution is limited by the bleak North Yorkshire Moors.

The associated grave-goods have now been listed, described and given some kind of context; most of the types represented are found elsewhere in southern England. The pottery might prove to be distinctive, and peculiar to Yorkshire, but the pots found with the burials belong to a single simple form, one element in the ceramic tradition, and only when the excavation of settlement redresses this imbalance will pottery play a part in the story of the Arras Culture. Of the metal types, some of the bracelets are distinctive and not represented in southern England, but one wonders how far that is due to the paucity of Iron Age inhumations south of the Humber. The archaeological evidence from the Arras Culture and from the rest of southern England comes from mutually exclusive contexts — entirely from burials in Yorkshire and nearly always from domestic and other non-funerary contexts elsewhere. The dangers of comparing evidence from these different sources is well-illustrated by an examination of the distribution of involuted brooches (Fig.35). These brooches are one of distinctive artefacts of the Arras Culture, found in four of the cemeteries, where some 50 examples are known. The type also occurs, but more rarely, south of the Humber — where it is widely distributed along the Jurassic zone, from Ancaster through Oxfordshire into Wessex and Somerset, and extending west into the Welsh Marches and south-west into Cornwall. Superficially there is a centre in Yorkshire and outliers scattered across the rest of the country. But if the distribution is divided according to contexts, the involuted brooches from burials are nearly all from Yorkshire, whilst those from other sites are found only in the south, never in Yorkshire. This cannot mean, surely, that in Yorkshire involuted brooches were worn only on corpses — a far more likely explanation is that no settlements have yet been excavated in Yorkshire. It follows that if in southern England at this time there had been a burial-rite which regularly left positive

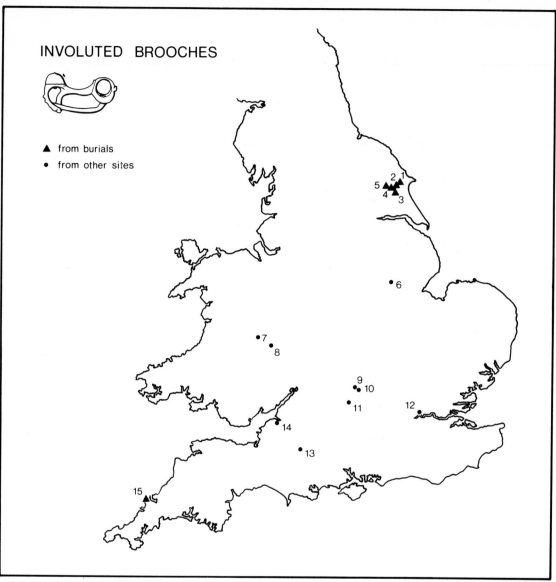

INVOLUTED BROOCHES

▲ from burials
● from other sites

35. *Distribution of sites which have produced involuted brooches: 1, Burton Fleming; 2, Danes Graves; 3, Eastburn; 4, Garton Slack; 5, Wetwang Slack; 6, Ancaster; 7, Twyn-y-Gaer; 8, Croft Ambrey; 9, Wood Eaton; 10, Beckley; 11, Frilford; 12, London (Prince's Street); 13, Cold Kitchen Hill; 14, Stokeleigh Camp; 15, Trevone.*

traces, as in Yorkshire, the distribution of involuted brooches might well have been weighted differently.

The involuted brooch can be used to demonstrate this point because it is a relatively common type, but there is no reason to suppose that the other artefacts of the Arras Culture do not fall into a similar pattern. There is little to connect the Arras Culture with the introduction of new metal-types, or with metal-working, still less with the production of major pieces of La Tène art. It is clear only that

there was a market for fine metalwork in Eastern Yorkshire. The distinctive feature of the Arras Culture is its peculiar burial rites, nothing more.

But the burial rites are distinctive and peculiar only when viewed in a British context. When the horizons are extended to Europe, features of the Arras burial-rites can be readily matched — the distribution of vehicle-burials and of square-plan barrow ditches has been discussed above in some detail, and Arras can be seen as one of a number of

La Tène cultures which employed these distinctive funerary practices. The ideas of vehicle-burial and square-plan barrow ditches might well have common origins, but in the areas discussed above it has been seen that in detail the practices vary considerably. To some extent this must be due to evolution within the various cultures — the Arras Culture, for instance, could have existed for about half a millenium and in that period of time there must surely have been some cultural change. In order to compare Arras with its continental kinsmen it is necessary to isolate the initial stages of the culture — a chronology must be devised.

In such a far-flung province of the La Tène culture, removed from any contact with the classical world, nothing can be expected from absolute chronology. But some form of relative chronology should be possible for a culture with a considerable assemblage of metal artefacts. Ideally, such a chronology should be based on grave-groups — considering artefacts associated in more than one grave-group and eventually arranging the grave-groups in a chronological sequence. The best example of this approach to relative chronology is Hodson's work on the cemetery at Münsingen (Hodson 1968) — where he had the added advantage of a horizontal stratification — but the method can also be applied to a larger area, using grave-groups from a series of cemeteries, as did Decker (1968) for the late La Tène period in the Neuwied Basin.

But this approach to Arras is not successful. Taking the cart-burials alone, there are only nine grave-groups; at a stretch one might define four, perhaps even six, of Hodson's "types of likely chronological significance", which would provide four of his "diagnostic tombs" with two or more types associated. Extending from the cart-burials to the other grave-groups produces an equally depressing list of material, for although perhaps 350 burials of the Arras Culture have been excavated (excluding Garton/Wetwang Slack and Burton Fleming) the vast majority have been unrecorded, without grave-goods, or with single artefacts. Less than 30 graves had two or more objects associated — and very few of those objects could be regarded as "types of likely chronological significance"; at most the number of diagnostic tombs, including cart-burials, can be no more than 15. The situation is not greatly altered by considering the recently-excavated sites, although at Wetwang Slack there is a possibility of some kind of horizontal stratification. At Burton Fleming so far 207 burials have been excavated, 113 without grave-goods, 52 with single artefacts, and only 42 with two or more types associated. Of these associations the majority comprise a pot and a brooch, and the pots can by no stretch of the imagination be regarded as of chronological significance. So far there are only 4 graves at Burton Fleming which could fall into Hodson's category of diagnostic tombs, and the results from Wetwang Slack are similar. Clearly there is insufficient evidence to construct a valid and independent relative chronology for the Arras Culture.

With the failure of this method, relative chronology can be tackled by direct reference to the continent — by establishing points of contact between the Arras Culture and the La Tène cultures abroad it should be possible to relate the Yorkshire material in a very general way to continental systems of La Tène relative chronology (Hodson 1964b:99-100). The earliest continental type found in the Arras Culture is the 'Marzabotto' brooch from Cowlam — a distinctive form which is the main characteristic of the earliest burials at Münsingen, in horizons A to D, and which in Champagne has been found with an Etruscan beaked flagon. On the continent this type should date before 400 B.C. One could argue for the Cowlam brooch being later in date than the continental 'Marzabotto' brooch, but such arguments are subjective. First, it may have had a British 'mock-spring' device (p.65), and second, the associated bracelet is extremely worn, which supports Greenwell's observation (1877:208) that these objects were found with "the body of an aged woman". The Cowlam brooch could have been old when it was placed in the grave, but even allowing for this, it would be difficult to put it later than *c.* 350 B.C., which is more than a century earlier than the next indication of continental influence (but see now p.94). The bracelet from Barrow L at Cowlam has been compared with continental pieces, including one with a 'Marzabotto' brooch at Yvonand; and both bracelets with this mortice-and-tenon fastening and large bead necklaces occur in horizons A to D at Münsingen.

The brooch from the Queen's Barrow, and that from Burton Fleming with a large ornamented foot-disc, display continental influence although they are obviously not imports. The makers of these brooches must have been influenced by the so-called Münsingen brooch, which also has a large decorated foot-disc. At Münsingen itself there is a restrained version of this brooch as early as horizon E, but the more flamboyant versions which more closely resemble those from Yorkshire are late in La Tène I. Furthermore, flattened bow brooches, such as that from Huntow, whose feet have been clasped to the end of the bow, must surely have been influenced by continental practice — that device is the classic diagnostic factor of La Tène II. In view of the isolated development which British metalwork displays, continental influence might best be seen on the most limited number of horizons — and both Münsingen brooches and those of La Tène II construction were in use at the same time (e.g.

Münsingen, grave 149, Hodson 1968: pl.65). This horizon would date c. 200 B.C. (Hodson 1964a: fig.6).

For the second and first centuries B.C. there is little sign of continental influence on the Arras Culture. Characteristic La Tène III artefacts, such as the long sword, make no appearance, and the brooches develop independently, with the exception of a simple late example from Burton Fleming. In fibula typology the next external influence is the appearance of Claudio-Neronian forms in immediate advance of the Roman conquest (Stead 1971:39-40). But it is to the second and first centuries B.C. that most of the artefacts found with Arras Culture burials would seem to belong; indeed the only positive evidence for an earlier phase is the single burial at Cowlam (see now p.94).

It could be argued that Cowlam was a phenomenon quite different from the Arras Culture: an isolated and unrelated group of barrows occupying part of the Arras area long before that culture became established. If this argument seemed unlikely on the grounds of similar grave-goods (bracelets and bead-necklaces) and the rite of crouched burial, it has now been firmly settled by the discovery of square barrows at Cowlam: Cowlam must represent an early stage of the Arras Culture. There must be other early sites, but the fact that none has yet been found suggests that they are rare. It may be that initially square barrows were employed by a small group, or perhaps at this early stage the burial-rite was reserved for only certain members of the community. The very fact that Cowlam is a small group of barrows, and not an extensive cemetery, may be significant here. Over the centuries the burial rite became more popular — either it was adopted by other groups or it was extended to other members of the groups — and it may be that by the time Burton Fleming and Danes Graves were flourishing all members of the community over the age of about seventeen were accorded burial in a square barrow. During this development, in the course of, say, four centuries, there is no evidence for contact between the Arras Culture and any other La Tène cultures with similar burial rites. What contact there was — and this is shown particularly in the metalwork — was with southern England. This strongly suggests that the rite of vehicle-burial was introduced at the same stage of innovation as the square barrows.

But the earliest stage represented on the Wolds already had an important non-continental element — the crouched burial — and the single early artefact has a characteristically British 'mock-spring'. Burials elsewhere in Eastern Yorkshire, although lacking reasonable chronology, may perhaps have closer links with the continent. At Skipwith, in the Vale of York, for instance, the rite of cremation invites comparison with the burials of the North Netherlands; but at the moment little is known about the Skipwith burials, and although cremation is referred to, the eighteenth-century account specifically mentions two crouched inhumations (Burton 1758:29-30). Far closer to the continent appears the burial at Pexton Moor, on the Limestone Hills, where the upright vehicle with separate holes cut for the wheels is closely comparable to the La Tène practice in Champagne, and in isolated instances in Germany and Czechoslovakia. Furthermore, no skeleton was found at Pexton Moor so that it need not necessarily have been a crouched inhumation. The upright vehicles buried at the nearby sites of Pexton Moor and Cawthorn Camps have been regarded as a regional trait, distinct from the dismantled vehicles of the Wolds; but it is also possible that they represent an earlier phase, with closer continental links, from which the tradition on the Wolds developed. The burial at Cawthorn Camps, with ribbed bronze nave-hoops, is unlikely to be early, but Pexton Moor could belong more or less anywhere within the second half of the first millenium B.C.

The earliest stage on the Wolds is represented by a single site, which might be a century earlier than any other known site, and which certainly has distinctive native features (see also p.94). Perhaps the Arras Culture started even earlier: items such as swan's-neck pins and ribbed/knobbed bracelets could indicate a Hallstatt phase of influence, and two-wheeled dismantled carts may occur on the continent in Late Hallstatt times. But so far square barrows have not been traced back to Hallstatt times except in the Low Countries, where the squares are not associated with cart-burials. A start early in La Tène I, and an origin in the mainstream of La Tène culture, seems more plausible.

Precisely where within the La Tène world the Arras Culture originated is obscure. So much of the surviving material belongs to such a late phase, when the Arras tradition had evolved considerably in Yorkshire, that it is hardly surprising to note major differences between Arras and the continent. The grave-goods are of little value in attempting to define a source, because they belong to a British tradition and are not restricted in distribution to the Arras Culture. As to the burial rites, the differences are perhaps no more marked than those between the various groups on the continent: Arras, Champagne, the Middle Rhine, Belgian Ardennes, and north-west France/Belgium — each area has two-wheeled cart-burials, each with slightly different aspects, and several have square barrows as well. Arras stands quite happily alongside the others as one member of a widespread family of La Tène cultures.

The start of the Arras Culture is perhaps best seen

in the context of the Early La Tène Celtic movements some of which were recorded by classical writers. The movements have been variously ascribed to internal quarrels and over-population, to Teutonic pressure from the north-east, and to a warlike element intent on plunder. Whatever the reason, Celtic movements to the south and east are well-documented from the early years of the fourth century, both in the form of the armed bands who sacked Rome soon after 390 B.C. and attacked Delphi in 279 B.C., and as immigrants who settled in lands adjoining the Romans and Greeks. Doubtless other contemporary movements took place in directions remote from the classical historians, and one such could have taken a tribe, group of tribes, or part of a tribe to Yorkshire.

The argument for linking the Arras Culture with a tribal name, the *Parisi*, is attractive, but speculative. The *Parisi* were established on the north bank of the Humber by the second century A.D. (Ptolemy, ii, 3, 10, links the *Parisi* with Petuaria, and the discovery of an inscription confirms that Petuaria was Brough, Corder & Romans 1937:229-32), and the tribe which gave its name to the capital city of France was settled there by Caesar's time. In both areas in the preceding centuries vehicle-burials were known — this and the similarity in name raises the possibility that the tribes were related, possibly derived from a common source. But the idea is incapable of proof — if the Yorkshire *Parisi* are to be linked with the Arras Culture then they arrived perhaps 500 years before their only mention in history, and who knows where the continental *Parisi* were in the middle of the first millenium B.C.?

The arrival in Yorkshire of artefacts from west-central Europe could be explained away by trade, but the arrival of ideas — complex burial rites — must surely mean the arrival and settlement of people. They could have been tribes, but they need not have been numerically strong: perhaps they were adventurers, mercenaries, evangelists, or a few farmers. There is no reason to suppose that they were a dominant element in the community, still less that they were the rulers, but their ideas about death and funeral ritual were influential, and they enable us now to recognise the Arras Culture.

ADDENDUM

The Arras Culture has so few artefacts of chronological significance that the recent discovery of two more warrants this post-script. In the 1978 season at Burton Fleming a bronze 'Marzabotto'-type brooch was found in a shallow double-grave at the centre of a barrow 9.5m square. The grave-group also included a bronze bracelet, two bronze rings (? ear-rings) and a jet toe-ring. The Burton Fleming 'Marzabotto' brooch (Fig.36, no.1) has a pin and one coil separate from the rest of the spring, linked by a solid bronze rivet through all nine coils — a method of construction recalling Cowlam and other British brooches but unmatched on the continent. The adjacent square barrow had a central grave with an iron La Tène II brooch — unique in Yorkshire in having a sphere instead of a disc on the foot (Fig.36, no.2). It seems to have had a three-coil mock-spring with a hollow rivet which passes through the coils and perhaps terminates at one end in a large disc. Further details may well be revealed when it is cleaned and conserved. The proximity of the barrows with these two brooches, and the complete absence of other early La Tène I material from Burton Fleming suggests that the British 'Marzabotto'-type brooch might have had a longer life than the writer has allowed. But even with these new discoveries our chronology rests on pathetically few objects.

The opportunity is also taken to draw attention to two additions to the bibliography: J.S. Dent's interim report, "Wetwang Slack", in *Current Arch.*, no.61, 1978, 46-50, and H.G. Ramm's important book, *The Parisi.*

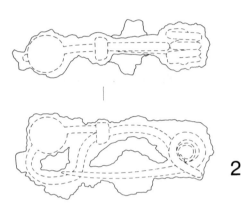

36. *Brooches found at Burton Fleming in 1978. Scale ⅔.*

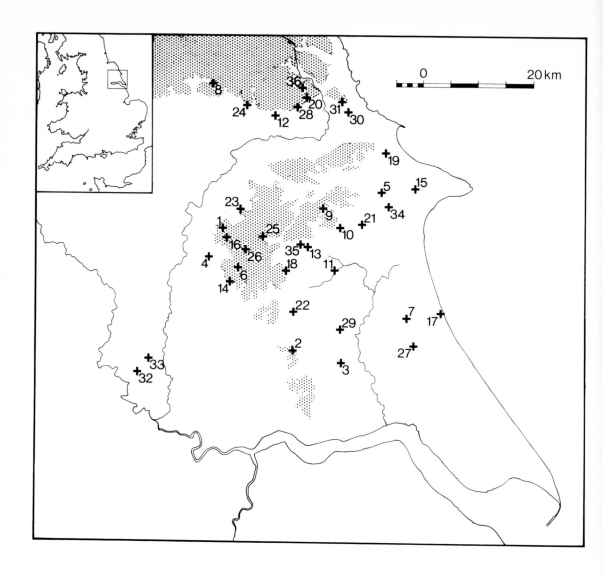

37. *Sites in Yorkshire and Humberside mentioned in the text: 1, Aldro; 2, Arras; 3, Beverley; 4, Bugthorpe; 5, Burton Fleming; 6, Calais Wold; 7, Catfoss; 8, Cawthorn Camps; 9, Cowlam; 10, Danes Graves; 11, Eastburn; 12, Ebberston; 13, Garton Slack; 14, Grimthorpe; 15, Grindale (Huntow); 16, Hanging Grimston; 17, Hornsea; 18, Huggate; 19, Hunmanby; 20, Hutton Buscel Moor; 21, Kilham; 22, Middleton-on-the-Wolds; 23, North Grimston; 24, Pexton Moor; 25, Raisthorpe; 26, Riggs; 27, Rise; 28, Sawdon; 29, Scorborough; 30, Seamer; 31, Seamer Moor; 32, Skipwith Common; 33, Thorganby Common; 34, Thorpe Hall; 35, Wetwang Slack; 36, Wykeham.*

APPENDIX

LA TÈNE BURIALS IN EASTERN YORKSHIRE

Notes:
1. Excluded from this list are the many sites known only from air photographs.
2. *Orientation* of a skeleton is recorded by giving the position of the skull (thus, a skeleton orientated north-east to south-west is recorded here 'NE').
3. *Position* of a skeleton: *contracted*, having the knees drawn up to the chin; *crouched*, femurs forming an angle of less than 90° with the vertebrae; *flexed*, femurs forming an angle of more than 90° with the vertebrae. These terms are used as consistently as is possible, but many of the nineteenth-century accounts are vague, with the skeletons merely "doubled up", and the older excavators were not consistent in their terminology (p.000).

Abbreviations:
A.M. Ashmolean Museum, Oxford.
B.M. British Museum (Department of Prehistoric and Romano-British Antiquities).
H.M. Hull Museum (not all registration numbers can be recorded — the register was destroyed during the 1939-45 War).
S.M. Scarborough Museum.
Y.M. Yorkshire Museum, York.

ALDRO North Yorkshire. (Leavening parish) SE. 798630.
Mortimer's Barrow 49, 30ft (9m) diameter and 1ft (30cm) high, had a central contracted inhumation on the old ground surface, NW., right side, no grave-goods (although flints and sherds were found). Mortimer (1905:79) recognised a ditch around the barrow and recent aerial photography has shown that it was square in plan and about 45ft (14m) across (Ramm, personal letter).

ALDRO North Yorkshire. (Thixendale parish) (i)SE. 807625, (ii) SE. 805625.
(i) Mortimer found no grave in his Barrow 117, then 45ft (14m) diameter and 1½ft (45cm) high (Mortimer 1905:80). Air photographs show a surrounding ditch 12m square (Ramm, personal letter).
(ii) Mortimer's Barrow 125, then 66ft (20m) diameter and 3ft (1m) high, had a grave but unusual soil conditions had destroyed any trace of a body (Mortimer 1905:80). Air photographs show a large rectangular-plan ditch, 20m by 16m (Ramm, personal letter).

ARRAS North Humberside. (Market Weighton and Sancton parishes) SE. 930413.
100 barrows can be plotted (Fig.1), using the Watson and Yorkshire Antiquarian Club MS plans (Pls. 1 and 2a), the 1855 and 1910 Ordnance Survey maps and air photographs taken in 1974. Nos.1 to 88 are numbered according to Watson — only those correlated with other sources are listed here; 89 to 100 are supplementary numbers used here for the first time. Grave-groups and single finds which cannot be correlated with barrows are listed below, A.1, etc.

W.2. Air-photograph (subsequently A-p).
W.3. 1855 and 1910 O.S.; A-p.
W.4. inscribed "excavations in rock" on Watson's plan; 1855 and 1910 O.S.
W.5. 1855 and 1910 O.S.; A-p.
W.7. inscribed "nothing" on Watson's plan; A-p.
W.8. A-p.
W.9. A-p.
W.11. A-p.
W.12. 1855 and 1910 O.S.; A-p.
W.13. A-p.
W.14. A-p.
W.17. Grave-group in Yorkshire Museum: two bronze rings (Y.M. 918.1 and 2.48; p.86).
W.22. A-p.
W.24. Grave-group in Yorkshire Museum: two bronze bracelets, one complete (Y.M. 921.1.48; p.73), and the other composed of two joining parts with different numbers (Y.M. 921.2.48 and 927.2.48; p.73).
W.28. inscribed "nothing" on Watson's plan.
W.32. A-p.
W.36. inscribed "the round thing" on Watson's plan; possibly the iron mirror, now lost, p.82.
W.43 Grave-group in Yorkshire Museum: two bronze bracelets (Y.M. 919.1 and 2.48; pp.73-5).
W.44. 1855 and 1910 O.S.
W.45. 1855 and 1910 O.S.; excavated in 1959 (p.10); iron penannular brooch in the University Museum of Archaeology and Ethnology, Cambridge (p.71).
W.49. 1910 O.S.; A-p.
W.50. ? A-p.
W.54. Probably the one on the Yorkshire Antiquarian Club plan; 1855 and 1910 O.S.
W.55. Probably the King's Barrow, see A.1. (p.98).
W.56. Probably the one on the Yorkshire Antiquarian Club plan; probably excavated in 1850 when it was found to have been previously excavated.
W.57. Excavated 2nd June, 1815; 1910 O.S. Grave-group recorded by Greenwell 1906:303, and note a; part of it survives: miniature bronze axe (Y.M. 922.1.48; p.84); bronze object possibly belonging to the group, now lost; broken jet bead, lost; piece of amber (Y.M. 922.3.48; p.86); blue glass bead (Y.M. 922.2.48; p.78); bronze ring, in two parts (Y.M. 922.4 and 5.48; p.86).
W.60. Near the chalk-pit, possibly Greenwell's 1876 cart-burial, see p.98.
W.61 1855 and 1910 O.S.
W.62. 1855 O.S., but the position relative to W.64 is odd.
W.63. 1855 and 1910 O.S. — the plottings differ slightly; excavated in 1959 (p.10) and the position of the 1959 barrow agrees with the 1910 O.S. plotting.
W.64. 1855 O.S., but the position relative to W.62 is odd.
W.67. 1855 O.S.
W.68. 1855 O.S.
W.70. 1855 O.S.

W.71.   1855 O.S.
W.72.   1855 O.S.
W.73.   1855 and 1910 O.S.
W.74.   1855 O.S.
W.79.   1855 O.S.
W.80.   1855 O.S.
W.85.   Bronze ring in the Yorkshire Museum (Y.M. 926.48; p.86).

In addition, 10 barrows are marked on the Yorkshire Antiquarian Club's MS plan — two are in the area plotted by Watson and probably correlate with W.54 and 56; the others are in Oaktree Close. Here they are given numbers following Watson's 88:

89.   Y.A.C.1; 1855 O.S.
90.   Y.A.C.2, excavated May, 1850; 1855 O.S. Produced a contracted inhumation, N., left side, accompanied by the skull and some bones from the foreleg of a pig. The human skull is illustrated and described by Davis & Thurnam 1865:pls.6 and 7.
91.   Y.A.C.3; 1855 O.S.
92.   Y.A.C.4; 1855 O.S.
93.   Y.A.C.5.
94.   Y.A.C.6 — noted as a barrow with a square-plan ditch; 1855 and 1910 O.S.; still visible in 1959.
95.   Y.A.C.7; 1855 O.S.
96.   Y.A.C.8.

Beyond these, there are four barrows marked on the Ordnance Survey maps but not plotted by Watson:

97.   east of W.61; 1855 and 1910 O.S. — the plottins differ slightly.
98.   south of W.72; 1855 O.S.
99.   east of W.63; 1855 O.S.
100. east of W.63; 1855 O.S.

The following grave-groups cannot be correlated with Watson's barrow numbers:

A.1.   King's Barrow, probably W.44; cart burial, p.22. About half the grave-group survives (surviving items given in brackets): two wheels (parts of one tyre and two nave-hoops, Y.M. 936.1 to 19.48; p.40); two linch-pins (one, Y.M. 901.1 and 2.48; p.45); two horse-bits (one, Y.M. 900.48; p.47); five terrets (two, Y.M. 902.1 and 2.48; p.50); two harness loops (Y.M. 902.3 and 4.48; p.52).

A.2.   Charioteer's Barrow; cart-burial, p.22. Grave-group (surviving items in brackets): two wheels (parts of a tyre and a nave-hoop, Y.M. 935.1 to 19.48, and one nave-hoop fragment, Y.M. 905.1 to 8.48; p.40); two antler ?linch-pins (one, Y.M. 903.1.48; p.45); two horse-bits (parts of one, Y.M. 905.1 to 8.48; p.47); bronze case (Y.M. 903.2.48; p.53); bronze disc — possibly more than one (one, Y.M. 904.1.48; p.53); small disc, possibly not part of the group (Y.M. 925.48; p.55); miscellaneous objects (Y.M. 904.5.48; 905.1 to 8.48; p.55).

A.3.   Lady's Barrow, possibly W.60; cart-burial, p.20. Two wheels (two tyres and four nave-hoops, B.M. 77.10 — 16.1 to 6; p.40); two horse-bits (B.M. 77.10—16.10 and 11; p.47); one terret (B.M. 77.10—16.9; p.50); bronze cap (lost; p.55); mirror (B.M. 77.10—16.8; p.81).

A.4.   Queen's Barrow, p.8. The grave-group comprised a brooch (Y.M. 907.48; p.66); pendant (Y.M. 906.48; p.84); two bracelets (Y.M. 908 and 909.48; p.73); gold ring (now lost; p.86); toilet-set (Y.M. 916.1 and 2.48; p.84); amber ring (Y.M. 915.48; p.86); bronze ring (Y.M. 914.48; p.86); necklace of glass beads (Y.M. and B.M., registration details on pp.78-9).

A.5   Group recorded by greenwell 1906:301–2, quoting Stillingfleet: a bronze torc (lost; p.80); wheel ornament (lost; p.84); 9 jet beads (Y.M. 928.1 to 9.48; p.80); from Hessleskew according to the register.

A.6.   Group recorded by Greenwell 1906:301: two bracelets; a brooch (p.73); and a ring (p.86); all now lost.

The following single finds cannot be correlated with Watson's barrow numbers.

A.7.   Possibly W.36. An iron mirror (now lost; p.82).
A.8.   Bracelet (Y.M. 927.1.48; p.75). The Yorkshire Museum register groups this bracelet with 927.2.48 — a half-bracelet which joins 921.2.48, from W.24. W.24 was on the Arras side of the road, but 927.1 and 2.48 are said to be from Hessleskew.
A.9.   Bracelet (B.M. 80.8—2. 137; p.75).
A.10   Bracelet (B.M. 80.8—2. 138; p.75).
A.11.   Bracelet (Y.M. 910.1 and 2.48; p.75). (Included by the Yorkshire Museum register and by Greenwell 1906: 298–9 in the Queen's Barrow grave-group, but Stillingfleet records only two bracelets in that grave which Davis & Thurnam 1865 describe as "massy bracelets set with paste" — a description which would fit Y.M. 908 and 909.48).
A.12.   Bracelet and an anklet (now lost; Oliver 1829: fig.7; p.75).
A.13.   Bracelet (now lost; Greenwell 1906: 300, note a; p.75).
A.14.   Jet ring (B.M. 80.8—2. 141; p.86).
A.15.   Bronze ring (Y.M. 920.48; p.86).
A.16.   Bronze ring (B.M. 80.8—2. 139; p.86).
A.17.   Piece of lead, with a bronze rivet through it (B.M. 80.8—2. 140; p.86).
A.18.   Spindle-whorl (Y.M. 923.48; p.86).
A.19.   Pottery (Y.M. 924.1 to 8.48; p.83).

BEVERLEY North Humberside TA.020390.
A small group of barrows, at least ten, and some undoubtedly have square-plan ditches. Two were excavated by Greenwell in 1875 (Greenwell 1877: 456; 1906: 278).

1.   Cart-burial, p.20. The grave-group comprises: two wheels (fragments of tyres and nave-hoops, B.M. 75.10 — 5.1 and 2; p.40); two horse-bits (B.M. 75.10 — 5.3; p.47); harness ring (B.M. 75.10 — 5.3; p.51).
2.   Nothing found.

BLEALANDS NOOK North Humberside. (Sledmere and Wetwang parishes). SE.920597.
Mortimer's 'Romano-British' cemetery had 12 skeletons, 11 with their skulls at the north or north-east end of the grave, and two cremations. There were no grave-goods. Romano-British pottery was scattered around the site but none came from the graves, so a pre-Roman date is quite possible. (Mortimer 1905: 194-98).

BUGTHORPE North Humberside c. SE.773580.
Burial found in or before 1860. Wood 1860:263; Thurnam 1871: 475; Greenwell 1877: 50, note. The grave-group comprised a sword and scabbard (B.M. 1905. 7—17. 1 to 3; p.60) and two discs (B.M. 1905. 7—17. 4 and 5; p.58).

BURTON FLEMING North Humberside (partly in Rudston parish). Between TA. 095692 and TA.094703.
An extensive cemetery, excavated 1967-78 (see pp.11-15).

CALAIS (CALLIS) WOLD North Humberside. (Bishop Wilton parish) (i) SE.831560
(i) Mortimer's Barrow C.72 was 25ft (7.5m) diameter and 1ft (30cm) high. The central grave had a crouched inhumation, NNW., left side, with the skeleton of a pig and two goats or sheep (Mortimer 1905: 163—4, and fig.411). A La Tène date is suggested by the size of the barrow, the position of the skeleton, and by comparison with Danes Graves Barrows 19 and 73. The date has now been confirmed on the ground by the Royal Commission on Historical Monuments (England) who recorded it as a 30ft (9m) square barrow, 1ft (30cm) high; subsequent air photographs also show the square-plan ditch (Ramm, personal letter).
(ii) A terret, apparently an isolated find, now in private hands (Clarke 1951:216; Macgregor 1976: no.47).

CAWTHORN CAMPS North Yorkshire (Cawthorne parish) SE.785899.
1. Cart-burial, p.22. The grave-group comprises: two wheels (two tyres and fragments of nave-hoops, Y.M.; p.40); horse-bit fragments (Y.M.; p.47); possible harness rings (Y.M.; p.51).
2. Square barrow (Stead 1961:47).

COWLAM North Humberside. (Cottam parish). SE.984667.
Five barrows excavated by Greenwell (1877:208—13); the site was re-excavated in 1969 when four of Greenwell's barrows were identified (Stead 1971: 22—4); and again in 1972 when two other barrows (apparently not excavated by Greenwell) and two flat graves were found (A.E. 1972:10). Greenwell's burials were all on the old ground surface.
1. Barrow L. 22ft (6·7m) diameter and 2ft (60cm) high. A crouched or contracted inhumation, NE., left side, with a bracelet (B.M. 79.12—9. 534; p.73); brooch (B.M. 79. 12—9. 535; p.64) and a necklace of 70 glass beads (B.M. 79. 12—9. 536; p.80).
2. Barrow LI, 24ft (7·3m) diameter and 1ft (30cm) high. A tightly contracted inhumation, N., left side, with a bracelet (B.M.79. 12—9.539; p.73).
3. Barrow LII, 32ft (9·7m) diameter and 2ft (60cm) high. A crouched inhumation, NE., left side, without grave-goods.
4. Barrow LIII, 42ft (13m) diameter and 1ft (30cm) high. A crouched or contracted inhumation, N., left side, without grave-goods.
5. Barrow LIV, 50ft (15m) diameter and 2½ft (75cm) high. A ?crouched inhumation, SSW., right side, without grave-goods.
(The four barrows excavated in 1969 had square-plan ditches enclosing barrow platforms between 10m and 14m

across — neither the measurements nor other details can be correlated exactly with Greenwell's account).
The following were excavated in 1972:
6. Square barrow, 9m across. No surviving burial.
7. Square barrow, 7m across, with a contracted inhumation of a child, N., right side, no grave-goods, in a shallow pit.
8. Tightly contracted inhumation in a flat grave only 70cm long; S., right side, no grave-goods.
9. Contracted inhumation in a very shallow flat grave; S., left side, no grave-goods.

DANES GRAVES North Humberside. (Kilham and Nafferton parishes) TA.018633.
Although barrows from individual seasons were numbered by the excavators those numbers seem never to have been plotted, so it is impossible to correlate any grave-group with any particular barrow. The barrow numbers given below were first listed in Stead 1965a: 105—10. 'Contracted,' 'crouched' and 'flexed' are not recorded here because it is obvious that the excavators were not consistent in their terminology; it is clear, however, that no skeleton was extended. Where grave-goods have been located their collection is recorded, otherwise they are presumed lost.
1. 1721. Barrow excavated, but no recorded grave-goods. Noted in the Kilham Parish Register, quoted by Mortimer 1899: 287, and Greenwell 1906: 254, note a.
2. Before 1830. Barrow excavated by Rev. W. Drake, of Northallerton, (Thurnam 1859). It produced a bronze bracelet (A.M. 1836.78); jet bracelet; and the "constituent parts of an iron comb".
3 and 4. 1834. Two barrows excavated by John Milner, of Kilham, and others; Mortimer 1899:289.
3. Burial with a pot.
4. Burial without grave-goods, in one of the largest barrows. Mortimer 1899:289 suggested that this might have been No.41, below.
5. c.1848. Four beads, two of amber and two of glass, "found about 1848 by Rev. W. Drake and Mr E. Tindall in Danes Graves" (B.M. Register) could conceivably belong to earlier excavations (No.2, above); but the glass beads are likely to be post-Roman (p.80) so the provenance is suspect (B.M. 76.2—12.10).
6 to 11. 1849. Six barrows opened by the Yorkshire Antiquarian Club; W. Proctor 1855. The barrows averaged 2ft (60cm) to 3ft (1m) high and 18ft (5·5m) diameter.
Some skull measurements of Nos. 6 to 10 are recorded by Greenwell, 1965, table, p.264.
6. (No.1) N. Burial with a pot by the skull. There is a drawing of this pot, and the one from the following barrow, in the B.M.
7. (No.2) N. Burial with a pot by the skull.
8. (No.3) SSW., left side, no grave-goods.
9. (No.4) NNW., right side, no grave-goods.
10. (No.5) N., right side, with a corroded, flat and semi-circular piece of iron, 2in (8cm) long, beneath the body.
11. (No.6) A large barrow, 5ft (1·5m) high and 25ft (7·6m) diameter. No burial was found, but Mortimer (1899:290) suggests that this might be correlated with No.43, below — the vehicle-burial!

12 to 14. 1849 or 1850. Three barrows opened by Thomas Kendall, of Pickering. In each of them he is said to have found a skeleton "accompanied by pieces of rusted iron" (Mortimer, 1899:291).

15 to 28. 1864. Fourteen barrows excavated by Greenwell (1865: 108—12). They were between 16ft (4·8m) and 24ft (7·3m) diameter and 2ft (60cm) to 4ft (1·2m) high, each with a crouched inhumation in a hollow in the old ground surface. Only five burials are noted individually (here Nos. 15 to 19). Of the fourteen burials excavated, Greenwell notes the positions of eleven (six on the left side, five on the right side; seven with the skull at the north end, two south-west, one west, and one east — the two sets of information are not correlated, except for No.19, below). Some measurements of six skulls are recorded in a table (Greenwell, 1865:264).

15. There was the burial of a child (about five years old) as a secondary in the mound.

16 to 18. Each had a skeleton with a pot.

19. W., right side, together with an iron brooch near the mouth (B.M. 79. 12—9. 2073; p.66) and the skeleton of a goat on each side.

29 and 30. 1881. Two barrows excavated by Mortimer when they were disturbed by trees blowing down; Mortimer, 1899:296—98.

29. The barrow was 15ft (4·5m) diameter and 2ft (60cm) high; the burial had been badly disturbed, and there were no grave-goods.

30. W., left side, with a pig-bone and a pot (H.M.; p.83).

31 to 46. July, 1897. Sixteen barrows opened by Mortimer, Greenwell and Boynton; Mortimer, 1897 and 1898. Some anatomical measurements given in a table, Mortimer, 1897, opp. p.8. Barrow No.31 was 13ft (4m) diameter and 18in (45cm) high; Nos. 32 to 40 were 10ft (3m) to 22ft (6·7m) diameter and 15in (38cm) to 30in (76cm) high; Nos. 41 to 46 were 15ft (4·5m) to 33ft (10m) diameter and 16in (40cm) to 3ft 6in (1m) high. The finds were given to the landowner (Mortimer, 1911:30) and some went to the Yorkshire Museum.

31. (No.1) N., right side, in a grave 7ft (2m) by 5ft 6in (1·6m) and 20in (50cm) deep; with a pot (H.M.; p.83); a pig-bone near it; and a corroded iron object.

32. (No.2) S., on its back, no grave-goods.

33. (No.3) S., left side, corroded iron object.

34. (No.4) N., left side, corroded iron object.

35. (No.5) N., left side, no grave-goods.

36. (No.6) The barrow had been previously excavated.

37. (No.7) N., left side, no grave-goods; an adolescent (c. 12 to 14 years old).

38. (No.8) N., left side, no grave-goods.

39. (No.9) W., left side, no grave-goods.

40. (No.10) S., left side, corroded iron object.

41. (No.11) The barrow was 33ft (10m) diameter, with a grave 7ft (2m) by 4ft 6in (1·4m) and 2ft (60cm) deep; SSW., left side, with a bronze pin (Y.M. 930.1.48; p.77).

42. (No.12) N., left side, with an iron object.

43. (No.13) Cart-burial, p.20. Two wheels (one tyre, one nave-hoop and fragments of other tyre and nave-hoops, Y.M. 937.1 to 3 and 7 to 9.48; also an iron rod, ? cleat, Y.M. 937.4.48; p.40); two linch pins (Y.M. 937.5 and 6. 48; p.45); two horse-bits (Fragments, Y.M. 937.13, 15 and 18.48; p.47); five harness rings (two, Y.M. 937.11 and 12.48; p.51); iron ring (Y.M. 937.17.48; p.55); bronze disc (Y.M. 937.10.48; p.55); bronze 'buttons' (lost; p.55); brooch fragments (Y.M. 937.14 and 16.48; p.55). The two skulls survive, Y.M. 933 and 934.48.

44. (No.14) NE., left side, no grave-goods.

45. (No.15) N., right side, with an iron object.

46. (No.16) Barrow 30ft (9m) diameter and 3ft (1m) high, with an oval grave 7ft (2m) by 5ft 6in (1·6m) and 2ft 6in (75cm) deep. There were five skeletons:
a. WSW., left side, a child (4 to 6 years old) with an iron bracelet.
b. A child (2 to 5 years old), no grave-goods.
c. N., on its back, an adolescent (15 to 18 years old) without grave-goods.
d. S., left side, with a bronze object on the right humerus and the remains of a bronze bracelet.

47 to 80. 1898. Thirty-seven barrows (three had been previously explored) excavated by Greenwell, Mortimer and Boynton; Mortimer 1911:30—7 (which gives barrow numbers); Greenwell 1906:258—9. The barrows were 10ft (3m) to 30ft (10m) diameter, 10in (25cm) to 2ft 6in (75cm) high, and the graves were 10in (25cm) to 3ft (1m) deep.

47. (No.i) NNE., left side, no grave-goods.

48. (No.ii) SW., right side, with a bronze brooch (B.M. 1918. 7—10. 1; p.68).

49. (No.iii) SSW., on its back, no grave-goods.

50. (No.iv) NNE., left side, no grave-goods.

51. (No.v) SSW., left side, no grave-goods.

52. (No.vi) SSW., left side, no grave-goods.

53. (No.vii) WSW., left side, with a pot (B.M. 1918. 12—11.1; p.83) and a pig-bone.

54. (No.viii) NE., left side, with a pot (B.M. 1918. 12—11.2; p.83) and a pig-bone.

55. (No.ix) NNE., left side, with an iron penannular brooch.

56. (No.x). Two skeletons, one above the other:
a. upper, NNE., left side, no grave-goods.
b. lower, NNE., left side, with an iron bracelet and another iron object.
(Nos. xi and xii had been previously excavated).

57. (No.xiii) NE., left side, with a bronze brooch (Y.M. 930.2.48; p.69).

58. (No.xiv) NE., left side, no grave-goods.

59. (No.xv) SW., right side, with an iron brooch (Y.M. 930.3.48; p.66).

60. (No.xvi) NE., left side, no grave-goods.

61. (No.xvii) NE., left side, with an iron object.

62. (No.xviii) NE., left side, with a chalk spindle-whorl.

63. (No.xix) NE., left side, no grave-goods.

64. (No.xx) NE., left side, no grave-goods.

65. (No.xxi) N., right side, with a corroded piece of iron, a pot (B.M. 1918. 12-11.5; p.83), and a pig-bone.

66. (No.xxii) N., left side, no grave-goods.

67. (No.xxiii) Two inhumations side by side in the same grave:
a. N., left side, no grave-goods.
b. N., on its chest — but which side the legs were drawn up on is not recorded; a pig-bone was found with this skeleton.
68. (No.xxiv) SW., left side, with an iron brooch.
69. (No.xxv) NE., left side, no grave-goods.
70. (No.xxvi) S., left side; an adolescent with a pot (B.M. 1918. 12—11.3; p.83) and a pig-bone.
71. (No.xxvii) NE., right side, no grave-goods.
72. (No.xxviii) SW., left side, no grave-goods.
73. (No.xxix) E., right side, with an iron brooch and the skeletons of two pigs and two goats (plan, Mortimer 1911: 35, fig.2).
74. (No.xxx) S., left side, no grave-goods.
(No.xxxi had been previously excavated).
75. (No.xxxii) NE., (side not recorded), with an iron brooch and a pig-bone.
76. (No.xxxiv) S., left side, with no grave-goods.
77. (No.xxxiv) S., left side, with no grave-goods.
78. (No.xxxv) NE., left side, no grave-goods.
79. (No.xxxvi) NE., left side, with a pot (?H.M., where there is a pot marked "xxxviii, 1898" — no barrow xxxviii was excavated; p.83).
80. (No.xxxvii) NE., left side, no grave-goods.
81-93. 1899. Twenty barrows, seven previously excavated, dug by Mortimer, (Mortimer 1911: 37—40). The finds were given to the land-owner "except the vase and the bones", and subsequently most of them went to the Yorkshire Museum. For a table giving some anatomical measurements of skeletons in Barrows 81—106, *Ibid.*: 46.

[There is some confusion about the 1899 finds from Danes Graves. A card in the Yorkshire Museum labelled "from excavations in 1899" has the following items inscribed:

a. 'No.II at the chest'
b. 'No.II on the wrist'
c. 'No.XII under the chin'
d. 'No.XIII at the chest'
e. 'No.XV under the chin'
f. 'No.XX, Body 1 at the knees'

This list includes all the grave-goods apart from the pots, which are now in Hull Museum. Some objects are threaded onto the card against the above inscriptions, but unfortunately there has been subsequent confusion. When first seen by the writer (Dec. 1976) there were three missing objects (against a, b and c in the above list) and a subsequent annotation with references to Greenwell's 1906 paper recorded that figs. 13, 15 and 17 had been removed. These three pieces are in the Yorkshire Museum collection, but were not found in 1899; it seems likely that the original 1899 finds were removed, these three pieces were substituted (perhaps when the collection was presented to the Yorkshire Museum) and then the same three objects were removed for display! Items d, e and f in my list tally with Mortimer's record of the 1899 excavations, but for the inclusion of an extra piece — half a penannular brooch — along with f. This penannular brooch is probably the 'harp-shaped fibula of iron' which should have been item c. If this explanation is correct, then the only missing grave-goods are those from Mortimer's 1899 Barrow 2 (my Barrow 81) and the bronze object from his Barrow 13 (my Barrow 89).]

81. (No.2) NNW., left side, with a blue glass bead, two tubular bronze beads, and a bronze bracelet (pp.80, 75).
82. (No.4) NNE., right side, no grave-goods:
83. (No.5) NNE., left side, no grave-goods.
84. (No.6) NNE, right side, no grave-goods.
85. (No.7) Two skeletons, an adult and a very small child.
a. adult, SW., left side, no grave-goods.
b. child, NE., right side, no grave-goods.
86. (No.9) SW., right side, no grave-goods.
87. (No.10) N., left side, no grave-goods.
88. (No.12) SSW., left side, in an exceptionally deep grave, 3ft 6in (1m), with an iron penannular brooch (Y.M.; p.71).
89. (No.13) NE., left side, with an iron involuted brooch (Y.M.; p.68) and a bronze object.
90. (No.15) NE., left side, with an iron object, possibly a toilet set (Y.M.; p.84), and two tubular bronze beads (Y.M.; p.80).
91. (No.18) NE., left side, with a pot (H.M.; p.83) and a pig-bone.
92. (No.19) NNE., right side, no grave-goods.
93. (No.20) Two skeletons side by side in the same grave.
a. NE., left side, with an iron involuted brooch (Y.M.; p.68), a pot (H.M.; p.83) and a pigbone.
b. NE., left side, with a pot (H.M.; p.83) and a pig-bone.
(Nos. 1, 3, 8, 11, 14, 16 and 17 had been previously excavated).
94-95. 1900. Two graves which Mortimer found by probing in the field to the west of the wood. Mortimer 1911: 40—2.
94. Previously excavated (but by whom?, because this was not a barrow) but an iron brooch (H.M.; p.67) had been left in the grave.
95. SW., "greatly decayed" and the position was not otherwise noted, found with a bronze brooch (H.M.; p.67).
96-98. 1902. Three barrows excavated by Mortimer (Mortimer 1911: 42—3).
96. (No.1) N., right side, no grave-goods.
97. (No.2) NW., right side, with the skeleton of a goat.
98. (No.3) NE., left side, no grave-goods.
99-106. 1909. Eight barrows excavated by Mortimer (1911:43—5).
99. (No.1) N., left side, with a pot (H.M.; p.83).
100. (No.2) N., left side, no grave-goods.
101. (No.3) NNE., left side, no grave-goods.
102. (No.4) SE., left side, no grave-goods.
103. (No.5) N., left side, no grave-goods.
104. (No.6) E., left side, no grave-goods.
105. (No.7) A child, aged about 4 years old, S., right side, no grave-goods.
106. (No.8) NE., left side, no grave-goods.

EASTBURN North Humberside. (Kirkburn parish) TA.007564.
50 burials excavated in an area excavation; one grave had an adult and a child, other wise they were single burials; Sheppard 1939: 36, fig., A—D. Grave-goods included: a brooch (H.M. 3029.42; p.68); remains of another (H.M. 3028.42; p.68); and a pot (H.M.; p.84). Other burials were excavated a year later, including one now displayed in Hull Museum, and the following items were recovered:

three pots, each with a pig humerus inside (H.M. 3036, 3037 and 3043.42; p.84); spearhead (H.M., p.64); sword (H.M.; p.63); bracelet (H.M. 3031.42; p.75); part of a brooch (H.M.; p.68); shield fragments (H.M. 3032 and 3033.42; p.57); piece of embossed bronze (H.M.); bronze toggle (H.M.; p.86).

GARTON SLACK North Humberside. SE.957596 to 953603.
(i) Cemetery excavated by C. and E. Grantham, who retain the finds in the their museum at Driffield. Grave-goods include: two iron involuted brooches, and fragments of two others (p.68); bronze finger-ring with overlapping terminals (p.86); bronze swan's neck pin (p.77); blue glass bead with white spirals (p.80); bronze bracelet with jet ring suspended (p.75); iron bracelet (p.75); and there was an iron spearhead in the shoulder of a skeleton.
(ii) Individual barrows and groups of barrows excavated by T.C.M. Brewster:
  a. Two square barrows 30ft (10m) across; one 20ft (6m) square; one skeleton with a bone pin (A.E. 1965: 8).
  b. Square barrow, central burial with iron brooch; three infants in ditches, one with a pot. Two flat graves, one with pig bones. (A.E. 1969: 13).
  c. *Area VII* Four square barrows, including: 1, central flexed burial with an iron mirror (p.82) and pig bones, and a secondary crouched burial in the ditch; 2, central extended burial, E., with a crouched burial, N., also on the barrow platform, and an adult and five infants as secondaries in the ditch; 3, no central burial, but two adolescents in the ditch.
  Area VIII Four flat graves, including a contracted inhumation with 35 blue glass beads (p.80) and an iron brooch.
  Area IX 20ft (6m) square barrow, with a crouched burial and a brooch. (A.E. 1970: 13—14).
  d. *Area XI* Cart-burial, p.20. The grave-group comprised: two wheels (two tyres and four nave-hoops, H.M.; p.41); possible pole-fitting (H.M.; p.53); two horse-bits (H.M.; p.47); five terrets (H.M.; p.51); two strap-links (H.M.; p.55); bronze pommel and strips (H.M.; p.55).
  e. *Area XIV* Square barrow, with ploughed-out grave (A.E. 1973:34).
(see also, Wetwang Slack).

GRIMTHORPE North Humberside. (Millington parish) SE.816535.
Four skeletons were found between 1868 and 1871 in three graves on the site of a hillfort. A fifth skeleton was found in the ditch of the hillfort in 1961; p.37 Mortimer 1869: 180—2; 1905: 150—2; Stead 1968: 166—73. Only the first burial had grave-goods.
1. Crouched skeleton, S., left side, with: shield (B.M. 76.2—8.1, 2, 6—8; p.55); disc (B.M. 76.2—8.3; p.57); sword and scabbard (B.M. 76.2—8.4, 5, 9, 10 and 12; p.61); spearhead (B.M. 76.2—8. 11; p.64); bone pegs (B.M. 76.2—8.13 to 25; p.86).
2. Inhumation, position not recorded, in a shallow grave.
3 and 4. Two successive crouched burials, both left side, N., in the same grave.

5. Crouched burial, SSE., left side, found in the hillfort ditch.

GRINDALE North Humberside. TA.155703.
Square barrow 13.5m by 15m with previously excavated grave and a pattern of nineteenth-century excavation trenches (A.E. 1972: 39). Probably a barrow excavated in 1857, see Huntow, below.

HANGING GRIMSTON North Yorkshire. (Thixendale parish) SE.810612.
Mortimer's Barrow 59, "a mere hillock", covered a grave 3ft deep with a contracted skeleton, SSE., right side, no grave-goods (Mortimer 1905: 102). Air photographs show a ditch 40ft (12m) square (Ramm, personal letter).

HORNSEA North Humberside. c. TA.210480.
A possible cart-burial mentioned in a MS account by William Morfitt (Stead 1965a: 93—4). No finds survive.

HUGGATE North Humberside. c. SE.920545.
Possible cart-burial(s), p.24; Mortimer 1905: 359. No finds survive.

HUNMANBY North Humberside. TA.101767.
Cart-burial, p.22. The grave-group comprised: two wheels (lost); possible linch-pins (lost; p.45); horse-bit (H.M.; p.47); terret (H.M.; p.50); harness-loop (H.M.; p.51); a possible shield (H.M. 3017 and 18.42; p.57).

HUNTOW North Humberside. (Bridlington parish) c. TA.155705.
Barrow excavated in 1857, Wright 1861; p.36. Three bronze brooches in the Ashmolean Museum (1927.877, 878a and b; pp.66 and 71). Probably the same barrow as that excavated by Manby in 1872, see Grindale, above.

HUTTON BUSCEL MOOR North Yorkshire. c. SE.959867.
Possible square barrows, Stead 1961:48.

MIDDLETON-ON-THE-WOLDS North Humberside c. SE.933482.
1. A possible cart-burial, Mortimer 1905: 359-60; p.24.
2. There is a linch-pin from this parish, but the circumstances of its discovery are not recorded (H.M.; p.45).
3. Contracted skeleton with an iron bracelet strung with two bone beads; two fragments of iron, possibly from a brooch; a pendant cut from antler; some sherds; (Sheppard 1923; H.M.).

NORTH GRIMSTON North Yorkshire. (Birdsall parish) SE.834668.
An extended burial discovered in 1902, Mortimer 1905: 354—7; p.37. Grave-goods: short sword (H.M.; p.61); long sword (H.M.; p.61) W bronze and iron rings (H.M.; p.62); fragmentary jet ring (H.M.; p.62); bronze fragments from a shield (H.M.; p.57). An iron spearhead found nearby about 30 years earlier (Mortimer 1905: 356) may have been from another grave, and there are square barrows in the vicinity (p.37).

PEXTON MOOR North Yorkshire. (Thornton Dale parish) SE.848853.

Cart-burial in a square barrow, p.22. The grave-group comprised: two wheels (one, excavated in 1911, now lost; the tyre and two nave-hoops of the other, Y.M.; p.41); horse-bit (Y.M.; p.47).

SAWDON North Yorkshire (Brompton parish) c.SE.940850.

The La Tène ornaments from this parish were not definitely found with burials. Two brooches acquired by Scarborough Museum in 1941 (pp.66 and 71) came from the collection of John Hopper, and were thought to have been found by him on the Old Farm, Sawdon, c.1910—18. Although they could have been found together, there is no proof of it (Watson 1947: 178). A ring-headed pin was acquired by the Yorkshire Museum with the Harland Collection in 1921, and is recorded as probably from Sawdon (Y.M.939.48; p.77).

SCORBOROUGH North Humberside. (Leconfield parish) (i) TA.017453, (ii) TA.012459.

(i) At least 120 barrows surviving in the cemetery, of which no fewer than eight have been excavated, but no grave-goods have been found. Mortimer 1895; Stead 1975. Mortimer dug six barrows, each with a contracted inhumation but no grave-goods:
  1. S., on its back (right side).
  2. N., left side.
  3. no bones survived.
  4. NNW., left side.
  5. SW., left side.
  6. N., left side.
(ii) An isolated square barrow, 9.5m by 10.5m, excavated in 1970 but no grave survived. Stead 1975: 8—9.

SEAMER North Yorkshire. (i) TA.033839, (ii) c.TA.020860.

(i) Possible cart-burial, Mortimer 1905: 358; Rutter & Duke 1958: 62. No finds survive.
(ii) Possible square barrows on Seamer Moor, Stead 1961: 48.

SKIPWITH COMMON North Yorkshire. SE.645377.

Square barrows, Stead 1961: 48—51.

SNILESWORTH North Yorkshire. SE.528950.

Possible square cairns, p.30.

THORGANBY COMMON North Yorkshire. (Skipwith parish) SE.666399.

Square barrows, Stead 1961: 51.

THORPE HALL North Humberside. (Rudston parish) TA.108676.

Sword, possibly found with a burial, Y.M. 938.48; p.62.

WETWANG SLACK North Humberside (Wetwang parish) SE.946601.

Excavations 1975 onwards still in progress. More than 200 graves excavated in 1975-7, with grave-goods including 30 brooches (including two penannular), 13 bracelets, 5 bead necklaces, 2 bead pendants, 2 ring-headed pins, 4 pots, 2 pairs of tweezers, 2 toe-rings, 1 sword, 1 amber ring, and 1 jet ring; information from the excavator, J.S. Dent, June 1977.

WYKEHAM North Yorkshire. SE.950881.

'Loft Howe' square barrow, p.30.

BIBLIOGRAPHY

A.E. 1965, etc. *Excavations Annual Report* (1968 onwards, *Archaeological Excavations*) Ministry of Public Building & Works (1970 onwards, Department of the Environment).

Agache, R., 1976 "Les fermes indigenes d'époque pre-romaine et romaine dans le bassin de la Somme", *Cahiers Arch. de Picardie,* 1976.

Alexander, J.A., 1964 "The origin of penannular brooches", *Proc.Prehist.Soc.,* xxx, 1964, 429-30.

Allen, J.R., 1906 "Notes on Archaeology and kindred subjects", *The Reliquary & Illustrated Archaeologist,* n.s., xii, 1906, 269-73.

Arrhenius, B., 1971 *Granatschmuck und Gemmen aus Nordischen Funden des Fruhen Mittelolters,* Acta Universitatis Stockholmiensis.

aus'm Weerth, E., 1870 *Der Grabfund von Wald-Algesheim.*

Barber, J., & Megaw, J.V.S., 1963 "A decorated Iron Age bridle-bit in the London Museum: its place in Art and Archaeology", *Proc.Prehist.Soc.,* xxix, 1963, 206-13.

Barfield, L.H., 1965 "Untersuchung von Grabeneinfriedungen bei Gut Dirlau, Kreis Duren", *Bonner Jahrb.,* 165, 1965, 167-76.

Bateman, T., 1861 (exhibit note), *J.Brit.Arch.Ass.,* xvii, 1861, 321.

Benadik, B., 1963 "Zur fragevon chronologischen beziehungen der keltischen Gräberfelder in der Slowakei", *Slovenská Arch.,* xi, 2, 1963, 339-90.

Bonenfant, P.P., 1961 "Sépultures Trevires à Tontelange", *Arch.Belg.,* 57.
　　1966 "A propos de deux usages funeraires des premiers siècles, avant et après Jésus Christ", *Arch.Belg.,* 95.

Boon, G.C., & Lewis, J.M., 1976 *Welsh Antiquity.*

Bosteaux-Paris, C., 1892 "Resultats de fouilles aux environs de Reims", *Ass. française pour l'avancement des sciences,* 1892, Pau, II, 613-18.

Bretz-Mahler, D., 1971 *La civilisation de La Tène en Champagne,* (Gallia supplément, xxiii).

Brewster, T.C.M., 1963 *The excavation of Staple Howe.*
　　1971 "The Garton Slack chariot burial, East Yorkshire", *Antiquity,* xlv, 1971, 289-92.
　　1975 "Garton Slack", *Current Arch.,* no.51, 1975, 104-16.

Brisson, A., & Hatt, J.-J., 1953 "Les nécropoles hallstattiennes d'Aulnay-aux-Planches (Marne)", *Rev.Arch. de l'Est et du Centre-Est,* iv, 1953, 193-233.
　　1955 "Cimetières gaulois et Gallo-Romains à enclos en Champagne", *Rev.Arch. de l'Est et du Centre-Est,* vi, 1955, 313-33.

Brisson, A., Hatt, J.-J., & Roualet, P., 1970 "Cimetière de Fère-Champenoise, Faubourg de Connantre", *Méms.Soc. d'Agric. ... de la Marne,* lxxxv, 1970, 7-26.

Brisson, A., Loppin, A., & Fromols, J., 1959 "Le sanctuaire celtique de Normée (Marne)", *Rev.Arch.,* 1959, II, 41-64.

Brothwell, D.R., 1961 "Cannibalism in Early Britain", *Antiquity,* xxxv, 1961, 304-7.

Buckman, J., 1851 "On the chemical composition of some ancient British and Roman beads", *Arch.J.,* viii, 1851, 351-4.

Bulleid, A., & Gray, H. St.G., 1911 *The Glastonbury Lake Village,* vol.1.

Burgess, C., 1974 "The Bronze Age", in Renfrew, C., ed., *British Prehistory, a new outline,* 1974, 165-232.
　　1976 "Burials with metalwork of the later Bronze Age in Wales and beyond", in Boon & Lewis, 1976, 81-104.

Burton, J., 1758 *Monasticon Eboracense: and the Ecclesiastical History of Yorkshire.*

Bushe-Fox, J.P., 1915 *Excavations at Hengistbury Head, Hampshire, 1911-12,* (Reports of the Research Committee of the Society of Antiquaries of London, iii).

Cahen-Delhaye, A., 1974 "Nécropole de La Tène I à Hamipré, Offaing: I, Trois tombes à char", *Arch.Belg.,* 162.
　　1975 "Tombes à char et buchers sous tombelles de La Tène I à Léglise-Gohimont", *Arch.Belg.,* 177, 1975, 17-21.

Challis, A., & Harding, D.W., 1975 *Later Prehistory from the Trent to the Tyne* Brit.Arch.Rep., 20).

Champion, S., 1976 "Coral in Europe: Commerce and Celtic ornament", in Duval, P.-M., & Hawkes, C.F.C., eds., *Celtic Art in Ancient Europe: Five Protohistoric Centuries,* 1976.

Chertier, B., 1972 "Les sépultures à char de La Tène I de Saint-Rémy-sur-Bussy, lieudit 'La Perrière,'" *Bull.Soc.Préhist. de France,* lxix, 1972, 130.
　　1976 *Les nécropoles de la civilisation des Champs d'urnes dans la région des marais de Saint-Gond (Marne). (Gallia Préhistoire,* supplément viii).

Cizmǎr, M., 1973 "Keltský kostrový hrob se čtvercovým příkopem z Domamyslic", *Arch.Rozhledy,* xxv, 1973, 615-25, 669-71.

Clarke, R.R., 1951 "A hoard of metalwork of the Early Iron Age from Ringstead, Norfolk", *Proc.Prehist.Soc.,* xvii, 1951, 214-25.

Clarke, R.R., & Hawkes, C.F.C., 1955 "An iron anthropoid sword from Shouldham, Norfolk, with related continental and British weapons", *Proc.Prehist.Soc.,* xxi, 1955, 198-227.

Clay, R.C.C., 1925 "An inhabited site of La Tène I date on Swallowcliffe Down", *Wilts.Arch.Mag.,* xliii, 1925-7, 59-101.

Collis, J.R., 1968 "Excavations at Owslebury, Hants.: An Interim Report", *Antiq.J.,* xlviii, 1968, 18-31.
　　1973 "Burials with weapons in Iron Age Britain", *Germania,* li, 1973, 121-33.

Corder, P., & Romans, T., 1937 "Excavations at Brough-— Petuaria", *Trans East Riding Ant. Soc.,* xxviii, 1935-9, 173-234.

Corot, H., 1905 "Le grand tumulus de Lantilly", *Rev.Préhist. illustrée de l'Est de la France,* i, 1905-6, 8-26.

Cowen, J.D., 1934 "The Cairnmuir gold terminal: a parallel, and a possible explanation of its use", *Proc.Soc.Ant.Scotland,* lxix, 1934-5, 455-9.
　　1967 "The Hallstatt sword of bronze: on the continent and in Britain", *Proc.Prehist.Soc.,* xxxiii, 1967, 377-454.

Coyon, C., 1924 "Fouilles dans un cimetière gaulois lieudit 'Le Montéqueux' territoire de Beine (Marne)", *Bull.Soc.Arch.Champenoise,* 1924, 30-2, and 61-2.

Crawford, O.G.S., 1921 "The ancient settlements at Harlyn Bay", *Antiq.J.,* i, 1921, 283-99.

Cunnington, M.E., & Goddard, E.H., 1934 *Catalogue of antiquities in the museum of the Wiltshire Archaeological and Natural History Society at Devizes*, part ii, second edition.

Curle, J., 1911 *A Roman frontier post and its people.*

Davis, J.B., & Thurnam, J., 1865 *Crania Britannica*, (plates 6-8, and the accompanying text).

Déchelette, J., 1913 *La collection Millon.*

1914 *Manuel d'Archéologie*, ii, 3me partie, Second âge du fer ou époque de La Tène.

Decker, K.-V., 1968 "Die jüngere Latènezeit im Neuwieder Becken", *Jahrbuch für Geschichte und Kunst des Mittelrheins*, i, 1968, 7-180.

Decker, K.-V., & Scollar, I., 1962 "Iron Age square enclosures in Rhineland", *Antiquity*, xxxvi, 1962, 175-8.

de Laet, S.J., 1966 *Van Grafmonument tot Heiligdom* (Mededelingen van de Koninklijke Vlaamse Academie voor Wetenschappen, Letteren en Schone Kunsten van België. Klasse der Letteren, xxviii, 1966, no.2).

de Navarro, J.M., 1966 "Swords and scabbards of the La Tène period with incised laddering", *Helvetia Antiqua* (Festschrift Emil Vogt), 1966, 147-54.

1972 *The finds from the site of La Tène*, volume 1.

Drack, W., 1958 "Wagengräber und Wagenbestanteile aus Hallstattgrabhügeln der Schweiz", *Zeitschr. f. Schweiz Arch. u. Kunstgesch.*, xviii, 1958, 1-67.

1974a "Die späte Hallstattzeit im Mittelland und Jura", in Drack 1974b, 19-34.

1974b *Ur- und Frügeschichtliche Archäologie der Schweiz*, iv, Die Eisenzeit.

Driehaus, J., 1966 "Zur Datierung des Graberfeldes von Bell im Hunsrück", *Bonner Jahrb.*, 166, 1966, 1-25.

Dudley, D., & Jope, E.M., 1965 "An Iron Age cist-burial with two brooches from Trevone, North Cornwall", *Cornish Arch.*, iv, 1965, 18-23.

Dunning, G.C., 1928 "An engraved bronze mirror from Nijmegen, Holland, with a note on the origin and distribution of the type", *Arch.J.*, lxxxv, 1928, 69-79.

1934 "The swans-neck and ring-headed pins of the Early Iron Age in Britain", *Arch.J.*, xci, 1934, 269-95

1976 "Salmonsbury, Bourton-on-the-Water, Gloucestershire", in Harding, D.W., *Hillforts*, 1976, 75-118.

Dupuis, J., 1940 "Une tombe à char gauloise de La Tène I", *Rev.Arch.*, 6me sér., xvi, 1940, 62-8.

Dušek, M., 1954 "Chotín I — skýtske biriruálne pohrebiste", *Arch. Rozhledy*, vi, 1954, 311-16, 329-31.

Duval, A., 1975 "Une tombe à char de La Tène III: Inglemare (Commune de Belbeuf, Seine-Maritime)", *Arch.Atlantica*, i, 1975, 147-63.

Duval, A., & Blanchet, J.-C., 1974 "La tombe à char d'Attichy (Oise)", *Bull.Soc.Préhist. de France*, lxxi, 1974, 401-8.

Duval, P.-M., & Kruta, V., 1975 *L'habitat et la nécropole à l'âge du fer en Europe occidentale et centrale.*

Dymond, D.P., 1966 "Ritual monuments at Rudston, E. Yorkshire, England", *Proc.Prehist.Soc.*, xxxii, 1966, 86-95.

Ellison, A., & Drewett, P., 1971 "Pits and post-holes in the British Early Iron Age: some alternative explanations", *Proc.Prehist.Soc.*, xxxvii, part i, 1971, 183-94.

Evans, Sir Arthur, 1915 "Late-Celtic dagger, fibula, and jet cameo", *Archaeologia*, lxvi, 1914-15, 569-72.

Favret, P.-M., 1913 "Cimetière gaulois de Mairy-Sogny", *Bull.Soc.Arch.Champenoise*, 1913, 109-20.

1929 "Le cimetière des Commelles; fouilles de G. Chance", *Bull.Soc.Arch.Champenoise*, 1929, 13-26.

1936 "Les nécropoles des Jogasses à Chouilly (Marne)", *Préhistoire*, v, 1936, 24-119.

Ferdiere, A., & al., 1973 "Les sépultures gauloises d'Allonville (Somme)", *Bull.Soc.Préhist. de France*, lxx, 1973, 479-92.

Filip, J., 1956 *Keltové ve střední Evropě.*

1960 *Celtic civilisation and its heritage.*

Flouest, E., 1885 "Le char de la sépulture gauloise de la Bouvandeau, commune de Somme Tourbe, Marne", *Méms.Soc.Ant. de France*, lxvi, 1885, 99-111.

Flouest, J.-L., & Stead, I.M., 1977 "Recherches sur des cimetières de la Tène en Champagne (1971-1976)", *Gallia*, xxxv, 1977, 59-74.

Fourcart, -., 1909 "Découvertes archéologiques regionales: à Juniville", *Bull.Soc.Arch.Champenoise*, 1909, 51.

Fourdrignier, E., 1878 *Double sépulture gauloise de la Gorge-Meillet, territoire de Somme Tourbe (Marne).*

Fowler, E., 1960 "The origins and development of the penannular brooch in Europe", *Proc.Prehist.Soc.*, xxvi, 1960, 149-77.

Fox, C., 1927 "A La Tène I brooch from Wales: with notes on the typology and distribution of these brooches in Britain", *Arch.Cambrensis*, 7 ser., vii, 1927, 67-112.

1946 *A Find of the Early Iron Age from Llyn Cerrig Bach, Anglesey.*

1949a "A bronze pole-sheath from the Charioteer's Barrow, Arras, Yorkshire", *Antiq.J.*, xxix, 1949, 81-3.

1949b "Celtic mirror handles in Britain, with special reference to the Colchester handle", *Arch.Cambrensis*, c, 7 ser., 1949, 24-44.

1950 "Two Celtic bronzes from Lough Gur, Limerick, Ireland", *Antiq.J.*, xxx, 1950, 190-2.

1958 *Pattern and Purpose.*

Fromols, J., 1955 "Recensement des tumulus et fouilles archéologiques dans la forêt des Pothées (Ardennes). Fouilles de MM. Brisson, Loppin et Hegly en 1938 et 1939", *Méms.Soc. d'Agric. ... de la Marne*, 2me ser., xxix, 1955, 5-32.

Giessler, R., & Kraft, G., 1941 "Untersuchungen zur frühen und älteren Latènezeit am Oberrhein und in der Schweiz", *Ber.RGK.*, xxxii, 1941, 20-115.

Goguey, R., 1968 *De l'aviation à l'archéologie.*

Goury, G., 1954 "Informations: IIIme circonscription", *Gallia*, xii, 1954, 146-55.

Gozzadini, G., 1870 *Di ulteriori scoperte nell'antica necropoli a Marzabotto nel Bolognese.*

Gray, H. St.G., 1910 "Notes on archaeological remains found on Ham Hill, Somerset", *Proc.Somerset Arch.Nat.Hist.*, lvi, 1910, ii, 50-61.

1912 "Additions to the museum", *Proc.Somerset Arch.Nat.Hist.*, lviii, 1912, ii, 104-23.

Gray, H. St.G., & Bulleid, A., 1953 *The Meare Lake Village*, volume ii.

Gray, H. St.G., & Cotton, M.A., 1966 *The Meare Lake Village*, volume iii.

Greenwell, W., 1865 "Notices of the examination of ancient grave-hills in the North Riding of Yorkshire", *Arch.J.*, xxii, 1865, 97-117 and 241-64.
1877 *British Barrows*.
1906 "Early Iron Age burials in Yorkshire", *Archaeologia*, lx, 1906, 251-324.

Guido, C.M., 1978. *The glass beads of the Prehistoric and Roman periods in Britain and Ireland* (Reports of the Research Committee of the Society of Antiquaries of London, xxxv).

Günther, A., 1934 "Gallische Wagengräber im Gebiet des Neuwieder Beckens", *Germania*, xviii, 1934, 8-14.

Haffner, A., 1971 & 1974 *Das keltisch-römische Gräberfeld von Wederath-Belginum*, volume i, 1971; volume ii, 1974.
1976 *Die westliche Hunsrück-Eifel-Kultur*.

Harbison, P., 1969 "The chariot of Celtic funerary tradition", *Fundb. aus Hessen*, i, 1969 (Festschrift für Wolfgang Dehn), 34-58.

Harris, A., 1973 "An East Yorkshire land surveyor: William Watson of Seaton Ross", *Yorks.Arch.J.*, xlv, 1973, 149-57.

Hawkes, C.F.C., 1946 "An unpublished Celtic brooch from Danes Graves, Kilham, Yorkshire", *Antiq.J.*, xxvi, 1946, 187-91.

Haworth, R., 1971 "The horse harness of the Irish Early Iron Age", *Ulster J.Arch.*, xxxiv, 1971, 26-49.

Hodson, F.R., 1964a "La Tène chronology, continental and British", *Bull. Institute Arch. London*, no.4, 1964, 123-41.
1964b "Cultural grouping within the British pre-Roman Iron Age", *Proc.Prehist.Soc.*, xxx, 1964, 99-110.
1968 *The La Tène cemetery at Münsingen-Rain* (Acta Bernensia, v)
1971 "Three Iron Age brooches from Hammersmith", in G. de G. Sieveking, 1971, 50-7.

Howarth, E., 1899 *Catalogue of the Bateman Collection of Antiquities in the Sheffield Public Museum*.

Hubert, H., 1900 "Sépulture à char de Nanterre", *Congrès int. d'anth. et d'arch. préhist.*, 12e session, Paris, 1900, 410-7.

Hughes, M.J., 1972 "A technical study of opaque red glass of the Iron Age in Britain", *Proc.Prehist.Soc.*, xxxviii, 1972, 98-107.

Jackson, C., 1869 *The diary of Abraham de la Pryme* (Surtees Society, vol.54).

Jacobi, H., 1912 "Die Ausgrabungen", *Saalburg Jahrb.*, iii, 1912, 6-71.

Jacobsthal, P., 1944 *Early Celtic Art*.

Jenkins, J.G., 1961 *The English Farm Wagon*.

Joachim, H.-E., 1969 "Unbekannte Wagengräber der Mittel- bis Spätlatènezeit aus dem Rheinland", *Fundb. aus Hessen*, i, 1969 (Festschrift für Wolfgang Dehn), 84-111.

Joffroy, R., 1958 *Les sépultures à char du premier âge du fer en France*.
1975 "Vix: habitats et nécropoles", in Duval & Kruta, 1975, 71-4.

Joffroy, R., & Bretz-Mahler, D., 1959 "Les tombes à char de La Tène dans l'est de la France", *Gallia*, xvii, 1959, 5-35.

Jope, E.M., 1954 "The Keshcarrigan bowl and a bronze mirror-handle from Ballymoney", *Ulster J.Arch.*, xvii, 1954, 92-6.

Keller, J., 1965 *Das keltische Fürstengrab von Reinheim*.

Kessler, P.T., 1930 "Eine neuartig Grabanlage der Latène-zeit im Wallertheim, Rheinhessen", *Mainzer Zeitschr.*, xxiv-xxv, 1929-30, 125-33.

Kimmig, W., 1970 "Zu einer verzierten Latène-Schmuckscheibe von Stedebergen, Kr. Verden/Aller", *Ber. RGK*, 51-2, 1970-1, 147-74.

Kirk, J.L., 1911 "Opening of a tumulus near Pickering", *Yorks. Phil. Soc. Report*, 1911, 62.

Klindt-Jensen, O., 1949 "Foreign Influences in Denmark's Early Iron Age", *Acta Arch.*, 20, 1949, 1-229.

Kossack, G., 1971 "The construction of the felloe in Iron Age spoked wheels", in J. Boardman, M.A. Brown & T.G.E. Powell, eds., *The European Community in Later Prehistory*, 1971, 143-63.

Kromer, K., 1959 *Das Graberfeld von Hallstatt*.

Kruta, V., 1971 *Le trésor de Duchcov*.
1975a "Les habitats et nécropoles latèniens en Bohême", in Duval & Kruta, 1975, 95-102.
1975b *"L'art celtique en Bohême"*

Kruta Poppi, L., 1975 "Les Celtes à Marzabotto (Province de Bologne)", *Études Celtiques*, xiv, 1975, 345-76.

Leeds, E.T., 1933 *Celtic Ornament*.

Lemoine, R., 1905 "Époque marnienne. Sépulture à char découverte du 10 mars 1904, à Châlons-sur-Marne", *Bull.Soc.Préhist. de France*, ii, 1905, 100-116.

Lethbridge, T.C., 1953 "Burial of an Iron Age warrior at Snailwell", *Proc. Cambridge Ant.Soc.*, xlvii, 1953, 25-37.

Lobjois, G., 1969 "La nécropole de Pernant (Aisne)", *Celticum*, xviii, 1969, 1-284.

Loughlin, N., & Miller, K., 1979 *A survey of the Archaeology of Humberside*.

MacAlister, R.A.S., 1929 "On some antiquities discovered upon Lambay", *Proc. R. Irish Acad.*, xxxviii, 1929, section C, 240-6.

Macdonald, G., & Park, A., 1906 *The Roman forts on the Bar Hill, Dumbartonshire*.

MacGregor, M., 1976 *Early Celtic Art in North Britain*.

Manning, W.H., & Saunders, C., 1972 "A socketed iron axe from Maids Moreton, Buckinghamshire, with a note on the type", *Antiq.J.*, lii, 1972, 276-92.

Mariën, M.E., 1961 *Le groupe de la Haine*.

May, J., 1970 "An Iron Age square enclosure at Aston upon Trent, Derbyshire: a report on excavations in 1967", *Derbys. Arch.J.*, xc, 1970, 10-21.
1976 *Prehistoric Lincolnshire* (History of Lincolnshire, i).

McDonnell, J., 1963 *A history of Helmsley, Rievaulx and district*.

McInnes, I.J., 1968 "The excavation of a Bronze Age cemetery at Catfoss, East Yorkshire", *East Riding Arch.*, i, 1968, 2-10.

Megaw, J.V.S., 1970 *Art of the European Iron Age*.

Menke, M., 1968 "Die spätlatènezeitlichen Jochbeschläge aus Karlstein, Ldkr. Berchtesgaden", *Bayer. Vorgeschichtsbl.*, 33, 1968, 58-81.

Minns, E.H., 1913 *Scythians and Greeks*.

Moosleitner, F., Pauli, L., & Penninger, E., 1974 *Der Dürrnberg bei Hallein*, ii.

Moreau, F., 1894 *Collection Caranda*, 1877-94.

Morel, L., 1898 *La Champagne souterraine*.

Mortimer, J.R., 1869 "Notice of the opening of an Anglo-Saxon grave, at Grimthorpe, Yorkshire", *Reliquary*, ix, 1868-9, 180-2.

1895 "The opening of six mounds at Scorborough, near Beverley", *Trans. East Riding Ant.Soc.*, iii, 1895, 21-3.

1897 "The Danes Graves", *Yorks.Phil.Soc. Report*, 1897, 1-10.

1898 "The opening of a number of the so-called 'Danes Graves', at Kilham, E.R. Yorks., and the discovery of a chariot-burial of the Early Iron Age", *Proc.Soc.Ant. London*, 2nd ser., xvii, 1897-9, 119-28.

1899 "A summary of what is known of the so-called 'Danes Graves', near Driffield", *Proc.Yorks.Geol.& Polytechnic Soc.*, n.s., xiii, 1895-9, 286-98.

1905 *Forty years researches in British and Saxon burial mounds of East Yorkshire.*

1911 "Danes Graves", *Trans.East Riding Ant.Soc.*, xviii, 1911, 30-52.

Moucha, V., 1969 "Latènezeitliche Gräber aus Sulejovice in Nordwestböhmen", *Arch.Rozhledy*, xxi, 1969, 596-617.

1974 "Príspevek k posnání štítu z doby laténské v Čechach", *Arch. Rozhledy*, xxvi, 1974, 445-53, 549-51.

Musty, J., & MacCormick, A.G., 1973 "An Early Iron Age wheel from Holme Pierrepont, Notts." *Antiq.J.*, liii, 1973, 275-7.

Nicaise, A., 1884 *L'époque gauloise dans le département de la Marne.*

1885 "Le port féminin du torque chez certaines tribus de l'est de la Gaul", *Méms.Soc. d'Agric. ... de la Marne*, 1884-5, 75-88.

Oliver, G., 1829 *History of Beverley.*

Parruzot, P., 1954 "Enceintes quadrangulaires découvertes par avion à Saint-Denis-lès-Sens (Yonne)", *Rev.Arch. de l'Est et du Centre-Est*, v, 1954, 71-3.

1960 "A la recherche des gisements protohistoriques dans le nord du département de l'Yonne", *Rev.Arch. de l'Est et du Centre-Est*, xi, 1960, 265-87.

Penninger, E., 1972 *Der Dürrnberg bei Hallein*, i.

Piggott, S., 1949a "A wheel of Iron Age type from Co.Durham", *Proc.Prehist.Soc.*, xv, 1949, 191.

1949b "An Iron Age yoke from Northern Ireland", *Proc.Prehist.Soc.*, xv, 1949, 192-3.

1950 "Swords and scabbards of the British Early Iron Age", *Proc.Prehist.Soc.*, xvi, 1950, 1-28.

1952 "Three metal-work hoards of the Roman period from southern Scotland", *Proc.Soc.Ant. Scotland*, lxxxvii, 1952-3, 1-50.

1965 *Ancient Europe.*

1969 "Early Iron Age 'horn-caps' and yokes", *Antiq.J.*, xlix, 1969, 378-81.

Probert, L.A., 1976 "Twyn-y-Gaer hill-fort, Gwent: an interim assessment", in Boon & Lewis, 1976, 105-19.

Proctor, W., 1855 "Report of the proceedings of the Yorkshire Antiquarian Club, in the excavation of barrows from the year 1849", *Proc.Yorks.Phil.Soc.*, 1855, 176-89.

Quatreville, A., 1972 "Les enclos rituels (époque de La Tène) dans les nécropoles de Manre et d'Aure (Ardennes)", *Bull.Soc.Arch.Chàmpenoise*, 1972, 13-55.

1973 "Les enclos rituels de l'époque de La Tène dans les nécropoles de Manre et d'Aure", *Bull.Soc.Arch.Champenoise*, 1973, 17-36.

Raddatz, K., 1967 *Das Wagengrab der jüngeren vorrömischen Eisenzeit von Husby, Kreis Flensburg.*

Ramm, H.G., 1971 "The Yorkshire Philosophical Society and Archaeology, 1822-55", *Yorks.Phil.Soc. Report*, 1971, 66-73.

1973 "Aerial reconnaissance and interpretation", *Yorks.Arch.J.*, xlv, 1973, 208-10.

1974 "Aerial reconnaissance and interpretation", *Yorks.Arch.J.*, xlvi, 1974, 151-3.

1976 "The origins of York", *Yorks.Phil.Soc. Report*, 1976, 59-63.

Reinecke, P., 1911 *Die Altertümer unserer heidnischen Vorzeit*, v, 1911.

Rest, W., 1948 "Das Grabhügelfeld von Bell im Hunsrück", *Bonner Jahrb.*, 148, 1948, 133-89.

Rest, W., & Roder, J., 1941 "Neue Wagengräber bei Kärlich, Landkreis Koblenz", *Bonner Jahrb.*, 146, 1941, 288-99.

Richmond, I.A., 1925 *Huddersfield in Roman times.*

1968 *Hod Hill*, ii.

Roder, J., 1948 "Neue Gräber der jüngeren Hunsrück-Eifel-Kultur in Kärlich, Landkreis Koblenz", *Bonner Jahrb.*, 148, 1948, 417-26.

Rosenberg, G., 1937 *Hjortspringfundet* (Nordiske Fortidsminder, iii, 1).

Rowlett, R.M., 1966 "Penannular fibulae in the Marne Culture", *Antiquity*, xl, 1966, 133-6.

1969 "Une tombe à char de Prunay (Marne)", *Bull.Soc.Arch.Champenoise*, 1969, 12-17.

Rozoy, J.-G., 1970 *Le cimetière du Mont-Troté.*

Rutter, J.G., 1959 "The Iron Age pits on Castle Hill, Scarborough", *Trans. Scarborough & District Arch.Soc.*, i, no.2, 32-44.

Rutter, J.G., & Duke, G., 1958 *Excavations at Crossgates near Scarborough 1947-56.*

Rybová, A., & Soudský, B., 1962 *Libenice: keltská svatyně ve středních Čechách.*

Rynne, E., 1976 "The La Tène and Roman finds from Lambay, Co. Dublin: a re-assessment", *Proc.R. Irish Acad.*, lxxvi, 1976, 231-44.

Scherer, J., Mordant, C. & D., 1972 "La nécropole I de La Tène de Gravon (Seine-et-Marne)", *Rev.Arch. de l'Est et du Centre-Est*, xxiii, 1972, 357-83.

Schiek, S., 1954 "Das Hallstattgrab von Vilsingen, zur Chronologie der späthallstattzeitlichen Fürstengräber in Südwestdeutschland", *Festschrift für Peter Goessler*, 150-67.

Schwarz, K., 1962 "Zum Stand der Ausgrabungen in der spätkeltischen Viereckschanze von Holzhausen", *Jahresber. der bayerischen Bodendenkmalpflege*, 1962, 22-77.

Scollar, I., 1968 "Iron Age enclosures in the Cologne basin", in J.M. Coles & D.D.A. Simpson, eds., *Studies in Ancient Europe*, 227-32.

Sheppard, T., 1907 "Note on a British chariot-burial at Hunmanby in East Yorkshire", *Yorks.Arch.J.*, xix, 1907, 482-8.
 1923 "Roman remains at Middleton-on-the-Wolds", *Trans.East Riding Ant.Soc.*, xxiv, 1923, 80-4.
 1939 "Excavations at Eastburn, East Yorkshire", *Yorks.Arch.J.*, xxxiv, 1939, 35-47.

Sieveking, G. de G., 1971 *Prehistoric and Roman Studies* (British Museum Quarterly, xxxv).

Smith, A.H., 1937 *The place-names of the East Riding of Yorkshire and York* (English Place-name Society, vol. xiv).

Smith, R.A., 1905 *A guide to the antiquities of the Early Iron Age. (British Museum).*
 1934 "Scarborough and Hallstatt", *Antiq.J.*, xiv, 1934, 301-2.

Snodgrass, A., 1973 "Bronze 'phalera' — a review", *Hamburger Beiträge zur Archäologe*, iii, 1973, 41-50.

Soudská, E., 1976 "Hrob 196 z Manětína-Hradku a další hroby z dvoukolovými vozy v Čechách", *Arch.Rozhledy*, xxviii, 1976, 625-54.

Spence Bate, C., 1866 "On the discovery of a Romano-British cemetery near Plymouth", *Archaeologia*, xl, 1866, 500-10.

Spratling, M. G., 1970 "The late pre-Roman Iron Age bronze mirror from Old Warden", *Beds.Arch.J.*, v, 1970, 9-16.

Stead, I.M., 1959 "A chariot burial on Pexton Moor, North Riding", *Antiquity*, xxxiii, 1959, 214-16.
 1961 "A distinctive form of La Tène barrow in Eastern Yorkshire and on the continent", *Antiq.J.*, xli, 1961, 44-62.
 1965a *The La Tène Cultures of Eastern Yorkshire.*
 1965b "The Celtic Chariot", *Antiquity*, xxxix, 1965, 259-65.
 1967 "A La Tène III burial at Welwyn Garden City", *Archaeologia*, ci, 1967, 1-62.
 1968 "An Iron Age hill-fort at Grimthorpe, Yorkshire, England", *Proc.Prehist.Soc.*, xxxiv, 1968, 148-90.
 1969 "Verulamium 1966-8", *Antiquity*, xliii, 1969, 45-52.
 1971 "Yorkshire before the Romans: some recent discoveries", in R.M. Butler, ed., *Soldier and civilian in Roman Yorkshire*, 21-43.
 1975a "The La Tène cemetery at Scorborough, East Riding", *East Riding Arch.*, ii, 1975, 1-11.
 1975b "Baldock", in W. Rodwell & T. Rowley, eds., *Small towns of Roman Britain* (British Arch.Rep.,15).
 1977 "La Tène burials between Burton Fleming and Rudston, North Humberside", *Antiq.J.*, lvi, 1977, 217-26.

Stillingfleet, E.W., 1846 "Account of the opening of some barrows on the Wolds of Yorkshire", *Proc.Arch.Inst.*, York vol., 1846, 26-32.

Sturt, G., 1949 *The Wheelwright's Shop.*

Talbot Rice, T., 1957 *The Scythians.*

Thurnam, J., 1859 (untitled note), *Arch.J.*, xvi, 1859, 83.
 1871 "On ancient British barrows, especially those of Wiltshire and the adjoining counties: part ii, Round Barrows", *Archaeologia*, xliii, 1871, 285-544.

Uzsoki, A., 1970 "Elözetes jelentés a ménfőcsanaki kelta temető ásatásáról", *Arrabona*, 12, 1970, 17-57.

Verwers, G.J., 1972 "Das Kamps Veld in Haps in Neolithikum, Bronzezeit und Eisenzeit", *Analecta Praehistorica Leidensia*, v, 1972.

von Weinzierl, R.R., 1899 *Das La Tène Grabfeld von Languest bei Bilin in Bohmen.*

Vouga, P., 1923 *La Tène.*

Wainwright, G.J., 1967 *Coygan Camp.*

Wainwright, G.J., & Longworth, I.H., 1969 "The excavation of a group of round barrows on Ampleforth Moor, Yorkshire", *Yorks.Arch.J.*, xlii, 1969, 283-94.

Wainwright, G.J., & Spratling, M.G., 1973 "The Iron Age settlement of Gussage All Saints", *Antiquity*, xlvii, 1973, 109-30.

Ward Perkins, J.B., 1939 "Iron Age metal horses' bits of the British Isles", *Proc.Prehist.Soc.*, v, 1939, 173-92.
 1940 "Two early linch-pins, from Kings Langley, Herts., and from Tiddington, Stratford-on-Avon", *Antiq.J.*, xx, 1940, 358-67.
 1941 "An Iron Age linch-pin of Yorkshire type from Cornwall", *Antiq.J.*, xxi, 1941, 64-7.

Warhurst, A., 1953 "A Belgic burial from Borough Green", *Arch.Cantiana*, lxvi, 1953, 157-60.

Waterbolk, H.T., 1962 "Hauptzüge der eisenzeitlichen Besiedlung der nördlichen Niederlande", *Offa*, xix, 1962, 9-46.

Watson, W., 1947 "Two brooches of the Early Iron Age from Sawdon, North Riding, Yorkshire", *Antiq.J.*, xxvii, 1947, 178-82.

Webster, R., 1970 *Gems: their sources, descriptions and identification.*

Wellbeloved, C., 1875 *A descriptive account of the antiquities in the grounds and in the museum of the Yorkshire Philosophical Society.*

Wheeler, R.E.M., 1943 *Maiden Castle, Dorset* (Reports of the Research Committee of the Society of Antiquaries of London, xii).
 1946 *London in Roman Times.*

Whimster, R., 1977 "Iron Age burial in Southern Britain", *Proc.Prehist.Soc.*, xliii, 1977, 317-27.

White, D.A., 1970 "The excavation of an Iron Age round barrow near Handley, Dorset, 1969", *Antiq.J.*, 1, 1970, 26-36.

Wightman, E.M., 1970 "Rhineland 'Grabgarten' and their context", *Bonner Jahrb.*, 170, 1970, 211-32.

Wild, J.P., 1970 "Button-and-loop fasteners in the Roman provinces", *Britannia*, i, 1970, 137-55.
 1976 "Loanwords and Roman expansion in north-west Europe", *World Arch.*, viii, 1976, 57-64.

Wilhelmi, K., 1971 "Ein vorgeschichtlicher Körper- und Brandgräberfriedhof bei Lengerich, Kr. Tecklenburg", *Arch.Korrespondenzbl.*, i, 1971, 207-14.

Wood, Sir Charles, 1860 (exhibit note), *Proc.Soc.Ant. London*, 2nd ser., i, 1859-61, 263.

Wright, T., 1861 *Essays on archaeological subjects*, vol.i.

Wurm, K., 1972 "Eine stilkritische Untersuchung über den frühkeltischen Bronzespiegel von Hochheim am Main (Main-Taunus-Kreis)", *Fundber. aus Hessen*, 12, 1972, 230-51.

Wyss, R., 1974 "Technik, Wirtschaft, Handel und Kriegswesen der Eisenzeit" in Drack 1974b:105-38.

York Catalogue, 1846 "Catalogue of Antiquities", *Proc.Arch.Inst.*, York vol., 1846, 1-25.

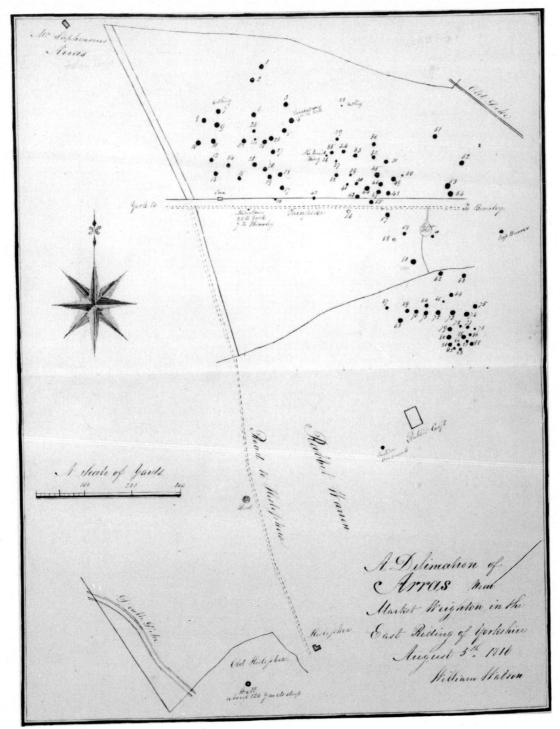

Plate 1. *Plan of Arras, by William Watson, 1816.*

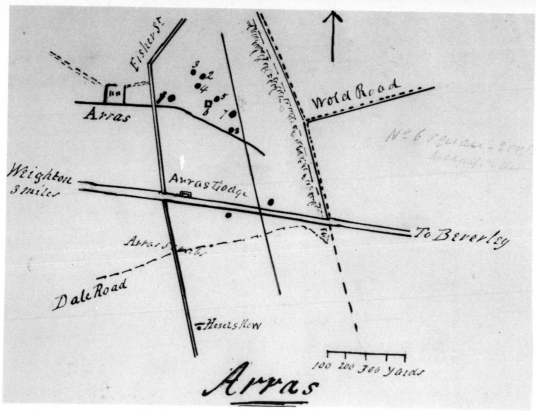

Plate 2a. *Plan of Arras, by the Yorkshire Antiquarian Club, 1850.*

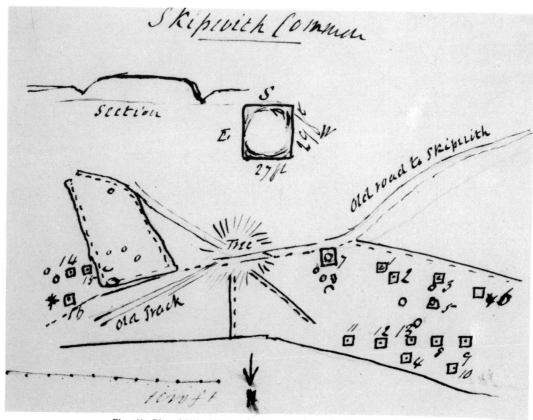

Plate 2b. *Plan of Skipwith Common, by the Yorkshire Antiquarian Club, 1849.*

Plate 3a. *Boynton, Mortimer and Greenwell at Danes Graves, 1898.*

Plate 3b. *Garton Slack cart-burial, 1971.*

a

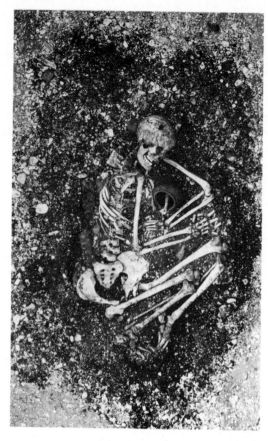

b

c

Plate 4. *Contracted (a), crouched (b) and extended (c)
skeletons at Burton Fleming.*

Plate 5. *Square barrows in the course of excavation at Burton Fleming. The grave in the larger central barrow is orientated north-south and those in the smaller barrows are east-west.*

Plate 6a. *Square barrows at Cowlam.*

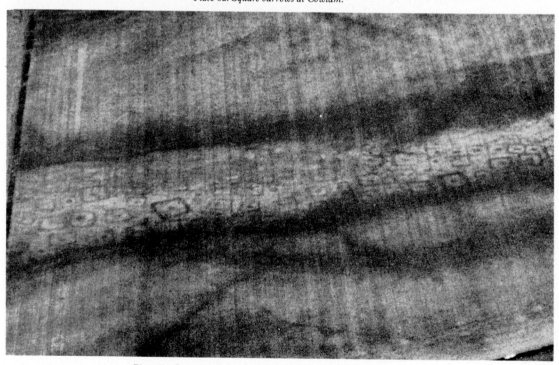

Plate 6b. *Cemetery of square barrows in the bottom of a slack at Grindale.*

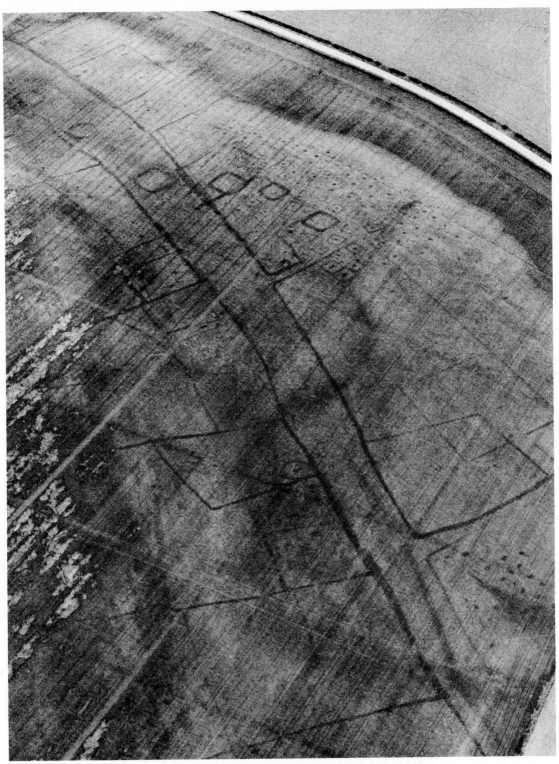

Plate 7. *Drove-way settlement and square barrows at Bell Slack, Burton Fleming.*

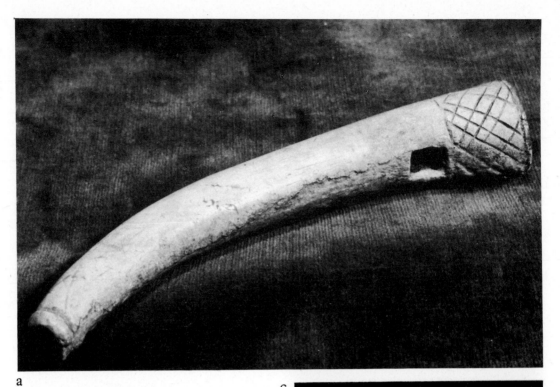

a

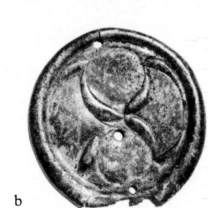

b

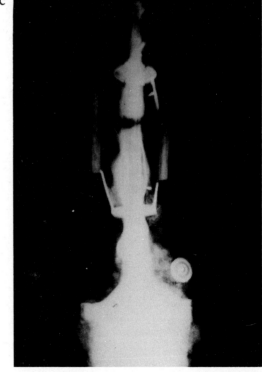

c

Plate 8a. *Antler linch-pin, Arras.*

Plate 8b. *Bronze disc, Grimthorpe.*

Plate 8c. *Radiograph of the hilt of a sword from Burton Fleming, showing the metal frame for the hilt and decorative bronze studs (a bronze stud over the left shoulder of the sword was removed in the course of excavation).*

Plate 9. *Hilt of the sword found at Thorpe Hall.*

a
b

Plate 10. *Scabbard chapes from Bugthorpe (a) and Grimthorpe (b).*

INDEX